D1027976

HITLER'S SOLDIERS IN THE SUNSHINE STATE

The Florida History and Culture Series

UNIVERSITY PRESS OF FLORIDA

Florida A&M University, Tallahassee
Florida Atlantic University, Boca Raton
Florida Gulf Coast University, Ft. Myers
Florida International University, Miami
Florida State University, Tallahassee
New College of Florida, Sarasota
University of Central Florida, Orlando
University of Florida, Gainesville
University of North Florida, Jacksonville
University of South Florida, Tampa
University of West Florida, Pensacola

Robert D. Billinger Jr.

HITLER'S SOLDIERS IN

UNIVERSITY PRESS OF FLORIDA

GAINESVILLE · TALLAHASSEE · TAMPA · BOCA RATON

PENSACOLA · ORLANDO · MIAMI · JACKSONVILLE · FT. MYERS · SARASOTA

THE SUNSHINE STATE

German POWs in Florida

14 13 12 11 10 09   6 5 4 3 2 1

First cloth printing, 2000
First paperback printing, 2009

Portions of several chapters in this book were published in slightly
different form in "With the Wehrmacht in Florida: The German
POW Facility at Camp Blanding, 1942–1946," *Florida Historical
Quarterly* 58 (October 1979): 160–73, which was reprinted in Lewis
N. Wynne, ed., *Florida at War* (Saint Leo, Fla.: Saint Leo College
Press, 1993), and "The Other Side Now: What Blanding POWs Told
the Wehrmacht," *Florida Historical Quarterly* 73 (July 1994): 62–78.
This book does not seek to republish these articles but is composed
of information and some wording taken in part from these published
articles. Permission to do so has been granted by Lewis N. Wynne,
executive director, Florida Historical Society.

LIBRARY OF CONGRESS CATALOGING-IN-PUBLICATION DATA
Billinger, Robert D., 1944–
Hitler's soldiers in the Sunshine State: German POWs in Florida /
Robert D. Billinger, Jr.
p. cm. — (The Florida history and culture series)
Includes bibliographical references (p.) and index.
ISBN 978-0-8130-1740-2 (cloth)
ISBN 978-0-8130-3441-6 (pbk)
1. World War, 1939–1945—Prisoners and prisons, American.
2. Prisoners of war—Germany. 3. Prisoners of war—United States—
Florida. 4. Florida—History, Military. I. Title. II. Series.
D805.U5B55 2000
940.54'7273'09759—dc21   99-31274

The University Press of Florida is the scholarly publishing agency
for the State University System of Florida, comprising Florida A&M
University, Florida Atlantic University, Florida Gulf Coast University, Florida International University, Florida State University, New
College of Florida, University of Central Florida, University of
Florida, University of North Florida, University of South Florida,
and University of West Florida.

University Press of Florida
15 Northwest 15th Street
Gainesville, FL 32611
www.upf.com

Dedicated to the Florida "alumni," especially
Gerhard Anklam, Werner Burkert,
Herman Finke, and Lüdeke Herder

CONTENTS

PHOTOGRAPHS FOLLOW PAGE 86

FOREWORD

Hitler's Soldiers in the Sunshine State: German POWs in Florida is the eleventh volume of a series devoted to the study of Florida History and Culture. During the past half century, the burgeoning population and increased national and international visibility of Florida have sparked a great deal of popular interest in the state's past, present, and future. As the favorite destination of countless tourists and as the new home for millions of retirees and other migrants, modern Florida has become a demographic, political, and cultural bellwether. But, unfortunately, the quantity and quality of the literature on Florida's distinctive heritage and character have not kept pace with the Sunshine State's enhanced status. In an effort to remedy this situation—to provide an accessible and attractive format for the publication of Florida-related books—the University Press of Florida established the Florida History and Culture series.

As coeditors of the series, we are committed to the creation of an eclectic but carefully crafted set of books that provides the field of Florida studies with a new focus and that encourages Florida researchers and writers to consider the broader implications and context of their work. The series includes standard academic monographs, works of synthesis, memoirs, and anthologies. And, while the series features books of historical interest, we encourage authors researching Florida's environment, politics, literature, and popular or material culture to submit their manuscripts for inclusion in the series. We want each book to retain a distinct "personality" and voice, but at the same time we hope to foster a sense of community and collaboration among Florida scholars.

In *Hitler's Soldiers in the Sunshine State*, Robert D. Billinger, Jr., examines one of modern Florida's least-known historical episodes: the incarceration of German prisoners of war in Florida during and immediately after World War II. Of the 378,000 German soldiers incarcerated in domestic American POW camps, approximately 10,000 spent part of their captivity in Florida. Two large sites—Camp Blanding, northeast of Starke, and Camp Gordon Johnston, on the outskirts of the isolated Panhandle town of Carrabelle—accommodated most of the state's German POWs, but at one time or another many prisoners lived and worked at one of the 25 smaller "side" camps that dotted the Florida landscape. Many POWs had little contact with American soldiers or civilians, but others had a more visible presence on the Florida home front. Working at a variety of jobs—from fruit picking and cane cutting to forestry and janitorial service—German POWs augmented several sectors of Florida's wartime economy and contributed to the growing diversity of the state. World War II brought major changes to Florida, and the infusion of German POWs was a significant, albeit atypical, part of this transformation.

Robert Billinger's extensive and imaginative use of archival and oral sources allows him to draw a richly textured portrait of the prisoners of war who labored under the Florida sun. His conversations with a number of former POWs—as well as his conversations with some of the Floridians who interacted with them—reveal a broad range of experience and a complex pattern of human behavior and intercultural contact. Told with verve and unblinking honesty, Billinger's stories of captivity and survival force us to reconsider facile generalizations about national character and comfortable stereotypes of Nazi war criminals. The flesh-and-blood human beings that populate the pages of his book are more interesting, and ultimately more believable, than the caricatured figures that often dominate the realm of popular history and memory. In this fine book, Robert Billinger not only illuminates a dark corner of Florida history; he also sheds light on the unintended consequences of war and the vagaries of the human condition.

Raymond Arsenault and Gary R. Mormino,
SERIES EDITORS

During World War II, many American captors learned that not all German POWs were alike, nor were they all Nazis. In fact, not all "Germans" were Germans. Most of the Wehrmacht were ethnically German, but many came from places like Austria, Czechoslovakia, Yugoslavia, Poland, and other countries within Hitler's sphere. Other prisoners were not Germans at all, but Baltic peoples coerced into Wehrmacht units, thus making German POWs in America and elsewhere more German in military uniform design than in ethnicity.

In Florida's prisoner of war camps, Hitler's soldiers, as well as their American captors, came to realize—to their amazement and sometimes horror—that differences of opinion and degrees of loyalty—to Hitler, to the Nazi government, and even to Germany—within the so-called German military were many and sometimes deadly. It was something that had to be dealt with on the national level, too, as some 378,000 German POWs reached American shores to be kept in 550 mostly small, rural, and isolated internment camps in forty-five of the forty-eight states.

For most of the German and American servicemen involved in the POW program in Florida, wartime was their first experience of the state. Their early contacts with the Florida environment and with each other were frequently not pleasant ones. Much later, the survivors of these early experiences would be left with mostly fond memories—memories that have led many veterans, American and German, to return with their families to the Sunshine State as visitors and residents in the postwar years. But the fond memories were usually the memories of advancing age among men—on both sides—who stayed in Florida camps long enough to remember some good times. German zealots of various political stripes, who made life in the camps a hell for their fellow prisoners and for their puzzled American captors, left Florida early, sent elsewhere by American military officers who could not tolerate "troublemakers," whether classified officially as "Nazis," "anti-Nazis," or just "troublemakers." The American army, trying to run a stable POW program on a massive scale, had little understanding of or patience for Germans who rocked the boat, no matter what the reason.

And the reasons were many. Underneath the uniforms of Hitler's military men lurked souls of diversity initially unimaginable to Americans and Germans alike. This diversity was bred by a variety of national, social, religious, regional, and ideological backgrounds. Divisiveness and alienation lurked beneath the surface of prison camp life outwardly regulated by their American captors, more immediately disciplined by a German command structure behind the barbed wire, and ultimately dependent on a mixture of immediate peer pressure and individual personality. Differences of military branch and experience also played a major role as well. Here, too, the differences were many, and they increased as wave after wave of Axis warriors arrived as captives on American shores between 1942 and 1945.

America's German wartime prisoners of war came to Florida as part of an international migration of captives that began to arrive in America almost as soon as the war began: first from U-boats sunk off the coast of North Carolina in 1942; then from Rommel's Corps, captured in North Africa in 1943; and, finally, from the Italian and French campaigns of 1944 and 1945. Ultimately, of the 378,000 German POWs in the United States, there were about 10,000 men in Florida's two major wartime base camps: Camp Blanding, near Starke, with nineteen smaller side camps holding a total of 7,500 men, and Camp Gordon Johnston, near Carrabelle, with three side camps of its own totaling about 2,500 men. The side camps of Camp Blanding included ones at Banana River, Belle Glade, Bell Haven, Clewiston, Dade City, Daytona Beach, Drew Field, Green Cove Springs, Homestead, Jacksonville, Kendall, Leesburg, MacDill Field, Melbourne, Orlando, Page Field, Venice, White Springs, and Winter Haven. For a brief period in April and May 1945 there was also a temporary Blanding work camp at Hastings. The side camps of Camp Gordon Johnston included Dale Mabry Field, Eglin Field, and Telogia. There were also POW camps in Florida that were side camps of out-of-state base camps. A temporary peanut-harvesting branch camp, set up at the Haag Show Grounds in Marianna, was a side camp of the base camp at Fort Benning, Georgia. Another POW camp was at the Naval Auxiliary Air Station Whiting Field. It was a branch camp of Camp Rucker, Alabama.

The POWs at these Florida camps were neither conquerors nor vacationers. But compared to the battle zones of North Africa, Russia, and Western Europe, their lives in Florida could have been and sometimes were experienced as "vacations." Nevertheless, they were put to work here, as elsewhere in the United States. Those who came to the Florida peninsula came as government-allocated fruit pickers and packers, sugarcane harvesters, potato diggers, pulpwood cutters, and custodial personnel for under-manned U.S. military bases. As replacements for an American civilian working population depleted by the draft, they served Uncle Sam and the American wartime economy.

My own exposure to German POWs did not occur first in Florida. It happened in Central Europe—in Austria and Germany. "You're an American, aren't you?" the desk clerk or barber or fellow train passenger would ask. "I used to work in America—for the American government. I harvested sugarcane [or picked fruit or did work in the motor pool] while in Florida [or Texas or Oklahoma or Arkansas] during World War II. Yes, I was a 'pensioned member of the Wehrmacht'—'Pensionierte Wehrmacht,' PW. It was marked on my clothing."

That was my first introduction to former Axis prisoners of war in America, and it came during the mid and late 1960s, when I was a student visitor in Austria and Germany. My interlocutors were usually men in their forties, friendly to a young American who spoke German—perhaps someone who looked about their age when they had first arrived in America between 1943 and 1945. They wanted to talk to someone who would express surprise at their stories, but they also wanted to talk about an experience that had, at least in hindsight, been among the best of their young lives.

Indeed, many of them had "grown up in America." They had been impressionable boys when drafted into the German army and became hardened war veterans—with experiences in Russia, North Africa, Italy, or France—before their capture. But they were still in their late teens or early twenties when they were introduced to the vastness, variety, and plenty of America. During their years in prisoner of war camps within the United States, they discovered many things. Most obviously there was America itself. It was an alien, bountiful, and materialistic land with its varied climates and peoples. In America—thanks to a carefully observed Geneva Convention—they had food, clothing, housing, and transportation like that received by America's own stateside GIs. What that meant, in effect, was generous meals with a daily meat ration for the first time since the beginning of the war, adequate housing, and comfortable transportation—passenger trains, not cattle cars. Also, along the way, the visitors discovered that America—far from exploding bombs and invading armies, except for the short but intense series of U-boat attacks off the Atlantic coast in the spring of 1942—was full of people, soldiers and civilians, who found it hard not to take them, the "enemy," into their lives and hearts. As one former POW wrote, he learned that "enemies are human."

Americans who experienced German servicemen on this side of the Atlantic frequently came to the same conclusion. That, too, is part of the story of German POWs in America, as I found out in Florida during my first college teaching years in West Palm Beach. There, like the German POWs of thirty years before, I encountered the former—and now older—little boys, farmers, preachers, and U.S. Army guards who had impressed and been impressed by their Wehrmacht charges. As among the former POWs, I found a warmth of memory and enthusiasm as these "older and wiser" Americans recalled with pleasure the lighter side of their contacts with their German "visitors." It turned out that the education had been mutual. These Americans, like the Germans I had met earlier, had also learned that "enemies are human."

But humanity has its drawbacks. Human individuality and intra- as well as intergroup diversity can make problems. Humans threaten other humans; countrymen injure and kill their countrymen; friends misuse friends. All of these aspects of humanity—the good and the bad—emerged as I examined the story of Hitler's soldiers in the Sunshine State. I have vivid memories of a middle-aged woman sharing a photo of a good-looking, friendly "Henri," who worked for the U.S. Corps of Engineers at Clewiston while detained at the Belle Glade camp. And I recall when a West Palm Beach judge, a former FBI agent, reached high on a bookcase to pull down a wartime diary, and we both watched as an old black-and-white photo fluttered to the floor. The photo, taken more than thirty years before, and forgotten over the years, revealed the hanging body of Karl Behrens. He was a young German escapee from the camp near Clewiston, who—in a state of depression—killed himself. The body was discovered by the FBI man and his partner those many years ago. The photograph was one taken to include in their official report of the escape and suicide. Later, I read with interest and horror U.S. military reports of protective segregation of prisoners within the POW compounds at Camp Blanding. Segregation was necessitated because of political differences that had been repressed within Nazi Germany and were revealed in brutal fashion in the interactions between the prisoners themselves. And, I began to consider the real possibility that not all of the German POWs who sought to escape the POW camps were fleeing their American captors; some were obviously fleeing the alienation and violence of their fellow captives.

On my journey through this study of wartime Florida, a journey that I began seriously in the late 1970s, I met many helpful and interesting people. I cannot begin to thank them all, because they have been so numerous and I so forgetful. Interviewees will be mentioned in the scholarly notes. But special appreciation goes to former Florida POWs who allowed me to correspond with them and interview them, repeatedly and in some detail. Gerhard Anklam, Werner Burkert, Herman (Horst) Finke, and Lüdeke Herder come foremost to mind. I am also grateful to the staff of the University of Florida Library and of the Modern Military and the Diplomatic Branches of the National Archives for their assistance on my many visits. Special thanks goes to Ken Schlessinger of Modern Military Records, National Archives at College Park, Maryland, for his help. For their help in obtaining interment records of Blanding's deceased POWs, I am grateful to the WASt people in Berlin and the personnel at the Fort Benning Post Cemetery. Special encouragement and assistance were also given by the nice people associated with the *Florida Historical Quarterly*, who published two of my articles on German POWs in Florida. Former editors Sam Proctor and Tony Pozzetta and assistant editor Mark Greenberg were particularly helpful. I must also thank my friend and colleague Professor Gary Mormino of the University of South Florida for his abiding interest in my study of Florida's German POWs. He has sent me copies of numerous useful newspaper clippings, new and old, over the years. Among these colleagues of the historical profession, I wish to thank Eliot Kleinberg of the *Palm Beach Post*. His interest in my research, use of it in his own articles, and persistent independent digging into the stories behind the POW stories have been an inspiration. I am also grateful to Peter Kehde of Lake-Sumter Community College, Martha Knapp, Eddie Herrmann, and Father Gregory V. Traeger, O.S.B., of Dade City, and Dr. Brian R. Rucker of Bagdad, Florida, for sharing information and contacts regarding the POW camps at Leesburg, Dade City, and Whiting Field. Finally, I want to thank my old friend, Austrian "brother," and historian colleague, Professor Siegfried Beer of the University of Graz. It was a summer with his family in Scheibbs, Austria, in 1965 that spurred my interest in Central European history. His own daring work in twentieth-century Austrian history has been an example and encouragement for my own research in this century. And, pleasantly, it was a reunion with him at Wingate University in the spring of 1997 that helped me develop a much better translation of the Bremer article presented in an appendix to this book.

I am also pleased to thank my colleagues at Wingate University for their interest and encouragement of my research over the years with their own scholarly examples, as well as through inquiries and words of support. Particularly I want to mention Professor Robert Doak, long-term friend and colleague from Florida and North Carolina days, who accompanied me on the early Florida lecture circuit. Also there has been the inspiration of my more recent colleague, Professor Scott Spencer, whose own special interests in the field of biblical studies have not prevented him from challenging me to a continuing scholarly and collegial dialogue. I also wish to thank the administration at Wingate University for their encouragement of my research. Particularly helpful have been a Jessie Ball duPont summer research grant in the summer of 1994 and a spring sabbatical in 1997. My undergraduate student co-researcher during the duPont research grant, Tomas Tolvaisas of Vilnius, Lithuania, was an enthusiastic and stimulating partner and has become a lifelong friend. Additional thanks to Sonny Baker, who helped me with a map, and to Lynn Moss, who gave my wife and me a hideaway in New Bern, North Carolina, while I revised this manuscript. Those revisions were greatly improved by the very helpful comments and suggestions of Philipp Gassert of the German Historical Institute and editors Meredith Morris-Babb and Judy Goffman and the staff and various anonymous outside readers for the University Press of Florida. I am most thankful for their efforts, which were prodigious and I hope not altogether futile. The improvements in the manuscript are chiefly theirs, the remaining faults my own. Two of the chapters appeared previously in the *Florida Historical Quarterly*, and I gratefully acknowledge their permission to use some of the same material.

Finally, and especially, I want to thank my wife, Chris, for all of her support. She has been my most receptive and interested audience and critic as the story of Hitler's soldiers in the Sunshine State developed. She, like most Americans, never realized that German prisoners of war had been held in the United States during World War II. And, she—like others involved in this tale—was pleased to conclude that enemies are human. But then, Chris knew, and she has taught me that all along.

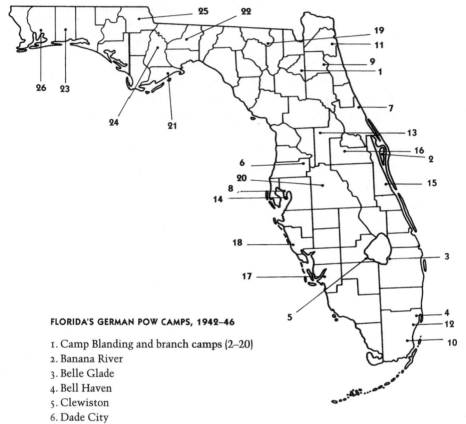

FLORIDA'S GERMAN POW CAMPS, 1942–46

1. Camp Blanding and branch camps (2–20)
2. Banana River
3. Belle Glade
4. Bell Haven
5. Clewiston
6. Dade City
7. Daytona Beach
8. Drew Field
9. Green Cove Springs
10. Homestead
11. Jacksonville
12. Kendall
13. Leesburg
14. MacDill Field
15. Melbourne
16. Orlando
17. Page Field
18. Venice
19. White Springs
20. Winter Haven
21. Camp Gordon Johnston and branch camps (22–24)
22. Dale Mabry Field
23. Eglin Field
24. Telogia
25. Marianna, branch camp of Fort Benning, Georgia
26. Whiting Field, branch camp of Camp Rucker, Alabama

Until the 1970s America's experience with large numbers of Hitler's soldiers on its shores was an untold story. The reason was simple: historians focused chiefly on the strategy and tactics of foreign battlefields, only later considering the implications of these developments on the home front. Even home front histories had little to say about German POWs in Florida or anywhere else. Amid the stories of death and destruction abroad and rationing, war brides, and the massive entry of women into the workplace at home, relatively small numbers of German, Italian, and Japanese prisoners of war on American shores were easily overlooked.[1]

They were overlooked by the wartime American public, too. This was not only because of their small numbers—378,000 Germans in mostly small rural camps—but it was also because of efforts by the American military authorities, whose goal was to limit popular knowledge regarding America's first large-scale POW program.[2] There were, of course, the provisions of the 1929 Geneva Convention regarding the handling of prisoners of war that were to protect prisoners, "particularly against acts of violence, insults and public curiosity."[3] But there was also the real concern that public awareness would bring either public fear or public criticism of government handling of the POWs and inhibit the most efficient use of POW labor within the United States.[4] Thus, the officially sanctioned and later tolerated press coverage of the POW program was relatively sparse. It took three forms: government-sponsored, and thus very positive, often pictorial, articles in national journals and newspapers; local newspaper coverage regarding the labor contributions, potential or real to local economies; and the relatively infrequent and brief physical descriptions and mug shots of escaped POWs, whose public identification and recapture was the official task of the FBI. The result was that few citizens in wartime America, with the exception of military guards and civilian employers of the POWs, were aware of their presence.

The earliest systematic American historical studies of the POW phenomenon began to appear in the 1970s. They were stimulated by a groundbreaking dissertation and by a helpful bibliographical essay that appeared in the journal *Military Affairs,* which set out the available parameters for research.[5] These parameters were being expanded at the time by the work of a German historical commission, which was created in 1957. With the support of the West German government it began the publication of a twenty-two-volume series dedicated to the fate of German prisoners of war on all fronts during World War II.[6] Shortly thereafter, there appeared a popular, and very professional, general study of the POW program, which has remained the standard work on the subject because of its particular emphasis on camp life and the internal conflicts within the camps.[7] It powerfully supplemented a slightly earlier study of the American government's attempt to reorient and "reeducate" the American-based prisoners.[8] The parameters for both sources and subjects were apparently set: government documents, interviews with prisoners and former guards, and contemporary publications were the sources, and the general subject of the nationwide POW program and specific aspects of that program—particularly the reorientation process—were the subjects. Further research and publication seemed merely duplication and explication of sources and themes.

By the 1980s there followed first a trickle and later a small stream of regional studies of the German POW experience in America that took the form of state and regional historical journal articles. Designed for a constituency of state and local historians and history buffs, they tended to focus on the experiences of Germans and Americans at some of the larger POW camps in places like Alabama, Louisiana, Virginia, North Carolina, and Indiana. Occasionally, they dealt with the impact of German POW labor on a sector of the wartime American economy such as the pulpwood industry.[9] My own first published study of German prisoners in Florida concerned the Camp Blanding POW story.[10]

In the last several years some of these state studies have developed from historical journal articles into book-length monographs. These works have focused either on unique camps or on the camps of an entire state.[11] Historians have begun to differentiate the complexities that faced both POWs and their American captors—subtleties of self-identification, allegiance, and motivation. There has also been an interesting book about the government's reorientation program. The author reached largely negative conclusions regarding its limited effectiveness.[12] Finally, there has been an oral history that has attempted to capture the memories and feelings of former POWs regarding various aspects of their internment experiences.[13] Thus, the historiographical trend has been from general studies to state, individual camp, and specific studies on particular aspects of the POW program.

Why write or read another state study when major aspects of the larger American POW experience have been covered in broader works or well illustrated in existing state studies in monographs and journals? And why Florida? The answer has both a unique regional component and a much more important generic one.

First, the regional component. Because of its climate and geography, conducive to agriculture, forestry, and military bases—as well as to tourism—Florida had an uncommon variety of locales, economies, and animal life for POWs to confront. Due to this variety, the Florida experience was the American POW experience in sunnier microcosm with additional unique factors thrown in. German POWs in Florida represented the wide variety of military formations, units, political factions, and nationalities found in Hitler's forces. They worked on military bases, in timbering, and in agriculture, just as POWs did throughout America. But they also picked citrus crops, harvested sugarcane in snake-infested fields, and worked in Miami Beach resort hotels like no other POWs did in America.

Still, Hitler's soldiers in the Sunshine State have received little attention from historians. Florida, after all, had neither the earliest large camps like those in Louisiana, Alabama, and Texas, nor major escapes such as occurred at Papago Park, Arizona, where some twenty-five prisoners staged a massive break.[14] Nor was it the scene of brutal murders of POWs by their comrades, such as occurred in Oklahoma, Arizona, and South Carolina, which led to courts-martial and death sentences for fourteen prisoners.[15] The last German POW escapee to turn himself over to American authorities fled from a camp in New Mexico, not Florida.[16]

But the Florida POW experience did have several features beyond exotic climate and animal life. For instance, Camp Blanding had the only officially designated "anti-Nazi" naval compound in the United States.[17] Additionally, Camp Blanding's separate German Army compound was the scene of open conflicts and riots in late 1943 that attracted official notice of both the American and German governments. They aroused the attention of those governments, and later of historians, because of the insights these conflicts uncovered concerning the wide diversity of political sentiments, allegiances, and even nationalities of Hitler's soldiers.[18]

It is attention to such Nazi versus anti-Nazi dynamics, the identification by repatriated Florida POWs of fellow prisoners as "traitors," and the problems faced by both American authorities and prisoners themselves with prisoner self-image that gives a study of the Florida camps a generic importance. National and specific camp studies have noted the existence of political conflicts within the camps. They have also focused on the American government's attempt to deal with "anti-Nazi" elements within the camps by setting up special anti-Nazi army compounds.[19] However, this study of Hitler's soldiers in Florida particularly highlights the political, moral, and national diversity among the prisoners themselves. Diversity runs like a red line throughout the story of German POWs in Florida between 1942 and 1946.

In POW camps in Florida, and particularly at the major base camp, Camp Blanding, the extreme diversity of the political and national allegiances, superficially concealed by the commonality of German uniforms, was clearly revealed. This revelation appeared to the horror of many of the German prisoners, even as it mystified and bewildered their American captors. For what was revealed was the difficulty for all concerned to identify and adequately classify the categories of diverse views. They were, in fact, often inchoate, overlapping, and more complex than official American intelligence categories like "Nazi" and "anti-Nazi." And, the application or misapplication of a categorical designation by fellow POWs could mean the difference between acceptance, ostracism, or even physical injury and death at the hands of self-appointed zealots who placed themselves in other categories. Such situations were vividly revealed by a series of separate incidents in both the naval and army compounds at Camp Blanding. These incidents in the two compounds will be the subjects of two separate chapters in this work.

However, conflicts—while the focus of this study—need to be seen in the context of a basically successful American POW program, in Florida as well as in the wider United States. To a large degree the success of the program had to do with the work program the government instituted in 1943. The use of POWs to replace sorely needed labor on American military bases and in the agricultural economy paid off. Uncle Sam got the labor he needed, and active POWs were relatively contented POWs. Furthermore, it was in their capacity as workers that the German POWs met American civilians—their fellow workers, supervisors, and employers. It was through such contacts that Americans and Germans began to discover their common humanity. It was also through these contacts at the workplace that individual personal idiosyncrasies, as well as political leanings, manifested themselves to the amazement, amusement, or anger of Americans, who were often more comfortable with the stereotype that "all Germans are Nazis."

Of course, the POW labor was not a total solution to problems that existed behind the wire. Therefore, the diversity of political opinions and allegiances within the camps arise again in two chapters devoted to escape attempts. Patterns among the identities and camp histories of would-be escapees indicate that a major factor in POW flight was alienation from elements within specific camps. Alienation rather than patriotism, the lure of freedom, or dissatisfaction with their American captors drove one man to suicide and motivated a significant number of the other thirty-two would-be Florida escapees.

The Florida press reported POW escapes and recaptures in varying degrees of detail. When the FBI was involved it controlled what appeared in the media. When local authorities were involved, the press was harder to control. Always ready for a story that would titillate readers and sell copy, the Fourth Estate plagued the POW program, which the government sought to keep low profile. One of the military's fears was that its adherence to the Geneva Convention would be misconstrued as "coddling." Indeed, in Florida—as throughout the United States—these charges arose in the press. It would take two studies and reports by the House Military Affairs Committee to satisfy critics. Two such press stories swept Florida, added to national concerns regarding "coddling," and had to be dealt with by the Military Affairs Committee. One story concerned elaborate-sounding menus at the POW facility at MacDill Field in Tampa. The other, which came on the heels of the first, was about a "strike" by German POWs at a bean-canning plant in Belle Glade. These stories, their impact, and their importance within the national context will be the focus of their own chapter in this book.

Moving beyond the stereotypes fed by the press, another chapter will deal again with the diversities of allegiances among the POWs, of which members of the press were unaware. These diversities did come to the attention of military authorities when they attempted to "reeducate" their captives. Original categories like Nazi and anti-Nazi sometimes had to be abandoned for the purpose of facilitating programs. A chapter on reeducation efforts will reveal some of these problems.

Finally, the concluding chapters discuss the fate of the POWs after their camps were closed in Florida in 1946. They left some of their number in Florida graves, but they left many fond memories in Floridian hearts. On the German side, later captivity in Britain and France and substandard living conditions in early postwar Germany deepened POW fondness for the "good times" in the Florida camps.

1

NATIONAL CONTEXT

Before one can focus on the unique and sometimes dangerously different personal and group identifications that German POWs assumed, it is necessary to know something of the contexts and settings in which this process of identification took place. World War II confronted the United States with a unique home front problem: what to do with thousands of enemy prisoners of war who, thanks to limited facilities in allied countries, would be sent to American shores. America's experience with foreign POWs was limited. There had been Hessians during the Revolutionary War, some Britains during the War of 1812, and a small number of German prisoners during the World War I. Initially, in World War II the number of POWs in the United States remained small. There were 32 POWs in the United States in May 1942—only 31 Germans and 1 Japanese. In November there were 380 Germans and 51 Japanese.[1] The problem of holding captured Axis soldiers still lay in the hands of Great Britain, an embattled empire with more than its share of home front concerns. Reluctant to enter the European war in the first place, the United States was hesitant to share Britain's POW housing problem. It was not without difficulty that in August 1942 Lord Halifax, the British emissary to the State Department, finally persuaded Washington to accept an "emergency batch of 50,000 enemy prisoners from Britain."[2] The really large numbers, however, began to arrive only after the defeat of Rommel's Afrika Korps in May of 1943. "On loan from the British and French government," about 135,000 of these men began appearing in the United States in June 1943.[3] The numbers continued to grow, until, as Arnold Krammer has pointed out, "by the late spring of 1944, the army found itself handling more German and Italian prisoners than there had been American soldiers in the entire pre-war U.S.

Army."[4] Ultimately there would be 378,898 Germans, 51,455 Italians, and 5,435 Japanese.[5] This study will focus on the largest group, the Germans, and of those only the 10,000 who were sent to camps in Florida. However, the big picture should be kept in mind in order to understand the development and evolution of the Florida camps.

Initially when large numbers of German POWs came to the United States the army used abandoned Civilian Conservation Corps camps, unused sections of regular military bases, and even fairgrounds and auditoriums to house POWs. These were located mainly in the rural South and Southwest so as to avoid potential Nazi sabotage. The sections of the United States chosen for POW camps were in areas commanded by the army's Eighth Service Command: particularly in New Mexico, Texas, Oklahoma, Louisiana, and Arkansas; the Ninth Service Command: especially in Arizona; the Seventh Service Command: particularly Missouri; and the Fourth Service Command: especially in Tennessee, Mississippi, and Alabama.[6] By September 1942, the War Department had nine camps in existence, eight in the building stage, five approved for construction, and ten provisional camps.[7]

Among these provisional camps was one at the American military base at Camp Blanding, near Starke, Florida. In September 1942, it began providing housing for U-boat captives. A separate compound, also within the large military installation, had earlier held civilian "enemy aliens" from several of the Central American states. They had arrived at Blanding in January.[8] The German Army compound at Camp Blanding that was activated in November 1943 would be the largest POW base camp within the state. It would be the administrative center for nineteen smaller side camps that would dot the peninsula. Most of these smaller camps would have only 250 to 300 men, compared to the 1,000 or so at the Blanding base camp. Later, beginning in March 1944, another base camp would be developed at Camp Gordon Johnston, near Carrabelle, and with three of its own side camps, it would bring a German POW presence to the western panhandle as well. The most important camp in Florida, however, would remain the POW base camp at Camp Blanding.

The U.S. military installation at Camp Blanding was located on property purchased by the Florida National Guard in 1939, when its former camp, Camp Foster, outside of Jacksonville, was turned over to the U.S. Navy for use as an air base. Named for Maj. Gen. Albert H. Blanding—World War I commander of the Thirty-first Dixie Division, later Florida National Guard bureau chief and Florida state defense chief during World War II—Camp Blanding was activated as a federal military facility on September 14, 1940. It was located on the east shore of Kingsley Lake, near Starke, about forty miles inland from Jacksonville, and it served as a major training depot for American troops during World War II. Its rural, isolated location and immense size—150,000 acres—made it an admirable place in which to hold prisoners of war easily and inconspicuously. Several thousand Germans could be overlooked by even the most inquiring eyes within a military reservation that could handle up to 75,000 American trainees at a time, had 125 miles of paved roads, and utilities equal to those of a city for 100,000. In fact, during World War II the U.S. military reservation at Camp Blanding was a community equivalent to Florida's fifth largest city.[9]

The German POW compounds—a small one for naval personnel and a larger one for army personnel—within the larger Blanding installation were located about a half mile from each other. Both compounds conformed to national standards at the time and were representative of the type of facilities that POWs inhabited. Four six-by-six-foot guard towers without catwalks stood at the four corners of the 200-man naval compound. But only two of the four towers were manned at all times. Different towers were occupied each day. From the towers, guards watched over the compound that lay within a double row of fencing constructed of cyclone wire, with a three-strand overhang of barbed wire. The inner fence was approximately seven feet in height and the outer fence a standard ten feet. Between the fences there was a "skinned area," which with the sod removed left a sandy area for easy escape detection.[10]

The majority of the buildings used for mess halls were old CCC barracks. The POWs' sleeping quarters were sixteen-by-sixteen-foot "victory-type hutments"—an improvement over the tents that housed the earlier enemy alien internees at the former U.S. military stockade about a mile away from the new POW compounds. The prisoners slept on canvas cots, but they were also issued mattresses. Naval officers had separate quarters within the same compound in which the naval enlisted men were confined. They also used the same mess and latrine facilities assigned for use by the enlisted men.

The larger army compound, like the naval compound, was described in a report by a State Department visitor as situated on a "slightly elevated tract of land" with a good number of "second growth white oak trees laden with trailing moss." Smaller blackjack oaks were also found in considerable numbers within the compounds. Both varieties afforded "comfortable shade during the heat and humidity of the summer months, especially enervating in August."[11] The buildings were old CCC barracks, but, painted olive drab and situated among the many pine trees growing throughout the compound areas, they presented "a very pleasing appearance."[12]

There was no doubt, however, that the army compound, with its "very pleasing appearance," was a prison that conformed to national standards. A visiting army inspector reported that all buildings within and outside the compound areas were at least seventy-five feet from the fences that surrounded the compounds. The fences were "standard double fencing with the inner fence constructed of hog wire." The lower half of the outer fence was of cyclone wire, with the upper part of hog wire and a three-stand overhang of barbed wire. There were eight six-by-six-foot guard towers, equipped with catwalks, around the perimeter of the army compound. Each tower, whose base was more than six feet above the fence, was equipped with a floodlight. Corner towers had machine guns mounted on the catwalks.[13]

Camp Blanding's compounds for enemy aliens, U-boat prisoners, and eventually POWs from the larger, earlier base camps in Aliceville and Opelika, Alabama, were part of a vast nationwide administrative program that had to be started from scratch with the beginning of the war in Europe. In anticipation of America's involvement in World War II, plans were developed for administration of enemy internees. Secretary of War Henry Lewis Stimson and the army's chief of staff Gen. George C. Marshall created a special division to deal with these problems. This new creation was the Office of the Provost Marshal General (PMGO). On July 31, 1941, Maj. Gen. Allen W. Gullion, the serving judge advocate general of American forces, was named to the post of provost marshal general.[14] Guarding interned enemies and later prisoners of war were to be only two of the PMGO's functions. The provost marshal general was also responsible for the organization and training of the military police and the protection of military and industrial installations from acts of sabotage.[15]

According to an agreement between the War Department and the Department of Justice of July 18, 1941, the PMGO became responsible for civilian internment camps as well as for internment camps for military prisoners of war.[16] Because in May 1942 the PMGO had only thirty-two POWs, its original detention concerns were with civilian internees. Initially, these were several thousand Japanese, German, and Italian aliens living in the United States who were investigated and ordered detained by the Justice Department.[17]

The War Department and Justice Department were not the only U.S. government agencies involved in the enemy alien and POW programs. Because of their international ramifications, the State Department was also involved. As provided for by the Geneva Convention, "protecting powers," including governments officially designated by belligerent countries and international organizations concerned with prisoners' welfare, such as the International Red Cross and the YMCA, were empowered to monitor the interests of POWs. Representatives of the U.S. State Department worked directly with these agencies. With the commencement of hostilities between the United States and Germany, in December 1941 the Legation of Switzerland, with its Department of German Interests, became the official "protecting power" of German citizens held in the United States. It continued in that role until the defeat of Germany in May 1945. After that, the U.S. government unilaterally declared that the German government no longer needed a third party to represent its interests in the United States. The result was that the International Red Cross (IRC) assumed most of the duties of the former Swiss representatives. Likewise, the YMCA continued its somewhat modified religious and recreational programs.[18]

It was through the good offices of the Swiss, along with those of the IRC and YMCA, that the German Foreign Office sought to protect its citizens. The process involved the Swiss government, acting through its legation in Washington—or the IRC or YMCA through their offices in Geneva and New York, respectively—working with the U.S. State Department. The State Department, through its Special Division, then communicated with the War Department and its Office of the Provost Marshal General, which was responsible for the German internees.

But the circuit for the passage of information was even more complicated, because the Office of the Provost Marshal General did not deal directly with the internees. The PMGO, originally under the army chief of staff, was placed, after a War Department reorganization of March 9, 1942, under a new division called Services of Supply. It was renamed after March 12, 1943, as Army Service Forces (ASF). In fact, until April 1943 the PMGO was not even directly under the commander of the ASF. The PMGO was one of nine administrative services of the ASF and did not report directly to the commanding general. Reports went indirectly through the chief of administrative services and the chief of staff of the ASF. However, after April 1943 the PMGO was placed under the Personnel Division, one of the staff of the commander of the ASF. After November 1943 the PMGO was ordered to report to the commanding general of the ASF through his deputy chief of staff for service commands. Finally, at the end of 1945 the PMGO reported directly to the commander of the ASF.[19] It was as complicated as it sounds.

In all of this bureaucratic hierarchy it was through the PMGO's Alien Division for civilians and the PMGO's Prisoner of War Division for military personnel that the State Department sought information about detainees or registered the complaints of the Swiss Legation. It was also in the company of a representative of the State Department's Special Division that the Swiss Legation and its representatives—as well as IRC and YMCA officials—visited internment facilities, spoke with internees and their captors, and reported its findings to the German Foreign Office, as well as to the U.S. State Department, and through the State Department to the U.S. War Department. Then the PMGO, on behalf of the War Department, worked through the Corps Area Commanders to contact local internment camp commanders.[20]

Florida, like most of the southeastern part of the United States was part of the Fourth Service Command, which had its headquarters in Atlanta. When contacted by the War Department and its

Office of the Provost Marshal General, the office of the Area Service Commander of the Fourth Service Command communicated with the appropriate military post commanders and their internment camp officers. That was the labyrinth of command structures that dealt with situations called to the State Department's attention through the visits of members of the Swiss Legation or through individual detainees, who, at the other end of the chain, contacted the office of the PMGO through camp, post, and service area commands.[21]

Meanwhile, at the POW camp level, a dual set of administrations existed, sometimes in active tension with each other: an American camp structure outside the wire and a German camp structure behind the wire.

While the larger POW base camps, like those at Camp Blanding and Camp Gordon Johnston, had a post commander from the larger military installation under whom a separate POW compound commander and command system had to function, smaller base camps, as detachments from the POW command structure of the larger compounds, often were commanded by an American first lieutenant, several sergeants, and a company of camp guards. Originally these guards came from specially formed military police escort companies (MPECs). As the war progressed, guards were introduced into military escort companies who had minimal or no military police training and were allocated to camps from ASF commands that selected "superfluous" personnel. These were men deemed physically or psychologically unfit for overseas service, recently retired officers or those with low achievement ratings, recycled combat veterans, and raw recruits.[22] The results frequently led to POW confrontations with American officers and guards who were aware of their own inexperience and lack of prowess compared to that of the real or imagined experience, prowess, and unit pride of their captives. This was particularly true of POWs from the German U-boats and Afrika Korps, some of the earliest and longest tenured German personnel in American camps.

The command structure behind the wire did little to smooth the potential problems. Prisoners were required to elect a compound spokesman to voice grievances and requests to the American camp authorities. Although the spokesman held his position at the discretion of the U.S. camp commander, he had a lot of leverage on his side. One reason was that the spokesman was usually the highest ranking prisoner in the camp. Because officers were separated from enlisted men and sent to separate camps, this meant most camps had spokesmen chosen from the highest ranking noncommissioned officers present in the camp, usually sergeants. This was true in all of the Florida POW camps and compounds, with the exception of the naval compound at Blanding, which for a while actually had a U-boat captain as the senior camp spokesman. However, despite the fact that spokesmen were not to exercise authority over fellow prisoners, German military traditions and command structures were retained within the camps. Additionally, camp spokesmen were empowered by the Geneva Convention to represent the prisoners when camps were visited by representatives of the Swiss Legation, IRC, and YMCA. This gave them additional influence among their comrades and with the American authorities. The spokesmen functioned as conduits of information to international channels that led directly to the German Foreign Office and Military High Command. Their communications had the potential to affect the German treatment of American prisoners in Europe. It could also determine the fate of German POWs when they returned home.[23]

Life behind the wire was officially regulated and monitored by the War Department, State Department, Swiss Legation, IRC, and YMCA on the macro level and by the U.S. camp commanders and German spokesman on the micro level. But the real influences on the lives of individual POWs came in their contacts with smaller, more immediate, and less official peer groups. It was fellow prisoners—with all their personal, political, and ideological idiosyncrasies—who impacted most directly on a German POW's life. Prisoners interacted in contexts that might be categorized as "the typical camp routine": recreation, work, and education. As the categories of work and education will be the focus of two later chapters, the focus here can be on "typical routine" and recreation within the Florida camps—as within every camp in America.

Daily routines began with reveille at 5:30 A.M., when the Germans were awakened in their American army tents or barracks by whistle-blowing American sergeants. Each prisoner pulled on his U.S.-issued navy blue fatigue uniform, pants and shirt each marked with the white letters PW. German-issued uniforms were kept for leisure time. Prisoners then headed for an American-style mess hall run by fellow German cooks, who served an American-style breakfast that often included cornflakes. Geneva Convention provisions provided for captives to be housed, clothed, and fed like garrison troops of their captors, and so it was throughout the war as the American government attempted to protect its own men in German hands by strict adherence to the high standards of the 1929 agreement.[24]

After breakfast and general policing of his living area, each German began his morning ablutions using soap, toothpaste, shaving cream, and a razor bought by himself with the ten cents a day he automatically received from the U.S. government in the form of canteen coupons. He would later receive an additional eighty cents per day in canteen coupons for work assigned around the American military base or from work done under government contract with local civilian agricultural or lumbering interests.[25]

Between 7:30 A.M. and 4:30 P.M., Monday through Saturday, the prisoner performed manual labor, unless he was an officer not required to work or a noncommissioned officer required only to do supervisory duties. He would do warehouse work, construction, or KP work at an American military facility, or he would be involved in timbering, agricultural labor, or possibly bean canning at a civilian-owned plant.[26] At noon he would get his lunch, most likely a bologna sandwich or soup sent along from the POW camp.

By 5 P.M. he was behind barbed wire again to take a shower, change clothes, and have dinner. In the evening, until lights out at 10 P.M., he could amuse himself with sports like soccer, table tennis, or Faustball; attend an English, math, or American history class in the camp; pay to see an American movie in the compound recreation hall; or relax at the POW-run compound canteen. Items available in the canteen could be bought with his hard-earned prison coupons. These items included soap, handkerchiefs, and writing implements, selected American newspapers and magazines, soda, and even tobacco and up to two bottles of beer a day when they were available. The POW canteen was administered by the prisoners themselves, and profits earned could be used by the POW community to purchase sporting equipment or musical instruments for communal free-time activities.

In short, every aspect of life behind the wire followed a routine established by the Geneva Convention, the American military, and equally importantly the discipline of the German army, which the prisoners generally imposed on themselves. Except in the case of a sit-down strike or a camp riot, when American guards went into the camps to maintain order, the German Army sergeants controlled their own men as though the camps were "ordinary Wehrmacht training camp[s] in Germany."[27] This fact caused immeasurable problems for both American guards and individual POWs when soldiers of both armies made the mistake of thinking that Americans controlled the camps. To their horror, they sometimes confronted the iron hand of Nazi-enforced ideological discipline. Even more perplexing, they found—in Florida and elsewhere—that not just Nazi and anti-Nazi conflicts simmered, but so too did conflicts between service units and individual personalities.

2

UNCLE SAM'S SMILING WORKERS

THE FIRST WAVE: CANE CUTTERS, PULPMEN,
ORANGE PICKERS, AND MILITARY BASE WORKERS

Healthy young men with smiling faces were working in the Florida sunshine. The faces were German. During the day their owners wore U.S. Army fatigues with distinctive white PW lettering, but at night they returned to variants of their weathered Wehrmacht uniforms. They were Americans—or almost—by day, Hitler's soldiers by night. They led two lives.

But it is the smiling faces that are most remembered by the "alumni" of the POW program in Florida. In light of the fact that Hitler's soldiers in Florida revealed the ideological, social, and psychological cleavages that ran deep below the veneer of Nazi ideological uniformity and German military discipline, it seems odd to focus first on a work program that provided Germans and Americans with happy memories and the idea that enemies are human. However, pleasant memories that effaced earlier adversarial stereotypes were part of an evolving cognitive process. It was a stage in the changing mutual perceptions that remained an important impact of the wartime experiences on the lives of participants. Preconceptions that all of Hitler's soldiers were Nazis were replaced in the minds of many Floridians with an equally generalized image of the smiling boy next door. A similar process took place among the POWs. Americans, particularly guards and American civilians with whom they had contact during work experiences, began to be seen as fellow workers, comrades, or even friends. The process was not uniform. Old stereotypes remained or could be easily revived, but a negative set of stereotypes began to be replaced by a set of more positive ones. Nevertheless they were still stereotypes. Coming to understand their development entails understanding the POW work program in the United States in general and in Florida in particular.

The prospect of large numbers of idle German prisoners of war within the United States presented a potential security problem. But there was a solution to that problem and to the wartime manpower shortage at military installations and in the civilian economy. It was a POW work program. As early as January 1943, long before the first major influx of German POWs onto American shores, Washington decided to use future prisoner labor on American military reservations. Only in April, however, was the decision made to allow their use in civilian contract work as well. It seemed logical that the German prisoners might fill the gaps. Additionally, in the case of civilian contract work off base, it was the federal government that received the normal wage rates for civilian labor. It banked the funds and provided the POWs only with a standard eighty cents a day.[1] At the same time, work took POWs' minds off boredom and troublemaking.

It was decided to disperse the prisoners throughout the United States to, first, furnish labor for military installations and, second, make them available for civilian contract labor where the need was certified by the War Manpower Commission.[2] In fact, on August 14, 1943, a new directive was issued by Army Service Forces that stressed maximum employment but established three priorities of work. Priority I was essential work for the maintenance and operation of military installations; priority II was contract labor for private employers certified as necessary labor by the War Manpower Commission of the War Foods Administration; and priority III was useful but nonessential work connected with U.S. military installations.[3]

So it was that large numbers of German prisoners of war came to the Sunshine State and the number and purposes of the Florida camps proliferated. In the process stereotypes began to disintegrate. Real cleavages within the POW population remained masked to Americans. They began to be repressed even in the consciousness of the prisoners themselves. They found exhilaration of common purpose and teamwork on the labor front as they had on the battlefront.

Fifteen POW camps in Florida were visited by representatives of the International Red Cross in the spring of 1945. Nine of these— of which the Camp Blanding and Camp Gordon Johnston POW base camps were the largest—were on or attached to military bases. Six other camps were located in farming regions and were specifically set up to provide labor to the civilian farming industry. In Florida this meant in the citrus, sugarcane, or truck gardening industries.[4] Yet the numbers of the camps, while representing the priority given by the military to providing their own installations with labor, is misleading in terms of the chronological proliferation of the camps. The early POW branch camps in Florida were a response to the labor demands of Florida's agricultural and forestry interests. Of course, major military reservations became the Florida base camps, and military labor requirements received first priority. Blanding received its first complement of German Army POWs in November 1943, and Camp Gordon Johnston got its first POWs in March of 1944. However, the first branch camps to be hived-off from these two Florida base camps were created as a response to civilian needs. In the case of Blanding, agricultural branch camps included Clewiston and Leesburg, developed in February and March 1944, respectively. There were additional branch camps at Dade City by April 1 and at Winter Haven by April 15. A branch camp for forest work at White Springs was also activated by May 1.[5] For Gordon Johnston, the first civilian contract camp was set up at Telogia in June of 1944 to supply wood for the pulpwood industry.[6] For a brief period, two other agricultural branch camps existed in Florida. One was at Marianna, in Jackson County, which functioned as a side camp of Fort Benning between August and October 1944. Its purpose was to assist with the peanut harvest. It was again set up to help harvest peanuts in Jackson and adjoining counties in the summer of 1945.[7] Another agricultural camp was at Hastings in St. Johns County. It functioned as a work camp of Blanding in April and May of 1945.[8]

In January 1944, Paul V. McNutt, chairman of the War Manpower Commission, informed Senator Claude Pepper of Florida that he had certified to the War Department the need for the establishment of seven auxiliary prisoner of war camps in Florida. McNutt said that the camps were being requested "in order to supply muchly [sic]

needed labor in pulp wood cutting and gathering of naval stores."
The seven locations certified and awaiting army approval were at
Cottondale, Live Oak, Wewahtoka, Worthington Springs, Telogia,
Tallahassee, and Clewiston. The regional WMC office in Atlanta
requested 2,000 war prisoners for harvesting sugarcane in Clewiston alone.[9] Of course, what was requested and received were two
different things. By April, the sugarcane cutting camp at Clewiston
had only 300 men.[10] As for pulpwood cutting, only Telogia, a
branch camp of Gordon Johnston, and White Springs, a branch
camp of Blanding, produced labor reports by mid-June 1944.[11] Many
of the original sites for camps were not chosen and others were
erected instead.

When delegates from the International Red Cross, Swiss Legation, and Special Division of the U.S. Department of State visited
the base camp at Camp Blanding in April 1944, the POW camp
already consisted of two separate compounds. The naval compound, which at the time of their visit held 76 men, had been in
existence since September 1942. The larger army compound, with
766 men, had been created in November 1943, when 1,000 POWs
from earlier base camps at Aliceville and Opelika, Alabama, were
transferred to the new Florida army compound.[12] The majority of
prisoners worked within or near the camp. They were involved
in upkeep of the land, buildings, and rolling stock. "Until the
dispatch recently of a number of prisoners to side camps 85% or
more of those available were working for the most part in Camp
Blanding activities."[13]

The former wartime American executive officer at Camp Blanding, Col. Harry A. Johnston, recalled that the German workers usually outdid themselves in their labor efforts. When watch repairs
were needed, the Germans were called on and their technicians
exceeded quotas achieved by previous American workers by 50
percent. In the motor pool, where Americans tended to throw away
old spark plugs, the Germans cleaned and fixed them in less time
than was usually taken by Americans doing only part of the job.
The colonel was particularly impressed by the work of the Germans at the officers mess, which was run during the war by Del-
monico, the famous Miami restaurant manager. The kitchen, Johnston recalled, was spotless. And, when through an interpreter he
commended the German NCO on duty, the German requested a

letter of recommendation so that he might secure a job with the merchant marine after the war.[14]

While Camp Blanding POWs continued throughout the war to concentrate primarily on post and military reservation tasks, the early branch camps were quite different. They were to become very important to the agricultural economy of Florida. The first of these branch camps was the sugarcane cutting camp at Clewiston. But it was only the first. By April 1944, 126 Germans had been sent from Blanding to the new branch camp at Leesburg. They were put to work in citrus fruit picking. An additional labor company of 250 Germans arrived at Blanding on March 28 from Fort McClellan, Alabama, to be sent to Winter Haven to work in fruit preserving plants. On April 1 still another company of 250 men, this time coming from Camp Gordon, Georgia, were sent directly to Dade City to help the citrus industry there. An additional 250 POWs due to arrive at Blanding on April 18 from Fort McClellan were to be sent to White Springs for pulpwood work.[15]

The sugarcane cutting camp set up at Clewiston in February 1944 was one of Florida's first branch camps. But, according to at least one IRC report, it was "the worst camp in America."[16] Memorable enough to have its own chapter, the Clewiston camp needs only brief mention here. Located at Liberty Point, just north of Clewiston and on the shores of Florida's largest lake, Lake Okeechobee, this camp required some of the most strenuous work and provided the harshest living conditions in Florida. The prisoners who arrived there, directly from the camp at Aliceville, Alabama, in February 1944, were all Afrika Korps men. Though later supplemented by captives from the Italian and Normandy campaigns, it was the Afrika Korps that dominated the camp and influenced its atmosphere. They were tough guys, and they were given tough work. Of the 293 men at the camp, 235 were involved in the sugar fields, working eight-hour days for eighty cents a day. In the eyes of both prisoners and a Red Cross visitor, the harvesting of sugarcane was certainly the most difficult and dangerous of jobs. Using machetes, they cut about 9,000 pounds of sugarcane a day. It often required working in clouds of dust in the dry season and in tropical temperatures, which in summer reached the 100-degree Fahrenheit range.[17]

Worse, in the view of a Red Cross delegate, was another problem. "The danger of snakes is constant and each day the prisoners or the

Negroes who work in the fields kill many."[18] On the other hand, a former American guard at the camp expressed his belief that the real danger in the fields was *to* the snakes. He remembered that many of the Germans enjoyed catching and killing the snakes, especially as the fields were burned over in preparation for harvesting. In fact, he noted, the Germans asked permission to stand at the edges of the burning fields so that they might catch the fleeing reptiles. The Germans' purpose was to tan the hides for souvenir belts, mementos of their days in Florida.[19]

Conditions were better for everyone in Leesburg. The POWs were engaged in more pleasant work in citrus groves, packing plants, and truck farms in a less isolated area of central Florida. They enjoyed weekly Sunday swims in a nearby lake. They even developed their own little menagerie of pet animals.[20]

On March 11, 1944, the *Florida Times-Union* of Jacksonville ran an article titled "Leesburg Is Site of New Camp for War Prisoners." It was only through articles such as this—along with occasional FBI announcements regarding escapes—that the American public learned of the presence of German POWs. In order to prevent unnecessary fears, information regarding the presence of POWs was kept to a minimum. The historian, like the wartime American public during World War II, could look long and hard in the newspapers of the period to find the few references to local POW camps. National periodicals were occasionally fed scripted generalized information about the POW program by the government, but regional and local papers usually confined themselves to POW stories of business interest. In the process, however, they revealed much about both the local economy and the perceived importance of German POWs to that economy.[21]

The March 11 article in the Jacksonville paper noted that the Leesburg camp, soon to be the home of 125 Germans, was named as one of five new camps announced by the Fourth Service Command in Atlanta. It was stated that the Leesburg camp was to help with harvesting the citrus crop. The other four camps—at Loxley, Alabama; Brookhaven, Mississippi; and White Springs and Telogia, Florida—were to accommodate 250 men each and were to be created to help the southern pulpwood industry.[22]

The *Leesburg Commercial* of Friday, March 17, expanded on the earlier Jacksonville article. It mentioned the arrival of 125 Germans at the Lake County Farm Labor Supply Center on Wednesday, March 15. Their job would be to help harvest the bumper grapefruit, orange, and tangerine crops in the Leesburg area. Actually, it was noted, there had been calls for about 375 POW workers. According to J. M. Campbell, president of the Growers Marketing Service, the plan was eventually to bring a total of 400 to 500 men to the area.[23] In March 1945 there would be 272 POWs in the Leesburg camp.[24] The Germans worked in citrus groves, packing plants, and truck farms in Leesburg, Eustis, Tavares, and Mount Dora. They helped Paul Miller's construction company building houses in Leesburg. They assisted in the construction of a bean cannery and a portion of a Minute Maid plant.[25]

Thirty years after the Germans' departure, Leesburg area residents had very positive views of their mutual experience. Karol Borodine, who used prisoners to pick fruit, said, "They were marvelous and honest workers." Paul Miller remembered only one minor problem. While helping to build some homes on South Twelfth Street in Leesburg, POW carpenters made latticework using the design of the German swastika. "It didn't stay up 24 hours; I told them to take it down and redo the work." Other than that, "I never had five minutes of trouble with them."[26] A former American officer at the camp said, "The worst offense committed by the prisoners was stealing watermelons."[27]

Another instance of German-American interaction was remembered by Nancy Miller of Leesburg. She was a twelve-year-old, living with her family in Fruitland Park, when an army guard asked her father permission to allow a gang of German fruit pickers to cool off with a swim in the family lake. A U.S. Army searchlight unit was nearby and soon Miller heard American and German voices down at Crystal Lake: "The POWs and American servicemen from the searchlight battery were down there splashing about, swimming, joking, laughing, just having a real good time together." She said she thought it a strange scene, "American soldiers and their enemy sharing such a good time with each other while a world war was going on."[28]

In March 1945 the Leesburg camp was moved seven miles from its original tent camp site to a new location just east of Leesburg. It was on a portion of the Florida Field Station branch of the Watson Laboratories (radar) of the Army Air Force. The land was later occupied by Lake-Sumter Community College, across from the Lees-burg Municipal Airport.[29] Delegates from the International YMCA and from the International Red Cross who visited the new camp location found a degree of good humor and goodwill not usual in other camps. No doubt, part of the reason was the relatively pleas-ant working conditions in the citrus groves, truck farms, and pack-ing plants of central Florida. Additionally, under the palm trees and live oaks covered with Spanish moss, there was a beer garden that the Germans constructed for their after-work relaxation. There seemed to be an easy working relationship between the American military and their captives. Guy Métraux, representing the Interna-tional Red Cross, noted that each Sunday, prisoners were taken by truck to swim in a lake about ten kilometers from the camp. About 250 of the 272 POWs in the camp went along.[30]

Métraux also reported that the prisoners had developed quite a menagerie. As was the case at the Clewiston camp, the American military personnel noticed that the Germans were particularly avid snake hunters. Probably because there were so few snakes in Germany, the POWs were intrigued by the variety they encoun-tered in central Florida.[31] The Germans' pet collection briefly in-cluded even a six-foot-long alligator, which they brought back from a work detail. The POWs said that they planned to tame it. When the gator took a bite at the leg of a prisoner, they decided to release it. They were encouraged in that decision by the American camp commander, Capt. Benjamin Painter. He told the German spokes-man, Sgt. Heinz Kuhn, that the next time an animal like that was brought to camp, the prisoner responsible and the alligator would be held in the same cell.[32]

Like the camp at Leesburg, another was soon constructed at Win-ter Haven. The 250 POWs, a standard-size POW company, who arrived at Camp Blanding from Fort McClellan, Alabama, on March 28, 1944, were held there only a week. Their destination was the citrus processing plants in Winter Haven, some 165 miles away.[33] The local newspaper coverage of the planning for their ar-rival revealed to Floridians the nature, purpose, and precautions associated with the POW work program in the United States. The Winter Haven Daily Chief announced on Wednesday, March 22, 1944: "250 Nazi Prisoners To Be Used in Citrus Plants In City."

John A. Snively, Jr., president of the Orange Festival Corporation, announced that plans had been completed to bring German POWs to work in citrus canning and packing plants. The Festival Corporation had leased to the army its grounds and buildings, which were normally used to house recruited farm labor. The military had already moved in and installed road blocks and begun to put up an electrified fence. The article explained that the plan to use POWs in the city's citrus packing plants had developed out of a public meeting that had discussed the use of POW labor. The result was that individual packers and canners had filed reports of their labor needs. Use of German POW labor was then approved by the Fourth Service Command in Atlanta. The agreement with the army, the *Daily Chief* explained, was that the army would pay for the maintenance of the prisoners, while the citrus group taking part in the plan would pay for the utilities and rent. The POWs would be paid scale wages, but the amount over the eighty cents a day that each POW personally earned would be turned over to the army to meet maintenance costs.[34]

Another article on March 28, 1944, set the stage for the arrival of the Germans. It explained the benefits of their labor, the nature of the expanding POW work program, and the security precautions that were being taken. The tone and content of the article reveal much about central Florida in the mid-1940s:

> The usually dependable darky laborer is no longer too dependable. He is here today and gone tomorrow, he makes enough money in two or three days to satisfy his needs, and takes time off the remainder of the week. Putting German POWs out to work in fields and groves, mine and forest, here and elsewhere, is only a logical development of the changed economy under which we live during war times. The people of Florida, and other southern states, can expect to see war prisoner labor camps dotted here and there about the country side. It is economic good sense to put German POWs to work where they will be most useful to our home economy and the war effort by taking the place of men who are called into the service. . . . Precautions will be taken, of course, to keep these war prisoners from escaping or coming in contact with the

public. There will be armed guards and concentration centers behind wire barricades, etc., and in time, no doubt, their presence in a given locality will be accepted as one of those war time developments.[35]

By the spring of 1945, the POW tent camp was located in a large park in the center of the "little town of Winter Haven," fifty meters from a beautiful lake. Its layout very favorably impressed a visiting delegate of the International Red Cross. He noted that in front of each six-man tent, there was a small garden with flowers and tropical plants.[36]

The citrus industry of central Florida was the major beneficiary of the first wave of branch camp expansion in Florida. In addition to the Leesburg and Winter Haven camps, there was soon a camp at Dade City. The branch camp of Blanding at Dade City was set up in April 1944. It received its own labor company of 250 Germans, who came by train directly from Camp Gordon in Augusta, Georgia. They were to work in a citrus packing plant of the Pasco Packing Association and at the lumber mill at Lacoochee, operated by Cummer and Sons Cypress Company. The need for their labor was certified by the Tampa office of the U.S. Employment Service.[37] On their arrival on Saturday, April 15, it was noted that most of the prisoners were young. And, they arrived singing. An American officer remarked that they "soon would be singing God Bless America."[38] That would not be totally true: the Dade City camp produced several of the numerous Florida POW escape attempts, which will be the focus of another chapter.

The Dade City camp also had an interesting civilian female fraternization problem that illustrated some of the potential complications associated with POW utilization. J. L. Toohey of the Department of State, who accompanied Paul Schnyder of the International Committee of the Red Cross on his visit to the camp on November 29, 1945, reported the problem. About a month before their visit one of the prisoners was threatened and mistreated by two American guards. Investigating the complaint, Toohey discovered the difficulty of determining what really happened.

He stated in his report that it seemed that both of the Dade City POW work details—at the Cummer Cypress Company and the Pasco Packing Association—worked with or near civilian women.

Prior to the November 1945 visit by the representatives of the IRC and State Department, the guards had made no attempt to segregate the prisoners from either firm's civilian employees during their lunch hour—something that had since been changed. There had been several instances of prisoners receiving notes, money, and cigarettes from American working women. And, while the Pasco Packing Association fired female employees discovered engaging in such practices, the Cummer Cyprus Company did not. On one occasion a letter from a female employee of that company encouraged a POW to escape by naming a specific rendezvous time and place. Toohey learned that the FBI had been called in, though it was not clear to him whether that had been the result of a request by the American commandant or because a jealous guard may have asked the local sheriff to do something.[39]

The State Department man reported that in the most recent case, it seemed that the brother of one of the women employees tipped off a guard that his sister was fraternizing with one of the prisoners. Indeed, the prisoner was found to have two letters from the woman, and a squabble between the guard and the prisoner resulted: "The guard, when questioned, denied having pulled a pistol and threatening him [the POW] with it, but seemed to have been lying on this point. It is uncertain whether or not he was telling the truth in denying that the prisoner was beaten up by himself and another guard. At any rate it appears that the prisoner was on quarters for one day and in the guardhouse for four more. It is understood that the husband of the girl was so aroused by the incident that he made her quit her job with the Cummer Company."[40]

The memoirs of a former POW held at the Dade City camp present an interesting angle on the fraternization issue. Werner Burkert, who served with the Afrika Korps and was captured in Tunisia in May 1943, acted as the translator at the Pasco Packing Association orange juice factory. One of his unofficial "duties" was to translate and distribute love letters between the Germans and some of the female employees with whom they worked, acting, as he said, as a veritable "postillon d'amour [cupid]." Through such interpreting he was aware, for instance, that "Fritz is to meet Mary at 3 o'clock in factory bay F." Particularly memorable was one occasion when Burkert found himself talking with one of the American guards while he knew that the guard's wife was having a rendezvous with one of the POWs. Suddenly a POW with lipstick on his face came into Burkert's view. Fortunately for the German, the guard was facing Burkert and away from the compromised man. The quick-thinking interpreter grabbed for his own handkerchief and rubbed his mouth in warning to his approaching comrade. He simultaneously suggested that the guard and he walk across the street to check up on the POWs there, who were engaged in auto repairs, while the offending German disappeared.[41]

Ultimately, the Dade City camp would prove to be one of the longer existing Florida camps because it furnished labor for the hard-pressed Florida citrus industry. It would serve the industry from April 1944 to March 1946. Dade City's last Germans left on a special train of the Seaboard Air Line Railroad for New York and repatriation to Europe on March 9, 1946.[42]

The last of the branch camps of Camp Blanding to be opened in the spring of 1944 was at White Springs in Hamilton County. The camp that opened there in mid-April was made up of POWs shipped from Fort McClellan, Alabama.[43] Like the POWs at Telogia, and many branch camps elsewhere in the Southeast, they were workers in the "piney woods."[44] They were employed exclusively in the cutting and loading of pulpwood and in the repairing of firebreaks for a New Orleans company, R. W. Hillcoat, which was slow in paying the government for its contracted services. Perhaps that was appropriate, for an army investigator who reported the problem also noted that the German POWs seemed to be slow at their work and were not meeting their quotas.[45]

In addition to Camp Blanding and its proliferating branch camps, there was another base POW camp in western Florida that would soon have its own branch camps. This POW camp was within the confines of the immense Camp Gordon Johnston military reservation located in Franklin County on the Florida panhandle. It was near the small town of Carrabelle. The nearest city was Tallahassee, about fifty-eight miles away. As a POW facility it became, after Camp Blanding, the second POW base camp in the state.

Like the POW base camp at Camp Blanding, the one at Camp Gordon Johnston was within one of Florida's larger wartime military reservations. Camp Gordon Johnston proper was second in size only to Camp Blanding. Created as an amphibious training center because of the miles of isolated beach available for exercises, the military began construction of the installation in July 1942. The government had purchased 10,000 acres from landowners and leased an additional 155,000, mainly from the St. Joe Paper Company. The training facility was originally designated as Camp Carrabelle; however, in January 1943 it became officially known as Camp Gordon Johnston. The designation honored Col. Gordon Johnston, a cavalry officer who earned a Medal of Honor while serving during the Philippine Insurrection. He later served in World War I with the Allied Expeditionary Force in France.[46]

Despite the distinguished name, Camp Gordon Johnston was more notorious than famous. Its crude living conditions and dangerous training programs led one American soldier to address his letters "Hell-By-The-Sea, Carrabelle, Florida."[47] The same impression permeated the observations of a State Department visitor who inspected the POW facility at the camp in the company of an International Red Cross representative in November 1944. He noted the isolation of the camp, the white sandy soil that made any kind of cultivation impossible, and the primitive sewerage system of the camp. Because the American camp was operated as a temporary post, the sewerage system used by both Americans and Germans did not provide for flush toilets. Buckets were placed under seats, and a sanitary company removed and recreosoted the buckets daily.[48]

Ultimately the base camp for three branch camps—Telogia, Eglin Field, and Dale Mabry Field—the German POW camp at Camp Gordon Johnston started out on March 21, 1944, as a small branch camp for a contingent of 250 Germans from the larger and earlier facility at Aliceville, Alabama.[49] As a branch camp, the POW facility at Camp Gordon Johnston was a tent camp. It stayed that way for several months, even as its branch status changed. When visited by Maurice Perret of the International Red Cross on June 29, 1944, the camp had already been designated its own base camp as of May 1. Moreover, as an independent base camp, it already was charged with administering a branch tent camp of its own. This branch camp was at Telogia, on the border of the Apalachicola National Forest, just west of Tallahassee.[50]

But Camp Gordon Johnston in June 1944 still consisted of just fifty tents quartering five to six men each. One large tent was used as a mess hall and kitchen. There were two latrines, a shower house, an infirmary, and a canteen. As the canteen was in two small tents, the mess hall—a larger tent—was the only place where prisoners could gather outside their own tents. Since the camp was located on very sandy soil it was not possible to establish a sports field. And, although this temporary POW base camp was only a few hundred yards from the sea, the prisoners were unable to bathe there because of the dangers of the ocean at that location. Perret, the IRC visitor, noted, "No courses have been organized for the men are all employed and when they return to the camp they have no wish to study." All of the German prisoners were currently being used for work in the American military camp: in the kitchen and cleaning up at the post hospital, in the warehouses, in repair shops for military equipment, and in a post garage and machine shops. Fourteen others were employed in drainage work for the prevention of mosquitoes. Perret's IRC report concluded that "Discipline is good. The prisoners are reasonable; but we found, however, that general conditions are rather mediocre."[51]

Conditions for the POWs at Camp Gordon Johnston soon improved—long before the Red Cross reports found their official way to Geneva, the State Department, and back to the PMGO on March 12, 1945.[52] On August 1, the Germans were moved from their temporary tent camp to buildings of theater-of-operations type originally occupied by American officers. These buildings were in the main U.S. military base camp area, centrally located about five blocks from the Camp Gordon Johnston post headquarters. The new POW camp, enclosed by a single wire fence and composed of only one compound—about 900 feet by 600 feet—had room for one regular soccer field and one Faustball field.[53]

By November 1944 Camp Gordon Johnston had a German POW population of 498. But what captured the attention of a State Department visitor was that such a relatively small camp had six guard towers, manned both day and night: "As it seemed unusual to have so many towers manned day and night this matter was discussed at the conference with the Camp Commander. The Camp Commander stated that it was not so much necessary to man these towers in this way from the point of view of the prisoners of war as it was from the standpoint of sightseers from the Post who had to be warned away."[54] This was an obvious and instructive example of the U.S. military's attempt to adhere scrupulously to the terms of the Geneva Convention. Article 2 of its general provisions specified, in part, that "They [prisoners of war] must at all times be humanely treated and protected, particularly against acts of violence, insults and public curiosity."[55]

While the work that POWs performed at Camp Gordon Johnston was almost exclusively on the large American military post—their chief occupation being warehousing—there were occasional other tasks. In November 1944, for instance, 10 men went out on a government contract to harvest peanuts. Very different work was done at the side camp at Telogia, 97 miles northwest of Camp Gordon Johnston. That camp of 250 men, which opened on June 1, 1944, was engaged in the pulpwood industry. Another of Gordon Johnston's branch camps at Eglin Field, established in the fall of 1944, would have more military-related employment. In mid-November 1944, 25 prisoners of war from the main camp at Camp Gordon Johnston were detailed to start work on the construction of this additional branch camp about 180 miles west of the base camp. The plan for the new camp was that it would hold 250 more POWs who would be engaged in warehouse work at the Air Force base.[56]

Work was something that was used by the American government not only to alleviate problems of wartime labor shortages, but to divert potentially troublemaking prisoners. Unfortunately, however, it was also a tool that could be—and was—used disruptively by the POWs. It was a means by which they could seek their own diversion and at the same time express stubbornness or contempt for their captors. They did this by work stoppages. The phenomenon manifested itself at the base camp at Camp Gordon Johnston and at its branch camp at Telogia. In October 1944 at Camp Gordon Johnston two prisoners were given fourteen days on bread and water for refusal to work. Six weeks earlier there had been a situation at Telogia, when the whole camp refused to do a required task and the entire camp was put on bread and water. After that there had seemed to be no further trouble.[57] An International YMCA visitor to the Telogia side camp in March 1945 noted that "This camp has a very good 'group spirit.' It is quite homogeneous [He meant all Africa Korps and all working in the woods, felling trees for pulp and paper mills.] and seems to be able to work and play in good teams." "The prisoners of war seem to enjoy the dense forest, where wild life (snakes, birds, deer) abounds." He noted, too, that the prisoners had a little "zoo" with an alligator caught in a nearby stream.[58] German POWs were obviously fascinated by alligators. One recalls the temporary acquisition of a similar pet at the Leesburg camp, which was mentioned earlier.

By the late spring of 1944 the first phase of the proliferation of German POW camps in Florida was at an end. This first phase had seen the creation of base camps at Camp Blanding and Camp Gordon Johnston and the development of the first branch camps spread out from these two bases. Except for the work on the two major military bases themselves, the only other work on a military post was done at Eglin Field. The rest of the branch camps were developed to respond to the needs of the Florida pulpwood, sugarcane, and citrus industries. While these agricultural branch camps would continue to fulfill their original purposes throughout 1944, 1945, and into 1946, a second wave of branch camps would be developed after the spring of 1944 that would employ German prisoners of war chiefly on Florida's wartime military bases. These bases, particularly those supporting the Army Air Force and the Naval Air Arm, were to furnish the employment and provide the location for the numerous branch POW camps that would be part of Florida's second phase of camp development.

SECOND WAVE: MILITARY BASE WORK
AND SUPPLEMENTARY CIVILIAN LABOR

A second wave of branch camps were established to serve the increased needs of the military at wartime Florida's airfields and military bases in the second half of 1944 and 1945. These branch camps of the base at Camp Blanding included one at Kendall in June 1944 and one at Drew Field in August. Side camps of the base POW camp at Camp Gordon Johnston were activated at both Eglin Field and Dale Mabry Field by January 1945. Additional Blanding side camps at MacDill Field and Orlando Army Air Base were also on the rolls by January 1945. Venice Army Air Base received a POW compound in February. Welch Hospital in Daytona Beach had a POW compound by March. In April Page Field at Fort Myers had its Germans as well. In June large numbers of German POWs were sent to the Jacksonville Naval Air Station. The Jacksonville branch camp shortly became the largest of Blanding's branch camps with as many as 1,614 POWs. With only 848 army and 356 naval prisoners, Camp Blanding lost its ranking as the largest camp in Florida.[59] At the army air bases at Orlando, Drew Field, MacDill Field, Venice Field, and Page Field, the Germans served in officers' clubs and enlisted men's mess halls. They also worked in camp laundries and hospitals.

This second wave of camp expansion was designed to help Florida's civilian agricultural economy as well. German POWs from the existing branch camps were transferred from time to time to various Florida locations when circumstances required. For instance, POWs were sent to Homestead, south of Miami, in the spring and fall of 1945 to help first with the potato harvest and later with a post-hurricane orange grove cleanup. POWs were also sent to Belle Glade for bean canning between March and September 1945. Some of this Belle Glade group were later transferred to work at Banana River Naval Air Station. Another group was set to work in food preparation at Bell Haven Park, Miami, in May 1945. Finally, the sugarcane-cutting contingent, which had been at Clewiston since the spring of 1944, were transferred to Green Cove Springs Naval Air Station in December 1945. These later moves were associated with the phasing out of the civilian contract labor program and the return of POWs to military bases in preparation for their repatriation to Germany.[60]

The most stereotypical "tourist-style" Florida POW branch camp was at Kendall, on the outskirts of Miami. The camp, which housed its 264 prisoners of war in four large barracks, guarded by thirty-one American enlisted men, was opened in June 1944.[61] The military facilities in the Miami area were very different from those at training camps like Blanding or Gordon Johnston. So too were its surroundings. Most of the prisoners at Kendall worked in the large hotels on Miami Beach, which had been requisitioned by the military for convalescent American servicemen. The Germans served these hotels as gardeners, mechanics, hospital workers, electricians, painters, and kitchen helpers.[62] Their work conditions were good, and so was the setting of their POW branch camp. It was described rapturously by a visitor from the International Red Cross:

This camp is located several kilometers south of South Miami, in a tropical region not far from the great bathing resort of Mi-

ami Beach. It is relatively isolated, in a very beautiful pine woods and among palm trees. The climate is mild in the winter and never too hot in the summer. . . . The prisoners' barracks are exceptionally well arranged in palm and pine woods. There are coconut and some orange trees growing in the camp. As a whole it is very well arranged; in view of its gardens and the arrangement of the barracks, this camp is the best looking we have seen. The prisoners are fully aware of the privileged situation of their camp and they take good care of it. Tropical flowers (hibiscus, gardenias) grow everywhere; the prisoners tend the flower beds with zeal.[63]

These conditions, however, did not lead to everyone's contentment. Even Kendall had its escape attempts. Willi Severitt and Rolf Schenkel both got their photographs in the *Miami Herald* on Sunday, September 3, 1944, because they decided not to stay in the camp. Their mug shots, which appeared in the Miami newspaper, were standard FBI usage and were accompanied by physical descriptions of the two corporals, one infantry and one air force.[64] They voluntarily surrendered to authorities five days later, after not having eaten for two days.[65]

Drew Field, which opened at the end of August 1944, had no attempted escapes but plenty of internal problems. Of course, the Drew Field setting was somewhat more "military" than that at the Kendall camp. The Drew Field POW camp that held 395 Germans between August 1944 and March 1946 was part of Drew Field Air Base. That air base, located about twelve miles from Tampa, trained about 1,000 combat bombing crews of ten men each during World War II.[66] The POWs worked on the Army Air Force post in the quartermaster's workshops, repair shops, kitchens, canteens, and warehouses.[67]

The POW camp itself was located in a wooded area three miles from the airfield and exposed to the breezes of the Gulf of Mexico. The Germans were housed rather comfortably in four large two-story dormitories that had formerly been reserved for personnel of the Women's Army Corps (WAC). Latrines, showers, and laundries were installed in the barracks themselves and there were even small bathrooms for the prisoners.[68] But a visitor from the International Red Cross, who inspected the Drew Field POW camp in

March 1945, noted that there were internal problems at the camp that had little to do with the camp's comforts: "From a material point of view, the camp creates a very good impression. The morale among the prisoners is not very good from the point of view of discipline; as a result of insignificant incidents several weeks ago, it was lowered, but the spokesman states that everything would be in order again soon."[69]

What the incident was is unclear. But it no doubt had to do with tensions within the camp and between the POWs and their American work supervisors. After a visit to the camp in January 1945, field liaison officer Maj. Edward C. Shannahan noted: "Discipline and courtesy of the prisoners very poor." Labor was poorly supervised. Several work details were overstaffed. "It was noted that the prisoners in many cases are worked without guard." Major Shannahan was not impressed: "The work schedule of the prisoners on the date of this visit was as follows: 0800—reported to work; 1145 left for lunch; 1330 returned from lunch; 1600 quit work for the day (some details were noticed quitting work at 1550)."[70]

The curtailed work schedule might be attributed to mere laziness. However, one former POW at Drew Field who came to the camp after a stay at Opelika, Alabama, recalled: "There was a very strange climate in the camp, soldierly songs were sung during free time, there were celebrations with National Socialist content. . . . The overwhelming spirit was, I would say, Nazi in the camp."[71] He reported how an American army chaplain came to the camp now and then and held lectures: "I remember that once he went away enraged because the extreme Nazis of the camp had cornered him on the race question."[72]

The camp at Orlando Air Base was another German POW facility to open in the second wave of expansions. It was set up at the edge of the big American military field in November 1944. This large prisoner of war camp had enough internees to be divided into four separate companies. Each had its own set of barracks—each building holding fifty men—its own mess hall, and its own latrines and laundry facilities. As a branch camp of Camp Blanding, its function was to provide employment and housing for about 636, later 756, POWs who worked in and around the American base.[73]

Initially there were problems. Maj. Edward C. Shannahan, who visited the Orlando camp, along with six other POW facilities in

Florida between December 27, 1944, and January 7, 1945, found that the POWs at Orlando were not utilized efficiently. This, he noted, was due to the overcautious predisposition of the director of intelligence and the provost marshal at the camp. Because of the numerous restrictions that they placed on the use of POW labor, that labor had been on "boondoggling jobs." Shannahan called a conference with these American base officers and persuaded them to rescind many of the restrictions. The revised policies even led Shannahan to recommend that the camp be "increased to 1000 prisoners" if all of the suggestions for new work by prisoners could be implemented.[74]

It appears that revisions in the restrictions paid off. An article in Tallahassee's *Daily Democrat* on Tuesday, January 23, 1945, proclaimed the POWs' contribution to the American economy under the title "War Prisoner Labor Keeps Plants Open." The article stated that the POW labor was "proving a boon to short-handed business men." It noted that more than 600 German POWs stationed at the AFTAC base in Orlando were working in groves, canneries, packing houses, building supply yards, and plant nurseries. "They are better workers than anything we can get right now. We couldn't operate without them," a cannery spokesman said.[75] By March, a completely revised and successful labor program for the Orlando POWs was in full swing. The prisoners were divided into thirty-four groups: twent-three dispersed throughout the American camp and employed in garages, clubs, and in gardening; eleven other groups worked under government contract for civilians in the orange groves, a cement plant, and a box factory.[76]

The proliferation of POW branch camps in eastern Florida, manned by Germans from the base camp at Camp Blanding, was not the only area of Florida influenced by the second wave of camp expansions. The camp at Eglin Field, on the Florida panhandle, was opened in December 1944 as a branch camp of the POW base camp at Camp Gordon Johnston. It was located near De Funiak Springs and Crestview, on the edge of a small aviation camp that was part of the extensive system of American military camps belonging to the experimental station of Eglin Field.[77] It had been set up at Eglin, about 180 miles west of Camp Gordon Johnston, by a detachment of twenty-five prisoners from that base camp during November 1944. It was expected that the new camp would—like the numerous other POW camps in Florida created during the last year of the war—provide unskilled labor for the military warehouses on a major military base.[78]

The prisoners, a mixture of captives from the African campaign and from the fighting around Cherbourg, France, lived in large two-storied barracks, previously the quarters for American aviation cadets.[79] There were five sleeping rooms, with sixty beds each. The twenty German noncommissioned officers had small private rooms. Because of the good housing and the location of the camp within a "beautiful forest," with the section of the camp surrounded by barbed wire being very extensive, an International Red Cross visitor said, "As soon as the entertainment program is established, this camp will be one of the best which we have visited."[80]

But the work at Eglin Field was hard. It was not primarily in military warehouses, but in the woods. Most of the 300 Germans worked on the vast military grounds at tasks more strenuous than normal buildings-and-grounds, carpentry, and auto-repair work—though gangs of POWs did that work, too. Two of the largest groups—sixty and forty men respectively—prepared ground for laying a railroad track and cleared fields for bombing practice. Because of the dangers of snake bite, the prisoners were given a "very complete course in ophiology before being sent to their places of work. Each gang takes along a first aid package, in case of serpent bite."[81]

The camp at Dale Mabry Field, like that at Eglin Field, was also a side camp of Camp Gordon Johnston. It was located just west of Tallahassee on the border of Dale Mabry Field. That military facility claimed to have given combat training to 10,856 Army fighter pilots before the American section of the base was inactivated in November 1945.[82] The POW camp was set up on the Army Air Force base in December 1944. As at other military bases, Dale Mabry Field's German prisoners functioned as the carpenters, painters, craftsmen, automobile mechanics, and electricians for the general upkeep of the base.[83] Later, the POWs were also used on farms in a local four-county area to help harvest silage, corn, sorghum, and peanuts and to help with soil erosion and pasture renovation work. They were also employed on the farm run by Florida State College for Women.[84]

A POW branch camp of Camp Blanding was set up in December 1944 at MacDill Field, near Tampa. The work at MacDill Field

POW camp was on the major air base, located at the point of the peninsula that separates Old Tampa Bay from Hillsborough Bay. It was a big facility for a large number of POWs. Its 500 residents in March 1945 made the camp at MacDill Field the fourth largest camp in the Blanding system—following Jacksonville's 1,616; Blanding's 848 army and 356 navy prisoners; and Orlando's 756 POWs.[85] The MacDill Germans slept in thirty-nine barracks, each of which held approximately fifteen men. They ate in three dining halls, each with seating for 250 men. Their work was janitorial, automotive repair, warehouse work, and mosquito control. There was also a high percentage of work in the kitchens of the American military hospital and regular American mess as well as in the American laundry.[86]

The POW camp at Homestead, about thirty miles south of Miami, was set up in February 1945 for the sole purpose of aiding the labor-shortage-plagued Florida agriculture industry. Two POW companies of 200 men each, one sent from Camp Blanding and the other directly from Camp McCain in Mississippi, were sent to harvest the rapidly ripening potato crop.[87] After completion of that task, the intention of the American authorities was to send them to harvest sugarcane.[88] The 400 Germans in the camp lived under rather primitive conditions, in some seventy six-man tents on the flat, treeless land of south Florida. Each prisoner was equipped with individual mosquito netting for sleeping. All of the tents, except those of a German medical officer and of the two German company leaders, were without electricity, so the prisoners used candles in the evenings. After work, they enjoyed soccer on a large but dusty field, and three times a week they had the opportunity to see movies. A March 1945 visitor for the IRC noted that despite the fact that the conditions in the camp were very primitive, he found the morale of the POWs to be excellent. He accounted for this by reporting that the American camp commandant was a good man whose treatment of the prisoners was both just and fair.[89]

Apparently after the completion of the potato harvest, the Homestead prisoners were sent to another camp—possibly to harvest sugarcane as planned. The Homestead camp was not listed among the Florida POW sites after April 1945 until the return of 407 POWs to Homestead in October. This time they came to help rehabilitate hurricane-damaged orange groves.[90] They arrived in seven Florida

East Coast Railway coaches. Transport from the railroad station to the labor camp was by army buses. Twenty-eight individual grove owners in the area had applied for their labor.[91] As the Homestead branch camp was only a temporary one, however, the POW grove workers were again transferred at the end of November 1945.[92]

Unlike the Homestead agricultural group, the POW side camp at Welch General Hospital, Daytona Beach, which opened in February 1945, was one of the military facility branch work camps. As such, it was set up in a portion of what had been a WAC training center.[93] Originally the number of POWs to be sent to do general work around the hospital was set at 100 men.[94] Later, the number of German POWs stationed there rose to 254. They were housed in five barracks with an average of fifty-one men each, and they were guarded by twenty-seven American enlisted men.[95]

The POW camp at Venice Army Air Field, south of Tampa, was opened at the beginning of February 1945. It was to provide workers for the Venice town hospital, which had been requisitioned by the military. They were also to work in an officers' club and the American canteen, as well as to be employed as carpenters and mechanics on the air base.[96] The arrival of the 200-man German contingent was announced to the public by Col. V. B. Dixon, the Venice Field base commander, with the assurance that "no prisoner of war labor is being used, nor will it be used to replace civilian personnel now employed at the base."[97]

These assurances by Colonel Dixon did not satisfy everyone. J. L. Barbee, commander of the Bradenton Veterans of Foreign Wars post, told newsmen of the *Tampa Morning Tribune* that his organization passed a resolution on February 27 complaining that Bradenton vets were replaced by German POWs at the Venice air base. They also had sent the resolution to Congressman J. Hardin Peterson in Washington. The result was that the army promised to investigate reports that American veterans were being ousted from their base jobs and that civilians were forced to take orders from the German prisoners.[98] In a report on March 31, however, the Tampa newspaper reported that Lt. Col. W. B. Hunt, the commanding officer of Venice Army Air Field denied the charge by the Manatee County post of the VFW that veterans of World War I had been ousted from their jobs in favor of German POWs. He also stated that POWs on the base were used only as helpers to civilian employees, had no authority, and could give no orders. Moreover, he asserted, the German POWs at the base spoke little English. Responding to the charge that William E. Fischer of Palmetto, a veteran of World War I, had lost his carpentry job at the base to Germans, Fischer's foreman said, "in my judgement Mr. Fischer was found not to be a finished carpenter and for that reason I did not recommend him for re-employment at some future date."[99]

The Germans had a good situation at Venice Field. An IRC representative who visited their labor detachments in March 1945 found the "working conditions excellent" and "good humor among the prisoners who all, without exception, told us that they are well treated by the American soldiers and officers. . . . The camp is, from the point of view of morale, one of the best that we have seen."[100]

Guy Métraux, the IRC visitor, was impressed also by the camp setting: the POW camp's buildings were widely dispersed in a sandy area covered with beautiful trees. These buildings included some forty-one small five-man barracks and additional larger barracks for latrines, mess hall, recreation hall, and infirmary. There was the added attraction of an open air "Bier-garten" whose outdoor tables and chairs were located at the center of the camp. Venice Field may not have been Venice, Italy, but Mr. Métraux certainly was able to make it sound more like a tourist resort than the rougher agricultural camps at Clewiston and Homestead, which he visited during his spring tour.

South of Venice another POW camp was set up in February 1945. This was at Page Field, the military airfield just outside of the little town of Fort Myers, on Florida's southwest coast, where the Caloosahatchee River meets the Gulf of Mexico. The POW camp there was started as a branch camp of Camp Blanding by a working detachment of twenty Germans who were visited by Eduard Patte of the International YMCA. When he stopped by the camp on February 24, he found them in the process of setting up the camp for the 200 men who were to follow.[101]

The 225-man POW contingent that IRC representative Guy Métraux found at Page Field in mid-March was by then housed in five standard American barracks. He noted that several of these barracks were of concrete and thus, he felt, "particularly pleasant in summer."[102] A sports field was under construction and an open-air theater had already been completed. He also approved of the "excellent work conditions" of the various working detachments that he visited. There was only one possible exception: there was a group of fifty "ditch-diggers," who were involved in mosquito control. They did their work in water most of the time. However, Métraux was consoled by the fact that the ditchdiggers were provided with rubber boots and colonial helmets (pith or sun helmets). Also, though the work was hard, they were permitted numerous breaks for rest and refreshment.[103]

The IRC man, who visited in March, did not know what other tasks lay ahead for the Page Field contingent. In October, fifty of the men were sent to Miami. There they helped remove debris in the aftermath of a hurricane that hit the area on September 15. While in the Miami area the Fort Myers-based POWs were quartered at the Bell Haven POW camp.[104]

Florida's bean canners were the beneficiaries of the temporary POW camp at Belle Glade, about thirty miles west of Palm Beach. This Blanding branch camp, which existed between March and December 1945, was located in the rich, dark truck-farming land of south Florida. Despite its brief existence, the branch camp at Belle Glade received national publicity because of a short strike that occurred in April 1945, shortly after the camp was set up. The strike and its national acclaim will be the focus of another chapter.

By late 1945 the POW branch camp at Jacksonville Naval Air Station would become the largest branch camp of the Camp Blanding base camp. It would house 1,614 Germans compared to Blanding's smaller contingent of 1,204.[105] That development took time. When the Jacksonville camp was opened in June 1945 it had a smaller contingent.[106] Initially only 500 Germans were assigned to the station, with Capt. George R. Gresham, formerly the commander of the POW camp at Kendall, in charge.[107]

The unique feature of the POW camp at Jacksonville was that, although administered by the army, it was housed on navy property. The POWs and their army guards used navy facilities, were employed in navy work, and served according to conditions specified by the navy. According to a State Department visitor in November 1945: "[The camp] has excellent Naval type buildings with superb equipment, including refrigerated water fountains, large mixing machines, pressure cookers and the like. The Navy refused to comply with the Army's order that such equipment be removed."[108]

There were, however, some problems noted by the man from the State Department: "Discipline and courtesy are very satisfactory and probably was better before the arrival of 476 non-commissioned officers from Aliceville. Morale is excellent. The work is very easy." These two things—excellent morale and easy work—were related, according to the army officer in command of the POW camp at the time, Capt. Robert N. Hancock. He felt navy complaints about delinquency and work shirking by the POWs were the direct result of the navy's own practices. He cited a case in which 108 POWs were assigned to work in one galley. Hancock felt that the army would have employed only 24. But, he noted, he had no control over how the navy allocated work to his charges.[109]

Far to the south, the next POW camp to be opened as a branch camp of Camp Blanding did not have such problems: it was an army camp on an army facility. The Bell Haven branch camp, Miami, was opened on May 23, 1945. By late November it had 461 prisoners of war guarded by 45 American enlisted men. Of the POWs, 423 worked away from the POW camp: 88 in American mess halls, 15 as auto mechanics, and 218 as unskilled labor, mainly at the Miami Air Base. The camp itself occupied several buildings and part of the area of the Bell Haven Trailer Park at Seventy-ninth Street and Thirty-second Avenue in northwest Miami. The park also housed the headquarters of the Miami Military Police Detachment. Before the arrival of the Germans the area was used by an American combat team. Their former kitchens became barracks for the Germans. As the earlier American unit had installed good hard surface roads and walks and had done some landscaping, the camp was described by a State Department visitor as "very attractive."[110] It was, after all, like the POW camp at Kendall, part of the army's greater Miami sprawl that had taken over one of the most famous tourist resort locations in the world. The area was a virtual wartime paradise for American and German soldiers alike.

Much less touristlike were the northeast Florida POW camps at active military reservations. Such was the case at Melbourne. The first labor report from the POW camp at Melbourne was made on August 16, 1945.[111] The camp was set up at the American air base there, and the POWs were housed in igloo-type buildings.[112] It was a relatively small camp, with only 148 POWs, who had been shipped to Florida from Camp Forrest, Tennessee. The Germans were guarded by 20 American enlisted men. In this small camp, only 18 of the Germans worked in the administration and mess halls of the POW compound and in the American administrative unit attached to the POW camp; 131 worked at the Naval Air Station. Of the latter, about 75 were part of a less than glamorous night-laundry detail.[113]

Not far from Melbourne, on the edge of the Banana River Naval Air Station, near Cocoa, was another small contingent of 148 German POWs, guarded by 20 Americans. It was set up in early August 1945 with inmates from Camp Blanding, whose traveling and processing kept them from work on August 1 and 2. Again on August 15, the American camp commander noted a lack of POW work. This time 63 POWs were idle because V-J Day celebrations made for a lack of civilian supervisors. Originally the POW camp was located on the naval base in naval buildings, but in mid-October 1945 it was relocated. The Germans were then housed in four temporary hutments.[114]

One of their guards was a nineteen-year-old from Tulsa, Oklahoma, Charles M. Blackard. After infantry replacement training at Camp Blanding, he was assigned to a POW guard detachment: guarding German POWs first at Camp Blanding, then at Belle Glade, and later at Banana River. Years later, he recalled that most of the Germans at the Banana River camp worked on cleanup details at the naval air station.[115]

Not far west of Banana River, another air field became the home for more German prisoners during the final days of their captivity within the state. The POW camp at Green Cove Springs was set up on September 8, 1945, by Capt. Dwight Field, with a contingent of 246 prisoners of war that he had supervised at the sugarcane harvesting camp at Clewiston. The transfer came as a great relief to all concerned. It represented a move from the Clewiston tent camp—described by an IRC visitor as "known to be worst perhaps in all America"—to one that Edouard Patte of the YMCA called a "very nice small camp." A State Department visitor in December said of the Green Cove Springs camp: "not quite up to the superb standard of Jacksonville, but it is an adequate, clean and comfortable installation."[116] Unlike the harsh work in the cane fields on the southern shore of Lake Okeechobee, that at Green Cove Springs Naval Air Station was as mess hall cooks and KPs, janitors and supply depot men, or auto mechanics, carpenters, and painters.

As at Jacksonville, where army officers administered POWs whose work was supervised by the navy, German morale was "excellent." But, again, that was largely due to the navy's laxity in work assignments and supervision: "The work is very easy here and morale seems to be excellent. Prisoners work only forty hours per week because they are under Civil Service supervisors. All Army inspectors protest this arrangement and the Navy as consistently ignores the objections."[117]

Also, a certain laxness of military discipline evident at the Clewiston camp continued at Green Cove Springs.[118] J. L. Toohey of the Department of State, who visited the Green Cove Springs camp on November 23, 1945, in the company of an IRC representative, noted: "Discipline and courtesy are as nearly non-existent here as poor leadership on the part of officers can make it. During the course of the visit the Commanding Officer (who seemed to be going through the prisoner of war section for the first time and having trouble finding the different rooms we asked about) was nearly knocked down by two prisoners running up the stairway. He seemed to be chagrined but not surprised when they grinned at him and walked away without a word. In the prisoners' day room the Spokesman's 'Achtung' had to be repeated and abetted with a little physical prodding to get one prisoner of war out of his chair."[119]

This kind of attitude seemed to permeate the camp, affecting both German and American personnel. It certainly seemed so to Mr. Toohey, who noted: "Although the morale of the American personnel is not a concern of this report, it is perhaps relevant to add that the summary in the headquarters office was somewhat difficult because of the loud dressing-down the Executive Officer was giving an American sergeant for what seemed to be a very trivial offense. The audience, of course, was rather large because it included three additional non-commissioned officers who did not seem to be concerned in the proceedings other than for reasons of their own interest."[120]

In addition to the branch camps of Camp Blanding and Camp Gordon Johnston, one more Florida branch camp should be mentioned. It is the POW camp at Naval Auxiliary Air Station Whiting Field, near Milton in Santa Rosa County on the Florida panhandle. It existed between July 1945 and March 1946. The camp was located in Florida, but the base camp from which the German POWs came was Camp Rucker, Alabama. Thus, although the Whiting Field POW camp was in the Sunshine State, it was a camp that might be overlooked as a Florida camp. Army, IRC, and YMCA visitors listed in their reports of visits to Florida camps only the branch camps of the two major Florida base camps, Camp Blanding and Gordon Johnston.[121]

The first 100 Germans of the later 225-man POW detachment at Whiting Field arrived from their base camp at Camp Rucker on July 12, 1945. They were under the supervision of Capt. Robert H. Fuller of the U.S. Army. The Germans were brought to Whiting Field through the cooperation of navy authorities at the Naval Air Training Base at Pensacola and the army authorities of Camp Rucker to perform the manual labor necessary for the numerous construction and soil erosion projects under way at Whiting Field. Although administered by the army, the camp's food, bedding, living quarters, and medical care were provided by the navy because the prisoners were assigned to work for the navy. [122]

Fifty years after the existence of the POW camp at Whiting Field, memories remained among local residents. A former American guard and later Milton City councilman, Byron Stewart recalled that he fell in love with the "great pastry" made by the German POW cooks. He also said, "They could take bologna and vienna sausages and make better food than the Navy."[123] A former air field secretary, Eulena Sheffield, remembered seeing the Germans muster before heading out to work at Whiting or off base: "I never tried talking to them, I was working. . . . They were nice looking young men. They went out into the Allentown Community and worked for the farmers."[124] Finally, an older gentleman who worked at Whiting Field during the war years told his grandson how he once watched the Germans as they were clearing a section of dense woods and underbrush: "All of a sudden there was some frantic yelling from the soldiers as they had come across a skunk. He [the grandfather] couldn't tell what they were yelling, but he said they were certainly concerned about that skunk!"[125]

Working on Florida's numerous military reservations and for the civilian agricultural economy as pulpmen, sugarcane cutters, citrus fruit packers, and potato harvesters, about 10,000 German POWs experienced the Sunshine State. In turn, Floridians and American service personnel stationed in Florida experienced the Germans. One encounters few bad memories on either side. There was a major contribution made to Florida's labor supply, both on military bases and in the civilian economy. There was also a major contribution made toward convincing both Americans and their German guests that enemies are human. There were some minor problems of fraternization when healthy young German males aroused the interest of American female civilian workers. There were incidents of overly playful POWs returning to camps with live alligators and snakes, though it was usually the cherished snakeskin souvenir that was the prize. For many Germans, as for many of their American guards, their wartime experiences in Florida reinforced the allure of the Sunshine State. It lived up to its reputation as an exotic land—part farmland, forest, and swamp; part cane field, citrus grove, and tourist resort. Finally, it would prove to be a popular tour destination in the decades after the war, when former POWs would return with friends and family to see where they had "worked for Uncle Sam." Most preferred not to remember those parts of their POW experiences that clashed with their own images of comradeship on the battlefield turned to comradeship in the labor force. Americans, too, found it easier to deal with the stereotype of Germans as Uncle Sam's smiling workers.

3

U-BOAT MEN AND OTHER NAVAL PRISONERS: SPECIAL BREED, SPECIAL PROBLEMS

Experiences on the POW labor front created very different images of wartime enemies. Enemies became fellow sufferers and even friends. Among Americans, personal experiences with POW labor units created entirely new images of Hitler's soldiers: images of the "nice-looking boys" next door, the industrious workers, and the cheerful wartime visitors who brought pet alligators back to the Leesburg camp or chased copperheads at Clewiston to make souvenir belts. For the German alumni of the camps, the labor program began to build postwar memories of efficient teamwork, benevolent older American civilian employers, and friendly guards.

The idea that the enemy was human, at least to those most directly involved in the POW program—the POWs, their guards, and civilian employers and fellow workers—represented major cognitive progress for all involved. The new images, while contributing more accuracy to the personal judgments of participants, still hid the complexities of the human spirit.

Human diversity and the complex nature of wartime loyalties exhibited themselves with the first POWs interned in the Sunshine State. They were active-duty military men from that branch of Hitler's armed forces that first arrived in internment camps in the United States, the navy. In fact, the first real POWs in Florida were fourteen U-boat men who arrived at Camp Blanding in September 1942.[1] Though the war seemed far away to many Americans, others knew from personal experience that it lurked dangerously near—in the waters off the Atlantic Coast. Since January 1942 German submarines had wreaked havoc with American shipping.[2] Though the

American navy was slow to mount an effective antisubmarine effort, there were kills, and surviving U-boat men began arriving on American shores. The first live submariners to be captured in American waters were the men of the U-352. Their vessel was sunk by the USS *Icarus* off the Outer Banks of North Carolina on May 9, 1942. Brought to shore at Charleston, they were temporarily housed at Fort Bragg in North Carolina.[3] Afterward many of the naval officers were sent to a camp in Crossville, Tennessee, their men distributed to other camps. In 1943 the U.S. Navy became concerned that military censors were inadvertently letting nautical secrets get back to Germany. It was decided in early 1944 to consolidate the 6,286 navy men into four camps: Camp Blanding, Florida; Camp McCain, Mississippi; Camp Beale, California; and Papago Park, Arizona. Blanding's naval compound was designated by American authorities as an anti-Nazi compound.[4] That would soon prove to be an awkward and uselessly vague and misleading designation.

Germans and Americans soon discovered—at Camp Blanding's naval stockade and elsewhere at POW camps throughout the United States—that American-selected designations like "Nazi" and "anti-Nazi" were neither accurate nor very useful. These designations, which led the Blanding naval stockade to be officially declared an anti-Nazi camp, did justice neither to the realities of the situations faced by naval prisoners nor to the complex loyalties—volunteered or coerced—of many Germans during the Nazi period. In short, the story of the naval stockade at Camp Blanding reveals the complex realities often overlooked by American authorities because of the uniforms and military experience of their wartime enemies. Historians, further from the heat and passion of the period, can observe more objectively the fascinating, but dangerous, realities that at the time caused alienation, threats, and even death behind the wire of America's German POW camps. American military authorities could only react with surprise and confusion to developments largely beyond their control. Such is the story of the naval compound at Camp Blanding. The Blanding story was complicated further by the professionalism of the special German naval personnel originally assigned to this Florida camp. The first POWs in Florida, Hitler's U-boat men were a special breed with special problems.

Blanding's first contingent of U-boat men arrived on September 24, 1942.[5] They were men from whom naval intelligence hoped to obtain information about German submarine technology and operations.[6] They were isolated at Camp Blanding's anti-Nazi compound so that they would not be "contaminated" by other German naval prisoners whose earlier interrogation had proved less useful. This became obvious when Blanding's original fourteen naval prisoners were joined in November by three specially chosen men from the U-162.[7] They were transferred to Blanding from the interrogation center at Fort Hunt because it was contemplated that they might be returned there at some future time for further interviews with naval intelligence personnel. Eleven others of the U-162 crew were to be sent elsewhere, suggesting that Camp Blanding was beginning to acquire a unique character.[8] It was becoming a camp where naval prisoners who could provide information for American intelligence might be readily available. The prisoners had no say in the matter. American military intelligence officers wanted to keep a keen eye on these U-boat men while preventing the Germans from having any unregulated contact with the rest of the world. The strictest secrecy was to be observed concerning the prisoners, and they were to be prevented from any communication with unauthorized parties. All written communications by these prisoners were to be forwarded to the director of the aliens division of the PMGO for censorship and information.[9]

With the three men from the U-162, the detention roster of naval prisoners of war at Camp Blanding at the end of January 1943 consisted of only fourteen men—two officers and twelve seamen.[10] The POWs came from four boats sunk off the coast of America during the summer of 1942: the U-701 (July 7), U-210 (August 6), U-94 (August 27), and U-162 (September 4).[11] Early in America's war with Germany, U.S. naval intelligence was particularly interested in picking the brains of these U-boat captives. Their indiscretions, affability, or unintentional revelation of German naval secrets aroused the interest of naval intelligence gatherers at Fort Hunt. And, prisoners seen as particularly helpful—even through their inadvertence—could, to their surprise and chagrin, be classified as anti-Nazis.

The fact that Capt. Horst Degen was the ranking officer and internment camp spokesman for the small contingent of U-boat men at Blanding in January 1943 is a clue to the early intentions that American military authorities had for the camp. Degen, of the U-701, became an early Fort Hunt "star." Captured off Hatteras on July 7, 1942, and after a brief stay at the Norfolk Naval Hospital, the twenty-nine-year-old German captain became Fort Hunt's first visitor.[12] Fort Hunt, seventeen miles from Washington, D.C., was the first of two sites—the other, on the West coast, at Byron Hot Springs, California—chosen for the interrogation of selected prisoners. Opened in August 1942, its operation and existence were a secret. Throughout the war, Fort Hunt interrogation center was known only as P.O. Box 1142.[13] At P.O. Box 1142, Captain Degen seems to have talked quite freely to his interrogators. He gave them, for instance, his estimate that the record for U-boat diving time was twenty-eight seconds. He also shared the insight that each German submarine skipper reported directly to Adm. Karl Dönitz after returning to Lorient, France, from patrol.[14]

The intent of American military authorities to use Blanding as an anti-Nazi camp, or at least as a small and secure one where subjects for later intelligence interrogation could be held, was further confirmed in February 1943 when two sailors from the U-595 were sent to Camp Blanding from Fort Hunt.[15] The orders accompanying their transfer indicated that it was the intention of the military authorities to return them to Fort Hunt at a later date. They were sent to Blanding because "we do not wish them contaminated with pro-Nazi submarine prisoners." Nor were the selected prisoners to be allowed to betray the existence of Fort Hunt's intelligence operation intentionally or unintentionally. Their transfer was to be undertaken in secrecy, precautions taken to prevent them from transmitting messages either "through the medium of United States personnel or by throwing messages from car window while in route." Indeed, the prisoners "shall not be informed of their eventual destination."[16]

They would not stay at Blanding long. Like Fort Hunt, Camp Blanding's naval compound was not originally intended as the permanent wartime home of German U-boat men once the Americans had learned all they wanted from them. Of the twenty-three internees in mid-June 1943, all but one was part of a new batch of prisoners received from Fort Hunt earlier in the month.[17]

The naval prisoners confined at Camp Blanding may have been sent there because of the intelligence information that American military men had extracted or hoped to extract from them, but the camp was not the secure camp that American intelligence designated it to be. Danger lurked in Blanding's naval compound for those who were identified by their fellow prisoners as traitors to the Fatherland. On February 3, 1944, the adjutant at Camp Blanding requested of the Security and Intelligence Division of the Fourth Service Command that two German navy prisoners of war be transferred to another camp. Because of differences of political opinion, these men were not associating with the other naval prisoners and showed a fear of their surroundings. Their fear seemed justified in light of the negative treatment that they were receiving from their fellow prisoners of war.[18] The response from the office of the provost marshal general to the commanding general of the Fourth Service Command, who forwarded the Blanding request, stated: "Prisoners of war referred to in basic communication were classified as Anti-Nazi by representatives of the Office of the Assistant Chief of Staff, G-2, and for that reason were transferred to Prisoner of War Camp, Camp Blanding, Florida. There is no other Anti-Nazi camp to which these prisoners of war can be transferred. If it is believed that there is sufficient justification to warrant a reclassification of these prisoners of war, it is requested that this office be furnished full particulars."[19]

The particulars were returned almost at once. The situation within the naval compound had deteriorated drastically. On March 4, 1944, not only were two intimidated and frightened U-boat men placed in protective custody, but a third man had been found lying half conscious. The senior German POW officer, Capt. Klaus H. Bargsten, told American authorities that the injured prisoner had just arrived in camp that day and was recognized by several other prisoners who had known him in prisons near Washington, D.C. His fellow inmates stated that the new man had been a trusty there and had gone around with an armband and without a guard. They claimed that he was spying on the other prisoners and reporting to the American authorities. According to the German captain, the wounded prisoner was the survivor of a submarine that had been sunk off the coast of Brazil. He and another survivor had been caught on deck when the sub dived and was later destroyed. After drifting in a raft for seven days, the two survivors were picked up and taken to Brazil and then to Camp Hunt. At Blanding, the new arrival had openly said, "To Hell with Germany and all of you," or words to that effect. Bargsten stated, "the men in this camp are all loyal Germans and resented traitorous talk." Indeed, an American officer reported that the captain seemed to accuse the attacked man of being a communist. Bargsten told the Americans that as long as the war lasted the POWs had to remain true to their country. He implied that things might be different after the war, but meanwhile he could not vouch for the safety of prisoners like the wounded man and the two other men who "shot their mouths off."[20]

The officer of the day at Blanding placed the two uninjured, though threatened, men in the camp prison, not for punishment but for their safety. He warned them to keep their mouths shut for their own good and not to call out to or answer calls from any other prisoners. He then went to the station hospital to inquire about the other injured sailor. The man from the U-164 was being x-rayed at the time, but the medical officer stated that the prisoner's skull was badly beaten and his back and sides badly bruised. The prisoner, who was conscious while being treated, spoke English. He told the officer of the day that he was an anti-Nazi and that about fifteen prisoners had beaten him with their hobnailed boots. The medical officer confirmed this by noting the shoe-heel marks on the wounded man's head and sides. Instructions were left to admit the prisoner to the ward with the other German prisoners, as no single room was available in the hospital prison; but the American guard was cautioned to see that other prisoners did not attempt further attacks.[21]

Under later questioning, Captain Bargsten explained how resentment had built up against the three nonconformists. They had previously announced themselves anti-Nazi and refused to eat in the compound mess hall. After the first attack on them, they were offered the privilege of eating there, but they again refused. They were therefore fed outside on the kitchen porch. They also declined to talk to the other prisoners, who, in turn, would not let the alienated men work with them. Therefore, the anti-Nazis did neither KP nor latrine duty. In fact, they did no work at all, except for keeping their own quarters clean. They had a hut all to themselves while the other men had to live five or six to a hut. In short, Bargsten explained, they were living the same life as officers, who had larger and more roomy quarters, did not have to work, and had their food served to them. Thus they had provoked the anger of their comrades.[22]

The U.S. Army did not know what to do with self-proclaimed anti-Nazis who were threatened by other American-classified anti-Nazi comrades. On July 3, Blanding officers contacted the commanding general of the Fourth Service Command in Atlanta with a list of ten Blanding POWs—a list including the names of two of the men reported threatened in March—requesting that they be transferred. It was noted that all ten were ostracized by fellow prisoners because of their political opinions. As a result, Blanding officers complained, the men had had to be quartered and rationed outside of the navy compound for the last two months, making supplementary security measures necessary.[23]

Obviously the PMGO was uncertain of what to do about the situation. One attempt at a solution can be seen in a G-2 (intelligence) memorandum of June 29 that led to July 7, 1944, orders for the removal from the Blanding naval compound of ranking officer and spokesman Capt. Klaus Bargsten and another officer. They were transferred to Camp McCain in Mississippi.[24] Beyond that, the uncertainty as to what to do was evident in a note sent on July 27, 1944, by the assistant director of the Prisoner of War Division to the Office of the Assistant Chief of Staff, G-2, of the War Department. He explained that the prisoners who Blanding administrative officers wished to transfer because of their anti-Nazi attitudes had been classified as anti-Nazi German navy prisoners and transferred to Camp Blanding for that specific purpose in the first place. What could G-2 recommend?[25] The archival materials do not reveal the response, but the documentary record does indicate that on August 24 the commanding officer at Blanding informed the PMGO that the approved transfer of the ten prisoners to Camp McCain was canceled with the approval of the Fourth Service Command, because seventy-eight anti-Nazi naval prisoners were in the process of being transferred to Blanding from McCain. That seemed to make the transfer of ten anti-Nazis to McCain "neither feasible nor plausible." It was hoped by Blanding authorities that "The arrival of the seventy-eight (78) Anti-Nazi prisoners of war at this station will equalize the Anti-Nazi and Nazi element within the Navy Compound."[26]

The problems at the naval compound at Blanding became more acute, not less, as additional naval prisoners were transferred in from other posts like Fort Devens, Massachusetts;[27] Papago Park, Arizona;[28] Camp Livingston, Louisiana;[29] Indiantown Gap Military Reservation, Pennsylvania;[30] Camp Edwards, Massachusetts; and Camp Bowie, Texas.[31] Loyal Germans began to fear for their reputations, the reputations of their families, and their lives. Some of the naval prisoners found their classification as anti-Nazis surprising, their new "traitorous" camp mates repulsive, their reputations as loyal officers and Germans impugned, and their future in the German Reich—as well as their families' future—endangered. Others found that their anti-Nazi stands alienated them from fellow prisoners and often—as noted above—caused life-threatening encounters with comrades who beat or even tried to kill them. The result was that naval prisoners in each of these extreme groups sought escape through transfers, self-imposed segregation, or flight from the camp. Still others found themselves "rescued," at least temporarily, from turbulent, antagonistic, and dangerous Germans when American intelligence officers decided they were not really Germans.

The categories of Nazi and anti-Nazi proved to be much too simplistic. Germans were not all "Germans." Only gradually did the American camp authorities begin to realize that besides Nazis, anti-Nazis, and German patriots, they were dealing also with prisoners of non-German ethnicity. Many men were drafted or otherwise inducted into the German Army who before March 1938 would have been considered citizens of another country. Such inductees were only gradually identified by American intelligence and separated from their German comrades as potential candidates for privileges, possible collaboration, and selective repatriation. In June 1944, Lieutenant Colonel Edwards, assistant director of the Prisoner of War Division of the Provost Marshal General's Office, requested of the commanding general of the Fourth Service Command that two German naval prisoners of Polish origin, then at Camp Blanding, be transferred to the prisoner of war camp at Camp Butner, North Carolina. There they were to be interned in the special 500-man compound for such non-German nationals.[32]

Self-imposed segregation was another way to avoid the hell within Blanding's German naval compound—a hell that Hitler's Germany and human nature rather than American authorities had conspired to conceive. By the end of 1944, twenty-four of Blanding's German naval prisoners separated themselves from their comrades because they claimed to be loyal Germans and did not want to be associated with the anti-Nazis. One of these men was Lt. Berndt von Walther und Croneck of the U-162. He was among nine officers and ten enlisted men whom an American naval intelligence officer, who visited the naval POW camp at Papago Park in the fall of 1944, had suggested would "be of invaluable assistance to the United States and Britain during the occupation of Germany."[33] Walther and his comrades from Papago Park, however, were shocked and stunned by the reception that they received at the new camp to which they were assigned. "I had a terrible time there," Walther later told historian John Hammond Moore. "The camp was full of Reds, criminals and traitors. I slept each night with a large stick by my bed, fearing for my life. We adamantly refused to go into the main compound and eventually persuaded the commanding officer to erect a 'dead line' separating us from the 'anti-Nazis' so-called."[34]

In a letter to the provost marshal general dated February 13, 1945, Walther and his comrades described their plight and appended to it the signatures of twenty-four men who made the request to be transferred to Camp McCain or "to any other normal P.W. Camp in which we would be willing to live in correct relations with the American authorities without the presence of treacherous elements."[35]

In their communication to the PMGO, the Germans noted that by a letter of January 13, 1945, they had asked the Legation of Switzerland for mediation in support of their request for a transfer to Camp McCain. The Swiss reply of February 6 was the advice to forward such a request directly to the Provost Marshal General's Office. This they were doing. They stated:

We consider it the duty of a soldier to remain faithful to his country under all circumstances, especially in regard to his relations with his nation's adversaries. Therefore, we strongly disagree with the men who give the Navy Compound of Camp

Blanding its special character. These men have, according to our opinion, heavily violated their duties by reneging on their allegiance to Germany and her armed forces. Some of them have betrayed military secrets. There was even the case of a man who, avowedly, declared himself ready to fight against Germany. Such men, in our opinion, acted in a manner which will be disapproved by many decent men all over the world, regardless of nationality.[36]

Maj. W. H. Lowman, commanding officer of the POW camp at Blanding, explained to the provost marshal general in a letter of February 23, 1945, that the twenty-four prisoners in question were self-segregated from the other prisoners of the 200-man naval compound, but that they were "not actually separated from the rest of the compound by a fence, but are assigned to one section of the compound. These prisoners of war are not non-cooperative and have never been reported as such, but were segregated at their own request. Reason for request to be segregated from other prisoners of war in compound was because subject prisoners of war claim to be Nazis and the other prisoners in the Navy Compound are Anti-Nazi."[37]

Capt. Robert L. Kunzig, of the War Department's Special Projects Division, who visited Camp Blanding's naval compound on February 11–12, 1945, had already noted the problem that existed in the 216-man naval compound:

The navy compound contains in addition to its 175 enlisted men and 25 noncommissioned officers, 16 German officers. One of these officers is a violent anti-Nazi, and lives with the enlisted men. The other 15 officers denounce the above mentioned anti-Nazis, and live at one end of the compound in absolute separation from their "comrades." The separation is purely voluntary and is evidenced by no wire or fence. Eleven of these 16 came from Papago Park. Their position is that they were in disagreement with the methods and ideas of the Nazi officers interned at Papago Park, but were shocked to find themselves in such a violent anti-Nazi camp, as in Blanding. They feel they are permanently branded, and fear for their relatives at home, and themselves after the war. They have requested transfer to Camp McCain, urging that their facilities as officers are not adequate at Blanding. Captain Kunzig discussed the matter at length with Major Lowman, Prisoner of War camp commander. The following is recommended: if transfer should be desired, it could probably be effected, but Major Lowman expressed complete willingness to keep the 15 officers there. If it is permanently decided that they are to stay, he will fence off the officer portion of the camp and let them have their own private little section. It is Captain Kunzig's recommendation that this be done. His opinion is that on V-E day these 15 officers will swing over to the anti-Nazi viewpoint anyhow. They are a more cautious group, not given to violent open denunciations at this time. But on the other hand, they are not strong Nazis of the Papago Park variety. They have been transferred to Blanding, and might well stay right there.[38]

In this respect a postscript should be added to the story of the "self-segregated" naval prisoners at Camp Blanding. The naval intelligence officer who was responsible for the transfer of Lieutenant Walther and several of his colleagues from Papago Park to Blanding unintentionally made life hell for them. But he served well the interests of the American government. Soon after V-E Day, Walther was transferred to Fort Eustis, Virginia. There, along with 130 Germans, he worked for nearly a year translating documents for the Americans. Among these documents were the notes of German rocket scientist, and later U.S. space program leader, Wernher von Braun. Walther was returned to Germany in July 1946.[39]

One additional way to avoid the problems within the naval compound was to escape. It is difficult to determine motivations for escape attempts. The evidence is often indicative, but hardly conclusive. Of the thirty-three German POWs who participated in a total of twenty escapes from Florida POW camps between May 1944 and March 1946, eleven of the fugitives were from Camp Blanding, and eight of these eleven were naval prisoners. None of them were U-boat men. Three were from the merchant marine and five (four, really, because one man escaped twice) from port guard and support units.[40] They were POWs transferred to the anti-Nazi naval compound at Camp Blanding from camps like Fort George Meade, Maryland; Fort Devens, Massachusetts; and Camp Edwards, Massachusetts.[41] Interestingly, six of the would-be escapees attempted flight after the end of the war in Europe: five took to their heels in June 1945 and another did so in October of that year.[42]

The German POW who had the second highest number of escape attempts while interned in Florida was Bruno Balzer of the naval compound. He had two separate attempts to his credit, in February and again in June 1945. A member of a port unit at Palmi, Italy, he had been captured on September 1, 1943. More significantly, he was among the ten men from the naval compound who, ostracized and threatened by their fellow prisoners because of their opinion that Germany would be defeated, were held in protective segregation and unsuccessfully sought transfer to another camp in July 1944. Almost certainly, for Bruno Balzer and for several other would-be escapees from Blanding's naval compound, escape was an attempt to avoid the political troubles within the camp—political troubles among the prisoners themselves. Yet despite Balzer's requests for transfer and his two escape attempts, his name still remained on a Blanding naval internees list in October 1945.[43] Along with his name were the names of his six fellow naval escapees who found life within the confines of the naval compound a horrid reflection of the divisions within Germany itself during the Nazi period. They found that they had not escaped those conflicts merely by becoming POWs in the Sunshine State. The detention rosters of the naval compound, compiled in October 1945, still registered the names of men who represented the extremes of political opinion that existed within the officially anti-Nazi compound. Among those names were Bruno Balzer's fellow "defeatists" and Lt. Berndt von Walther's "loyalists."

Also, among those detained in the naval compound in October 1945 was a prisoner who particularly aroused the sympathetic interest of a YMCA visitor, himself a native of France, Edouard Jean Patte:

> Among the Navy officers interned I met a young man who was of German descent but had spent most of his life in Switzerland and in France, where he had married a French woman, had been interned by the French Government in 1939, by the German Government in a concentration camp in 1940 and 1941, was then drafted, taken prisoner by the Americans, so

that during this war he had already been the prisoner of three different nations. The most surprising thing was for me to talk with a German Prisoner of war who spoke French rather than German, and that with the most authentic southern French accent.[44]

The four-year history of the naval compound at Camp Blanding is one that reveals the political and emotional complexities and difficulties faced both by American military authorities and by their German prisoners. These complexities reflected those that the POWs had left at home in the Third Reich, an empire that after 1938 included not only a variety of anti-Nazi German groups but peoples of diverse subject nationalities as well. Along with these reluctant "Nazis" were also those German nationalists who, though opposed to Hitler, felt that loyalty to the Fatherland meant upholding its honor against its enemies during war time. It was a hard time for men of honor seeking to be true to themselves, their families, their military comrades, and their nation while being confined in a foreign land whose soldiers were killing Germans in order to overthrow the power of a despicable Nazi dictatorship.

4

WHEN THE AFRIKA KORPS CAME TO BLANDING: RIOTS AND REPATRIATIONS, NOVEMBER 1943–FEBRUARY 1944

If the problems and contradictions of group identification and loyalties were evident in Camp Blanding's small naval compound, they would be even more evident in the army compound established at the camp in November 1943. But the construction of an army compound at Blanding almost did not happen. On January 9, 1943, Brig. Gen. B. M. Bryan, director of the Aliens Division of the PMGO, directed a proposal to the Requirements Division, Services of Supply of the War Department. It called for the construction of a 3,000-man internment camp at Camp Blanding, Florida, subject to the approval of the commanding general, Eastern Defense Command.[1] The response of the Eastern Defense Command, however, was negative: "In reply to your inquiry to Operations Division, War Department General Staff, construction is not recommended for a 3,000-man internment at Camp Blanding, Florida, or any other site in the Eastern Defense Command."[2] The result was that on January 15, 1943, by command of Lieutenant General Somervell, commanding general of the Services of Supply, the provost marshal general and the chief of engineers were informed that "the construction of an internment camp at Camp Blanding, Florida, is not favorably considered."[3]

But things changed. There were massive numbers of arrivals of German prisoners of war on American shores as a result of the collapse of Rommel's Afrika Korps in May 1943. The number of German prisoners in the United States escalated from 990 in January 1943 to 123,440 by December.[4] This was because of the surrender of Rommel's forces to the British in Tunisia and the earlier American decision in November 1942 to take "British-owned"

German prisoners to the United States.[5] The decision to expand the number of camps throughout most of the United States led to approval of construction of an army POW camp at Camp Blanding on October 6, 1943.[6]

The German army compound, located about a half mile from the existing naval compound, opened on November 5, 1943, to hold 1,000 Afrika Korps men. On that day, the compound received 500 prisoners: 250 each from camps in Aliceville and Opelika, Alabama. An additional 500, again 250 from Aliceville and 250 from Opelika, arrived on November 12.[7] The camps from which the first German army POWs at Blanding came were among the early large camps, holding about 5,000 men each, which had been created in late 1942. Beginning in June 1943, American camps would begin to receive the first large influx of German prisoners of war to arrive in the United States, men of the famed Afrika Korps.[8] Ultimately about 135,000 of them would be sent to camps in the United States. Their large numbers, about a third of the German prisoners held in America, early arrival, and immense self-confidence influenced the life of all the American camps for much of the war.[9] The Afrika Korps men, known for their pride, discipline, and haughtiness, gave the American officers at Camp Blanding a severe baptism of fire within the first two months of their arrival. But that baptism, which was occurring at many of the American camps, also revealed the internal weaknesses within the famed Afrika Korps and within the German Reich itself.[10]

The troubles at Blanding began at once. One of the new arrivals, Alfred Paschke, called all the Germans together and told them that he was going to run the camp. He insisted that they should do as little work as possible for the Americans, sabotage government property, and "ride" the sick report.[11]

Problems mounted with the arrival of the additional POW contingents from Opelika and Aliceville. It seemed as though most all of the 250 from Aliceville were "either wounded or trouble makers."[12] Then, on November 15 a strike occurred, involving all but about fifty men. The German leaders claimed that the work they were being required to do on the American military base was aiding the American war effort. Paschke and others wrote to the Swiss Legation and the International Red Cross protesting the American work requirements. Only the intervention of the commanding general of Camp Blanding, Brig. Gen. L. A. Kunzig, who explained that the work the POWs were assigned was not contrary to the Geneva Convention, and a letter from the Swiss Legation to the same effect, returned the Germans to work.[13]

But it did not increase their efficiency or eliminate their inclination to test the limits of American military forbearance. Even after the American authorities declared Alfred Paschke an agitator and troublemaker and transferred him on December 7, his followers continued his policies. American officers noticed that work details did little work and German interpreters failed to properly translate conversations between American authorities and the workers. Rumors had it that the men were being told to destroy government property and that POWs who worked too well for the Americans would be removed from the work details and their lives threatened.[14]

Then, suddenly, Blanding's guards faced open riot. Capt. Edward C. Shannahan, who was making an inspection tour for the PMGO and was to report on the POW facilities in Florida, arrived at Camp Blanding late in the evening of December 26, 1943. He was told by the POW camp duty officer that he was "certainly glad to see me." Shannahan later reported that "No attention was paid to the remark until the following morning when, upon meeting Major Woodruff Lowman, the camp commander, it was discovered that there was a very tense situation existing within the prisoner of war compound."[15] The visiting captain found himself both reporter and participant in the settlement of the situation.

Shannahan found that a riot had occurred in the German army compound on December 22. He reported that "a reign of terror" had been instituted by "flying squads" that roamed the compound armed with clubs, threatening the lives of men who were denounced as traitors to the Fatherland. The Americans removed thirty prisoners for their own protection and placed them under guard in an abandoned mess hall about a half mile from the compound. During the next few days the terror behind the wire caused additional groups of two and three prisoners to flee to the guards. Soon a total of sixty-five men were segregated for their own protection.[16]

On December 25, when two additional prisoners were removed during the daily count, further protests broke out. In the evening, prisoners began gathering around the main gate of the army compound demanding that the two men taken into protective custody that day be returned. When the group failed to disperse, guards used tear gas. But "the guards had not placed the grenades accurately and the Germans were able to bury them, meanwhile shouting 'sieg' (victory)." At about 10:15 P.M. Major Lowman, the American POW camp commander, instructed the officer of the day to remove the German spokesman and eight other leaders—all high-ranking noncommissioned officers. He had them placed in two cells in Camp Blanding's U.S. military garrison prison. There they stayed until Captain Shannahan's arrival. The PMGO inspector had to explain to Blanding officers that use of the American garrison prison for disciplining POWs was contrary to the terms of the Geneva Convention. After that, the obstreperous German compound leaders were moved to a hut outside of the prison.[17]

During the next several days Captain Shannahan tried to help the Blanding authorities quiet the camp. One problem was dealing with the German spokesman, Stabsfeldwebel (master sergeant) Kaemmer. He was a former Opelika prisoner who had no real experience as a compound leader but who had lots of complaints he wanted to send by telegram directly to the Swiss Legation. Shannahan tried to get him to reconsider his complaints while he sought to establish the real causes of the discord at the camp and seek solutions.

The heart of the German spokesman's concerns was the presence of "traitors" among the German POWs and the indignities their comrades faced through association with them. Kaemmer charged that German POW cooks had to "wait on traitors" because self-segregated "traitors" were fed in the dining hall by regular POW kitchen personnel. The spokesman also complained that he could no longer control his German interpreters. They seemed not to be translating things properly. An additional complaint was that Gen. L. A. Kunzig, the American commander of the Camp Blanding garrison, had threatened the prisoners with a "no work, no eat" policy. Finally, and most provocatively, Kaemmer claimed that he had documentary proof that the sixty-five men, whom the Americans had placed in protective custody, were traitors. He asserted that several traitorous letters were found among the papers of men who had been removed from the compound. The only letter that he actually produced, however, was one from prisoner Helmut Gosse to a captain in the French Foreign Legion. It requested that the captain obtain Gosse's release so that once more he could fight for France against the Nazis.[18]

Helmut Gosse's letter, which Major Lowman sent through the Fourth Service Command to the assistant chief of staff, G-2 [intelligence], War Department General Staff, on January 4, 1944, reveals the cause of the German spokesman's concerns and some awful secrets about both the German army and the Third Reich:

> Dear Capt. You most likely expected to hear from me. After my departure from Midelf I was sent to the Libres Kadron [sic] with the S.B.A. where I stayed till the defeat of France. You surely remember Article #13 of the treaty. The paragraph in which France had to turn lose all political emigrants. I was sent to Germany then, and went to a C.C. Concentration Camp where I spend [sic] six months. After that I was sent to a prison and charged with being a traitor to the German Government. They couldn't prove that I was a member of the French Foreign Legion and a member of the democratic party. I was sent away but not freed. After a few weeks they asked whether I wanted to stay or join the German Army. I chose the German Army, and I believe that you could understand my choice if you have heard what is happening behind the barb wire fence of a concentration camp. The day I was accepted into the German Army I found out that my brother has been killed by the Gestapo at Oranenburg in the year of 1939. Dear Captain, can you understand the angry feeling which I had against those bandits. When I asked you today what the possibilities are to join your ranks again so is it only my free will to help voluntarily to chase away that regime of terror. I therefore ask you my dear Captain to answer me. I already had asked the Americans to let me join their Army for the very same reason, but didn't receive any answer. In the hope to receive a favorable answer from you, I am respectfully yours. s/ Helmut Gosse[19]

Captain Shannahan, the visiting military inspector turned negotiator, concluded that there might be one or two anti-Nazis in the group of segregated prisoners, but the balance merely rebelled against the actions of their leaders. General Kunzig, the Camp Blanding base commander, agreed and accepted Shannahan's suggestion that the Fourth Service Command be requested to issue orders transferring the agitators to an infamous Nazi camp in Alva, Oklahoma. Kunzig also said that he would request a transfer of the anti-Nazis to Camp McCain, Mississippi.[20]

While Shannahan was trying to deal with problems in the army compound, he found that he had an additional source of information and assistance in the German naval compound. Hearing that the naval compound was becoming restive due to rumors that they were hearing from the army compound, the American inspector decided to have a conference with the senior naval officer and compound spokesman, Kapitanleutnant Klaus Bargsten.[21]

Shannahan found that the U-boat captain knew just about everything that had happened in the army compound. He received his information from naval prisoners whose work details took them in the vicinity of the army prisoners. The German captain accepted Shannahan's explanations of the problems and of the actions he proposed to take. Captain Bargsten told the American that he was sure that all sixty-five men who had fled the army compound in search of protective segregation could not be traitors. In fact, he knew one of these men, a former professor, a man with whom the captain had been detained at Fort Hunt when they were being questioned by American intelligence officers. Bargsten maintained that the man "was a party member and definitely not a Communist or a traitor."[22]

Shannahan then interviewed Bargsten's friend, who said, "he and most of the men had rebelled against the orders to slow down, go on sick call and in general fail to cooperate with the American officials. He stated he and the majority of the men wished to cooperate to show the Americans that the German people are not the barbarians they are being painted."[23] After Shannahan allowed the former professor to converse with Captain Bargsten, the American not only received confirmation of the professor's comments but also learned through Bargsten the names of the chief German agitators.

When Shannahan again interviewed the pugnacious spokesman, Feldwebel Kaemmer, from the army compound, he did so with Captain Bargsten present. During that conference, Kaemmer produced a letter he intended to send to the Swiss Legation. In it he complained of being confined "in an American military prison, in the same building with a Negro awaiting the death sentence for mutiny. However, he and the rest of the leaders were removed to another building the following morning." Shannahan told Kaemmer that he was subject to the Articles of War and that he was suspected and accused of actions prejudicial to good order and discipline and charges might be filed against him. The American officer also, somewhat disingenuously, explained away the original detention of Kaemmer and the other German agitators in an American military prison. He told the German army spokesman that in the U.S. Army a man could be confined by an officer who stated that charges were to be filed against him. According to Shannahan's explanation, Blanding's POW camp commandant, Major Lowman, had considered filing charges, but had since reconsidered. That explained the original military prison confinement and the Germans' later removal to a separate building outside the prison. Of course, the American did not repeat what he had told Lowman about such confinement being contrary to the Geneva Convention.[24] After the interview, Kaemmer was returned to his separate confinement with the other agitators until they could be transferred away from the camp.

As Captain Shannahan was preparing to leave Camp Blanding on December 30, there was one last incident that he witnessed. A thirty-seven-man POW detail refused to walk to a job site, claiming that walking to work was not prescribed in the Geneva Convention. When they were informed that if they did not walk the short distance to the post dump they would not eat, thirty-three decided to walk. Four others were confined between the fences. From there they proceeded to denounce the American guards with "all the vile English words they knew." By the time Shannahan left Blanding that afternoon, they had already missed one meal because of their refusal to go to work. The PMGO visitor was sure that the incident was a test of the post commander's "no work, no eat" policy. He was equally sure that the policy, one followed throughout the United States during this time, would work.[25]

What had been learned by the Americans at Blanding, and what did they do to restore order at the camp? While they had the opportunity to see the divisions within the German army, they had a more pragmatic interest in getting rid of troublemakers, whether

Nazi or anti-Nazi. Blanding's problems were made the problems of other POW camp commanders. Following Shannahan's advice, Blanding officials initiated efforts to transfer both anti-Nazis and Nazis. The Nazis were the first to go. They were sent to the Nazi camp in Alva, Oklahoma. Orders for their transfer were issued on December 31, 1943.[26] The anti-Nazis were to go to Camp McCain, Mississippi. Approval for the transfers came from the PMGO to the commanding general of the Fourth Service Command in a letter dated January 18, 1944.[27] In requesting transfers for thirty-seven of the sixty-five men who had received protective segregation at Blanding, Major Lowman explained that two had come from Aliceville and the rest with the two groups from Opelika. Their background explained their alienation from fellow prisoners: "It is our understanding that the 962nd Regiment was more or less an Anti-Nazi or Communist Regiment, the 361st Regiment is a French Foreign Legion Regiment and some of these men are Austrians, Poles and Czechs. Some of these men served prison sentences in Germany because they did not believe in the Nazi party."[28]

An alternative and complementary, though not complimentary, perspective on the December 1943 troubles at Camp Blanding's army compound can be gleaned from reports by four German POWs who were repatriated through a wounded prisoner exchange in March 1944.[29] As repatriated prisoners they were required to respond to a German government questionnaire entitled "Report regarding treatment in British or American prisoner of war captivity."[30] The Wehrmacht's questionnaires and the stenographic records of the supplementary statements of the repatriated Blanding prisoners disclose another side to the incidents at Blanding.[31]

The four repatriated Germans were among an early contingent of POWs who had been transferred to Blanding from Aliceville, Alabama. It was the shipment of prisoners who had been described to the December 1943 PMGO visitor, Captain Shannahan, as consisting entirely of "either wounded or trouble makers."[32] From what they told the Wehrmacht it can be seen that they were probably both—wounded troublemakers. The stories that each told—to court stenographers in different German cities—had only two things in common: all four had been soldiers in Tunisia when the Afrika Korps was defeated in May 1943, and each was already wounded when captured. Beyond that, their individual stories differed somewhat. One soldier was a twenty-two-year-old private first class, in the tank corps of the Hermann Göring Division, another a private in the 962 Infantry Regiment, a third a forty-year-old private in the 665th Pioneers, and the fourth a twenty-year-old signal operator on a patrol boat. They were all captured by the British between May 7 and May 11, 1943. Shortly thereafter they and their fellow captives were turned over to the Americans in Oran, Algeria, transferred to Casablanca, Morocco, and shipped to Boston. There they were put on a train to Aliceville, Alabama, a large POW camp that held 6,000 prisoners. By their own admission they were transferred to Camp Blanding because of the trouble they caused in Aliceville.[33]

According to the private of the Hermann Göring Division, their problems at the Aliceville camp started when American officials asked them to pick cotton. Sergeant Warnstedt, the German prison camp spokesman, prisoner company leader, and former official of the propaganda ministry—later a troublemaker at Camp Blanding as well—refused on the prisoners' behalf. The POWs considered the work to be a part of the American war effort. Their resistance to the cotton-picking order first led to their segregation in a branch camp of the Aliceville base camp and subsequent transfer to Camp Blanding.

The soldier from the Pioneer regiment told a similar story, but from a different angle. He claimed that while he was in the camp hospital in Aliceville, he saw a German POW admitted who had received a shotgun blast to the chest and face. Reportedly, the wounded man, who died several days later, had been shot twice by a Jewish guard. The guard had bragged that he would kill a Nazi. According to the Pioneer, the POWs at Aliceville reacted to this situation by refusing to work for a month and by demanding that Jewish guards be removed. However, the Jewish guards were still there and the Pioneer's whole company was transferred because of the problems they caused the Americans. Some went to a disciplinary camp in Oklahoma, and the Pioneer and the other wounded men in the POW company were sent to Camp Blanding.

As though to suggest the harshness of this transfer, two of the transferees described Camp Blanding as a place of unbearable heat, infested with snakes and deadly scorpions. The camp, one complained, was a training area for white and black American troops, but the Americans were rotated every three months while the Germans were not. Able-bodied German prisoners were required to do rough work, such as loading coal and ashes, cleaning streets, and cutting trees. He did note, however, that the food at Blanding was no worse than at Aliceville and rations were not cut when the Germans resisted American attempts to propagandize them for democracy.

The repatriated Panzer soldier spoke of conflicts between communists and national socialist-thinking prisoners both at Aliceville and Blanding. He warned the German military that in the future they should be sure that *Bewährungsbataillone* (probationary battalions) not be used against the English or Americans. It was his view that such troops—"composed mostly of political prisoners and to a lesser extent other criminals"—deserted too readily to the enemy. Then they were given preferential treatment in the American camps. He claimed that in Aliceville and Blanding, conflicts occurred when members of these disloyal units separated themselves from their fellow prisoners, formed soldiers' councils, and attempted to replace camp leaders. He asserted that at Blanding there were sixty communists who went over to the Americans after one of their number was nearly beaten to death by "loyal" Germans. The returnee had been told by another Blanding comrade that there were as many as 120 more prisoners at Blanding who had secretly agreed to help the Americans.

The Panzer soldier claimed that he and his comrades attempted to find out who belonged to this disloyal group; but while loyal Germans gathered and rejoiced that the sixty communists had been taken away, guards suddenly put on gas masks and threw tear gas grenades into the crowd. Later, an American general threatened to withhold the German prisoners' food and pay because of their open hostility, but Sergeant Warnstedt pointed out that this action contravened the Geneva Convention. The American response, the informant told the Wehrmacht, was that they removed the prisoners' spokesman, three company leaders, and four sergeants from the camp and confined them in a barracks together with Negroes awaiting the death penalty.

The German army camp spokesman at Blanding had asked the Panzer soldier to particularly report an incident concerning the mistreatment of several wounded men. According to the spokesman, the prisoners in question had always been driven to their work site, but one day they were told to walk instead. When three declared they could not walk because of foot wounds, they found no sympathy. Instead they were locked up for twenty-four hours without food, although they expressed the wish to American officers that they be examined by a doctor. When the doctor did see them the next day, they were declared unfit for work and better food was ordered for them.

Obviously the German and American points of view differed on the stories of the men behind the wire and the incidents Captain Shannahan reported during his December visit to Camp Blanding. These incidents reveal the nature of the early American experience with German POWs in microcosm. Discipline within the camps was generally upheld, though sometimes ineffectually. American authorities insisted on a "no work, no eat" policy and segregated Nazis and overzealous anti-Nazis. Despite what loyal Germans reported, anti-Nazis, or communists, were not particularly privileged. Nor were they usually allowed to enter American service.[34] Indeed, it was not unusual for anti-Nazis to receive treatment that was as harsh as that meted out to the Nazis.[35] The solution sought by local camp authorities to problems caused by political diversities within their camps was to transfer troublemakers to other camps.

German reports concerning the events at Camp Blanding did not indicate that the Americans were as frustrated by anti-Nazi elements as by Nazi ones.[36] Because discipline and cooperation within camps depended largely on the existing German military hierarchy among prisoners, individuals who bucked that system were unwelcome—even to the Americans. This was true whether they were Nazis resisting American efforts or anti-Nazis resisting both German and American military authorities. Sometimes, camp commandants classified any troublemaker as a Nazi, thus hopelessly confusing the segregation program.[37] Only later in the POW experience in America did camp administrators get assistance from trained intelligence officers who could help segregate and reeducate POWs. These officers—interested in showing growth of anti-Nazi sentiment—used what they thought were anti-Nazi elements as part of their propaganda efforts to prepare repatriated POWs to be the leaven of a democratic post-Hitlerian Germany. Small numbers of these anti-Nazis were selected and sent to training schools for early postwar repatriation.[38]

Slowly American intelligence officers began to recognize the massive cleavages within the ranks of Hitler's armies, even if that recognition still tended to conform to existing Nazi and anti-Nazi preconceptions. They found that even the famous Afrika Korps, reputedly the most patriotic and fanatical of Hitler's legions, suffered from disunity that came from mixing elite military units with those whose purpose was primarily penal. Probationary battalions, made up of concentration camp inmates, were among those German units captured by the Allies when German forces collapsed in Tunisia in May 1943. The appearance in American POW camps of men from these unique units mixed in with those from more elite units of the German army divulged the serious political tensions within the Wehrmacht. Captives and captors came to realize that the German military uniform concealed, but it did not efface, differences that divided and separated Germans from each other. Communists, democratic socialists, labor leaders, and democrats found themselves incarcerated at Camp Blanding—as elsewhere within America—with obedient military men and "patriotic Germans," some of whom were real Nazis. Others were just nationalistic Germans who refused to cooperate with the "enemy" and despised those who did.

What was manifested between November 1943 and February 1944, when the Afrika Korps came to Blanding, was the complexities of European nationalism, racism, and totalitarianism of the 1940s. The POWs had witnessed these tensions in their homelands, seen the horrors of war, and finally found themselves far from the front but hardly safe from the hatreds that divided the German Reich. They were less endangered by the Americans than by each other. In the relative tranquillity and security of the Florida interior, the devils that the German POWs brought with them from Europe broke forth to afflict what could have been a peaceful paradise in the midst of a world at war.

THE "WORST CAMP IN AMERICA":
CLEWISTON ESCAPES AND A SUICIDE

Sometimes the physical conditions of a POW camp, combined with the psychological tensions among its disparate inmates, created in individual prisoners the desire for escape at all costs. One risk was death at the hands of trigger-happy guards, frightened local civilians or lawmen, or members of the FBI. While the U.S. Army had immediate responsibility for capturing fugitive POWs, it was ultimately the Federal Bureau of Investigation that took over if the escapee got beyond the grasp of the local military. It was not unusual for military authorities to warn new arrivals in American POW camps that their ultimate pursuers would be the FBI. The reputation of Hoover's G-men, made famous in numerous American prewar movies, combined with German assumptions that the FBI might handle its responsibilities like Hitler's dreaded Gestapo, was used as a potential deterrent to would-be escapees.[1]

Still, such a deterrent was not foolproof. Escape attempts could be used to prove bravery, prowess, and individuality, as well as to seek temporary freedom. Even unsuccessful escape attempts could lead to transfer to other camps where physical and psychological surroundings and labor responsibilities might be more congenial. Another form of escape was more permanent: suicide. While from the national perspective the number of escape attempts and suicides was lower than among similar-sized civilian populations in the United States and Germany, both phenomena occurred at Camp Blanding's first branch camp, Clewiston.[2]

Perhaps more accurately the camp should have been called the Liberty Point camp, because it was located at Liberty Point Plantation Village in Glades County near Moore Haven, just north of Hendry County and its county seat, Clewiston.[3] But Clewiston was the nearest large town. The camp was located not far from the dike on the southwest shore of Lake Okeechobee. When visited by Guy Métraux of the International Red Cross in March 1945, the Clewiston camp received a very mixed review. The small white wooden barracks with green roofs made a "good impression at first look."[4] But a longer look, combined with the weather on the day of the visit, led to further comments in the IRC report that suggested a far different story. The camp, Métraux noted, was in a flat treeless region and very dry. "There had been no rain for six months." The heat was described as "continuous"—103 degrees Fahrenheit on the day of the visit. Moreover, the camp, located in the middle of a sugarcane field, held prisoners engaged in the incredibly hard work of cutting cane in snake-infested fields.[5]

Due to the harsh working conditions in the camp, a number of the German inmates made desperate efforts to be transferred. According to the German doctor, Dr. Franz Josef Lang, prisoners often wounded themselves with knives or feigned hysteria in order to obtain medical transfers.[6] The IRC man concluded his report with the telling phrase, "This camp is known perhaps as the worst in all America."[7]

What Guy Métraux did not write in his report was that the reputation of the Clewiston camp had already been confirmed by an escape-suicide and three other unsuccessful escape attempts in the months before his visit. It is to these acts of desperation, as well as to more mundane tales of the "worst camp in America," that one must turn in order to sample the extremes of the German POW experience in Florida.

The Clewiston camp was set up in February 1944 in response to the U.S. Sugar Corporation's need for labor in its sugar fields. This was usually the labor of local blacks and West Indian migrants imported for the purpose. Wartime conditions, the draft, and higher pay in other occupations led the sugar company to contact the army for use of German prisoner-of-war labor. As Jay W. Moran, general manager and vice president of the U.S. Sugar Corporation told the *Clewiston News:* "We feel that we are cooperating with our government in making easier its task of handling the war prisoners in this country." He also admitted that the POWs were to provide a "partial solution of labor difficulties which the United States Sugar Corporation in common with all farmers in the country have been experiencing in recent months."[8]

Despite reassurances in the Clewiston newspaper that the POWs had "been together in a prisoner of war camp in the south [Aliceville, Alabama, though that was not mentioned in the article][9] and their camp routine and organization was well established," the fact was that the operation at Clewiston initially had a make-do atmosphere. David Forshay, the company clerk of the American guard unit at Clewiston and a Lake Worth native, recalled the establishment of the camp as being rather casual—as had been the army's whole approach to the POW program from his point of view. As he noted tongue in cheek some forty years later: he was selected as a guard at the POW camp at Aliceville "because of his ability with languages"—he had had some Spanish in school. While home on leave in Lake Worth in early 1944, he received orders to meet 1st Lt. Dwight Field at the West Palm Beach Post Office and assist him in the establishment of a branch camp at Liberty Point, near Clewiston. According to Forshay, Lieutenant Field was an old National Guard master sergeant who had been promoted from the ranks and assigned to the Aliceville camp.[10]

While the U.S. Sugar Company set up the camp, as required by government contract, things like office equipment were scarce. Before the Germans arrived, Forshay set up his own typewriter from home on an apple crate and hammered out Field's first orders. When the U.S. guard detachment under Capt. Robert J. Arnold came by train from Aliceville, Lieutenant Field and his clerk were already ensconced at the old sugar camp at Liberty Point, around which the U.S. Sugar Corporation had built the required wire fence. Parenthetically, Forshay noted that Lieutenant Field and Captain Arnold did not get along well. Arnold was a younger man and an OCS graduate. Later, when another Blanding branch camp was set up at White Springs, Arnold was transferred there and a freshly promoted Captain Field ran the Clewiston camp alone.

Captain Arnold told the Kiwanis Club at Clewiston in June 1944 that his men at the camp were elements of the 572d Prisoner of War Detachment and they guarded 310 German POWs. His charges were all from Rommel's Corps, of high intelligence and fine physical fitness, and considered themselves Hitler's elite. As such, they rejected American news of German setbacks. According to Arnold, there was not an anti-Nazi in the batch in the spring of 1944.[11]

An unusually extensive and informative article on the Clewiston camp in the *Miami Daily News* proclaimed the same message: "Arrogant Nazis Still Laud Hitler."[12] The article displayed photographs of camp commander Capt. Robert J. Arnold and four pictures of various groups of German prisoners. They were shown jauntily marching off to work with shovels, riflelike, over their shoulders; arriving on a truck for work in the sugarcane fields; playing chess; and purchasing a candy bar in the stockade canteen. The news reporter tried to capture the attitudes of the prisoners, yet reassure the public that they were well guarded and secured. Their attitude, as described by Milton Sosin, the *Miami Daily News* reporter, was soldierly and self-assured:

> *They are jaunty, confident, and arrogant members of the fuehrer's forces—not cowed and beaten soldiers of a nation being pushed into a tighter and tighter circle. . . . On 'D' day, they arrived in camp from the sugar cane fields in good formation under the watchful eyes of the guards. Their shovels were swung over their shoulders all at the same angle, as if they were still carrying rifles. They were in step as they marched down their company street within the barbed wire compound. At the command of their elected company leader, a bronzed Viking giant who held a post in the German army comparable to our sergeant-major, they halted near one of the plantation cottages owned by the sugar company, where a Miami Daily News reporter, photographer, and Captain Arnold watched them.*

According to Sosin: "All look healthy and are deeply tanned. Some of them were tanned when they arrived in the United States—tanned by the sun of the African desert, where many of them were captured. They are young. Even now, some of them, veterans of five years in Hitler's army are only 23 or 24. Most of them range in ages from 25 to 30, although one man, seen coming in with a work gang, was much older and sported a bar of mustaches of the 'handlebar' variety." Farther on in the article the themes of soldierly pride and self-assurance continued: "no matter from what walk of life they came, what their rank in the German army (there are no commissioned officers among the Clewiston prisoners) or what may have happened to them or their families, they are all Nazis and proud of it. When one talked, the others in the group listened, waiting to pounce on any word that might be taken for a criticism of Hitler or a phrase that might be interpreted as an admission of defeat or defeat to come."

The Miami reporter's description and evaluation of the situation among the POWs at Clewiston was accurate—but amazingly more detailed and revelatory about a specific camp than government officials usually allowed.[13] The earliest large group of German prisoners to arrive in Florida, as throughout America, were members of Hitler's elite Afrika Korps. Generally in their twenties, these young men were—and certainly perceived themselves to be—the best of the German army. Captured relatively early in the war, while Germany was still on the offensive, they considered their own capture in May of 1943 a fluke. In their minds, theirs was a winning cause. Reports to the contrary, whether in the American press and radio or in the perspectives of later arrivals, were considered propaganda at best and treason at worst.

After D-Day there came to the POW camps in America new captives who had experienced a different, if not yet defeated, Germany. These later arrivals were usually younger or older than the earlier camp inmates and came from units that were less distinguished than the Afrika Korps. In many camps, the new arrivals were greeted not as long-lost brothers but as suspected traitors—or as undesirable, distinctly "unmilitary" additions to the camp scene.[14] This was the case at the Clewiston camp as well. Thirty years later a former guard at the camp noted that unit pride created problems between the Afrika Korps men and the post–Normandy invasion newcomers. He also inadvertently revealed the extent to which the prejudices of the Afrika Korps were picked up by their American guards. He commented that by 1944 the Americans felt themselves to be "old soldiers," like the Afrika Korps men. He admitted that both the Germans and the Americans at the camp referred disparagingly to the more recent arrivals as "young punks."[15]

This situation, characteristic of many POW camps after the summer of 1944, almost certainly played a role in a suicide mystery at the Clewiston camp at the end of 1944. It is a mystery that, though well investigated, is still not fully explained.[16] And, it is one that leads to divergent suspicions that still exist on both sides of the Atlantic. A young POW, Karl Behrens, apparently escaped from the camp and was later found hanging by FBI searchers in early January

1945. A brother in Germany has accepted a depression-suicide explanation. At least one former Clewiston prisoner wonders about foul play by the Americans. Some Americans suspect the work of German zealots.[17]

Karl Behrens was eighteen years old when he was taken prisoner in Cherbourg, France, on June 27, 1944. He was one of 25,000 new prisoners captured by the Americans that day. Shipped to the United States shortly thereafter, he arrived at Camp Blanding on July 19. He was transferred to the Clewiston branch camp on August 16. The youth from Oberneuland, near Bremen, in northern Germany, had obtained a diploma as a machine fitter in 1942, at the age of sixteen. He was then inducted into a paramilitary labor battalion, which worked on repairing fighter planes near his hometown. In April 1944 his unit was ordered to France. Within two months he was in captivity and within another six weeks facing the strains of an unfamiliar Florida and a world of strenuous labor in the cane fields among hardened older soldiers who considered recent captives from the French campaign to be "punks."[18]

In September and October 1944, the American military, in an effort to "sell" the presence of German POWs in America and place developments in the camps within the best possible light, explained to the newspaper-reading public that 243,848 prisoners were already in the United States in some 126 base camps and 400 work camps. Amid a general description of the work programs was the suggestion that while the fanaticism of the early POWs was rather high, the arrival of Normandy prisoners was helping to prove to Afrika Korps members that American news concerning German defeats were not lies. The army admitted that there had been murders and that there had been a particular rash of recent suicides, but said that insurance actuaries showed that the rate was lower than in a normal city of comparable size to that of the current POW population in America.[19] Within a few months Karl Behrens's name would be added to those listed in the suicide statistics.

What did Behrens experience during the fall of his first and last year in Florida? For one thing, flight from a hurricane. In late October 1944, when a major hurricane threatened Florida, schools were closed, civilians were urged to take precautions, and the Clewiston POWs were moved from their fragile internment camp near the shore of Lake Okeechobee and taken by train to Camp Blanding to ride out the storm. Though there was major damage to the Florida citrus and vegetable crops, the storm's effect on the Clewiston area was rather slight: sixty-eight-mile-per-hour winds at the peak and less than an inch of rainfall, though area residents were without electrical power and water for a short time during the night of October 19–20.[20] What Behrens and his Clewiston comrades experienced at Camp Blanding was more of a disturbance than the gale they missed at Clewiston. The temporary arrivals at Blanding faced all kinds of friction while living briefly with their inconvenienced, cramped, and less-than-hospitable countrymen at the Blanding base camp. As one American guard from the Clewiston camp put it: "Both groups got into fights: Germans from the two camps fought, the American guards from the two camps fought, and even the pet dogs from both of the camps did not get along."[21]

And then there was the hard work of the sugarcane fields that began almost as soon as the Germans returned to Clewiston. On the first of November, harvesting began on a wide front of some fifty-two miles around the southern shores of Lake Okeechobee. While most of the labor used by the U.S. Sugar Corporation was provided by a large number of Jamaicans, "in addition, the company has a contingent of German war prisoners, who have proved satisfactory in field operations."[22] Finally, there was even a cold spell. On December 13, 1944, the temperature at 8 A.M. in Clewiston was thirty-two degrees.[23]

There were other things going on within the camp that indicated subtle games of "catch me if you can" were being played around the camp by both the U.S. military and their German prisoners. A report to the director of the Prisoner of War Operations Division on visits by Maj. Edward C. Shannahan to several Florida camps during late December 1944 and early January 1945 discloses some insights in this regard.[24] For one thing, the camp's commanding officer—by then, apparently Capt. Dwight Field, though the report does not mention a name—impressed Shannahan as being "extremely capable and desirous of getting all the work he could out of the prisoners." When Shannahan suggested that prisoners be used as KPs in the American mess hall, the "Camp Commanding Officer stated he could not do this as he had to have 90% of his available strength on contract work." However, Shannahan's report hints that the commanding officer was less than attentive to prisoner welfare. For instance, the visitor noted that there was no hot water in several of the POWs' washrooms; there was no recreation area— "Prisoners are hauled to a field about 8 miles from the camp every Friday (they work Sundays)"; and there were problems in securing cigarettes and beer for the POW canteen. There had not been any cigarettes for almost two months when Shannahan visited. The post exchange officer at Morrison Field in West Palm Beach would not provide cigarettes because he claimed his distributor would cut off the supply to his base if any of his cigarettes went to the prisoners. The same problem existed regarding beer. A solution to that problem was found, however, when the post exchange officer at Camp Blanding sent a carload of beer to the branch camp.

But the Germans seem to have played the game, too, though Shannahan thought that could be remedied. On the day of his visit, thirty men were on sick call, and the records indicated that during the last two weeks the average daily sick call list included 23–24 names. The American inspector noted the source of the problem at once: sick call was held at 7:45 A.M. and work details left the camp at 7:30 A.M. He suggested that the sick call hour be changed.

All was not well at the Clewiston camp: the events of the next four weeks confirmed this. On Monday morning, January 1, 1945, the *Miami Herald* published a mug shot of Karl Behrens with a short note of his "escape" under the heading of "War Prisoner Hunted in Glades." Following standard procedure, the regional FBI agent in charge of the Miami office, Richard G. Danner, announced that Karl Behrens, eighteen, a six-foot, 155-pound, brown-eyed, fair-complexioned German with light brown hair, wearing blue or khaki denim with the letters *PW* on the back, had escaped from the Clewiston camp.[25] The next day, a follow-up story on page 1 said, "Fugitive POW Found Hanged." The story told how FBI agents and military personnel had found the body of the German hanging from a tree two miles northwest of Clewiston. Agent Danner indicated that while there was no suicide note, circumstances indicated that the German had taken his own life.[26]

An FBI report on the incident is tantalizing because, while it reveals more about the escape and suicide, it alludes to some unsettling possibilities, especially through a mysterious note that was found with Behrens's effects. The official report also indicates in its form, language, and subject matter how the FBI performed its task as the agency responsible for apprehending escaped prisoners of war.

The FBI report presented first a synopsis of the facts of the case: "Karl Behrens, a Prisoner of War, 18, escaped on the afternoon of December 30, 1944, from the Branch P.O.W. Camp, located seven miles Northwest of Clewiston, Florida, while working in the sugar cane field. Immediate search instituted on 12-30-44 and on 1-1-45 subject found dead by Special Agents Hugh MacMillan and George Brouillard hanging from a tree at a point approximately 75 yards South of dike bordering Lake Okeechobee, Florida. Army authorities advised stops canceled. Description set out."[27]

The details of the investigation as it developed toward its conclusion and to the final FBI field agent report are presented in seven pages of good bureaucratic style, some of which is worth summarizing. Other portions of the report call for direct quotation in order to capture the flavor of the report, the lax situation that existed in the POW camp, and the air of mystery that hung—and still hangs—over the incident.

The FBI investigation began with a 9 P.M. telephone call on December 30 to Agent MacMillan in West Palm Beach from the American commander of the Clewiston prison camp. He informed MacMillan that a prisoner, Karl Behrens, had escaped from a sugar-cane field sometime between 3 P.M. and 6 P.M. that day and that a check of the prisoner's clothing revealed that some items were missing. He also told the FBI man that a preliminary check to locate the prisoner in the vicinity of the camp had failed to bring the desired result. According to MacMillan's report: "Upon receipt of this information stops were immediately placed with all law enforcement agencies throughout the State of Florida and in addition appropriate publicity was released pertaining to his escape."[28]

MacMillan drove west that night to Clewiston, arriving at 11 P.M. On the way out to the camp, he looked under the bridge at Twenty Mile Bend and stopped to alert owners of several filling stations along the way. Once at Clewiston, he was joined by fellow agents Jack Borden and George A. Brouillard, and also by Agent John Lomme, who was stationed in Fort Myers.[29] MacMillan coordinated and directed the extensive search in cooperation with the chief of police of Clewiston and local patrolmen and constables from Belle Glade, Pahokee, and Fort Myers, as well as with patrolmen from the Florida State Highway Patrol. Additionally, the prisoner of war camp made available a detail of six men. All of these individuals were assigned to strategic points on highways and roads adjacent to the camp and on the dike adjoining Lake Okeechobee. MacMillan then tried to keep warm by sitting near the fireplace in the Clewiston Inn during the very cold night of December 30 while he awaited the results of the search efforts.

As the investigation developed, MacMillan learned from an American sergeant that about 5:30 P.M. on December 30, 1944, a German prisoner, the company leader, informed him that Behrens had not reported to the compound after finishing his work in the sugarcane fields with work group Number 2. The American sergeant went to the area where Behrens had been working, one-quarter of a mile west and about one-half a mile north of the camp, accompanied by two German POWs, one of whom acted as an interpreter. Not finding Behrens, they returned to the camp and reported the incident to the camp commander. Then they checked the POW compound. Finally, the sergeant returned to the original work area for an extensive search with the help of another American guard and three German prisoners. This continued until dark.

Interviews with German prisoners, which Agent MacMillan related in his report, reveal a certain laxity in Clewiston POW camp life that was not atypical of situations in many of the POW camps throughout wartime America. Certainly the absence of close supervision by armed American guards became obvious, though it was not directly mentioned or criticized in the FBI report.

MacMillan learned through interviews with the German company leader, whom he questioned through the efforts of both a German POW interpreter and an American army interpreter, that Behrens had been last seen in the compound around noon on December 30. The German camp leader told the FBI man that he knew of no plans that the young soldier may have had to escape. Instead, he suggested, that Behrens might have fallen asleep in the cane fields and then later left the field to take a swim in the nearby canal and drowned. Other prisoners in Behrens's work group had stated that he liked to swim.

Interviews with other German POWs further reveal both the laxness of the camp and the apparent alienation of Behrens from his fellow inmates. It is remarkable how no one seemed to notice his absence from work groups. For instance, Behrens's work group leader told the FBI that the young man sat down for a rest in the cane fields at around 2 p.m. His group had been cutting weeds along a lane cut between two forty-acre fields of cane. The group leader then left the immediate area with about six members of the group in order to work elsewhere, leaving Behrens and eight others to work near the end of the lane. The work leader told MacMillan that Behrens could not speak English, was quiet, in good health, and a good worker. Behrens's German work leader and the other members of his work detail did not think that Behrens would attempt to escape, rather they believed that the young man may have had some accident.

Another prisoner volunteered that he considered himself a good friend of Behrens and had been the one who reported his absence from the camp. The prisoner told MacMillan that he was from the same area of Germany as Behrens, though they had not known each other before coming to the camp. He was positive that Behrens had no plans for an escape and feared that his absence was due to an accident. He said that Behrens enjoyed swimming, was "rather childish," and "liked to play." On the other hand, the American private who acted as an interpreter for the camp told the FBI man that he gathered from the statements of various prisoners interviewed that Behrens was "rather of a despondent and quiet nature."

Then, there was a mysterious note among Behrens's effects. It was "an undated letter in German addressed, 'Lieber Karl,' and signed in German 'The Christmas-man.'" The American interpreter at the camp prepared a translation for the FBI. "It is to be noted the letter is unintelligible and that the original letter in question was transmitted on January 5, 1945, by the Miami office to Major _____, Prisoner of War Camp, SCU 441, Camp Blanding, Florida."[30] Whether the note was written by a friend or foe is unknown. Its impact on Karl Behrens's behavior also remains an open question. But it was one that did not trouble the FBI for long. Their job was to find their man. The army could worry about the escapee's personal life.

On January 1, 1945, at about 5 p.m. FBI agents Brouillard and MacMillan found Karl Behrens. He was hanging by the neck from a small tree. The location was about seventy-five yards south of the dike bordering Lake Okeechobee, about two miles northwest of the

Clewiston POW camp. They immediately informed the American officers at the camp and returned to the body accompanied by two American captains, a sergeant, a detail of soldiers and two German prisoners. The sergeant took several pictures of the hanging prisoner; four sets of three different views were attached to the official FBI report.

The rest of the FBI report goes into the rather graphic details of the condition of the body and the conclusions of the American POW camp doctor and the FBI agents regarding the apparent suicide. "There was no indication that a struggle of any kind had taken place in the immediate vicinity of this tree." The Medical Corps captain who was at the scene examined the body after it was lowered from the tree and reported that he found no evidence of violence or injuries. Death appeared to be by strangulation. He estimated that death had occurred the same day that Behrens had been reported missing.[31]

For the FBI and the army the case was closed. The story of the discovery of the body of the apparent suicide was reported the next day in a brief front page notice in both the *Palm Beach Post* and the *Miami Herald*.[32] Meanwhile, Karl Behrens's body was returned to Camp Blanding for burial in the POW graveyard at the camp on January 5, 1945. After the war and the reversion of Camp Blanding from a federal base back into a Florida National Guard facility, the body was transferred and reinterred in the POW graveyard at Fort Benning, Georgia.[33]

Bernhard Behrens, the surviving brother of Karl, who forty years later continued to live in the family home in Oberneuland, Germany, "thinks he understands what drove Karl to take his life: His father had tried to kill himself several times in the 1930s and Karl never got over the shock. Bernhard also says his brother had difficulty dealing with the hard labor, the homesickness, and the intolerable heat."[34] Some Clewiston locals still wonder if Behrens was killed by diehards within the camp.[35] At the time, officers at the camp said that there was no substantiation for the belief that Behrens had been done in because of anti-Nazi beliefs. As a cause for his suicide, they noted that he had not heard from his family since his capture.[36] Another Clewiston German POW escapee, whose fate was different than Behrens's, blamed the camp administration. Although without direct knowledge of the Behrens affair, because he arrived in the camp shortly after it occurred, Gerhard Anklam claims that he and his fellow escapee, Wilhelm Stüttgen, had their own feelings: "Wilhelm Stüttgen and I saw a reason, as Karl Behrens probably did, to leave due to the terrible treatment of the POWs by the camp commander."[37]

Gerhard Anklam was one of four men who attempted to escape from the camp within a little over a month's time: Karl Behrens's flight and suicide were on December 30, 1944; then Gerhard Anklam and Wilhelm Stüttgen attempted escape on January 23, 1945; and finally Gottfried Pernull made his attempted flight on January 27. The later, more temporary, escapes will be explored in the next chapter. They are mentioned here only as indices of problems at the Clewiston camp and of the kinds of solutions that were sought by individual POWs. What were they fleeing? Certainly there was the hard work in the sugar fields that was mentioned by every visitor to the camp.[38] There was the brusque manner of the commanding officer who showed more interest in work than in the welfare of his prisoners.[39] There was also the Afrika Korps.

The haughty and jaunty unit pride the Afrika Korps men displayed at the Clewiston camp impressed Capt. Robert Arnold, the first American commander of the camp,[40] and a *Miami Daily News* reporter who visited the camp.[41] And, that haughty pride persuaded even the camp guards that the later arrivals in the camp were merely "young punks."[42] Karl Baum, one of the Afrika Korps prisoners at Clewiston and a postwar immigrant to California, denied that his comrades at Clewiston mistreated other German prisoners.[43] But they may not have been overly friendly or attentive to captives who appeared in America after they did. Certainly no one seemed to know or care a lot about Karl Behrens. Afrika Korps men generally had their own unit loyalty and tended to think of themselves as the only good and true Germans. This was the case throughout most of the war, even when they might claim other national identities after the war was over. Karl Baum's name, for instance, is found in a July 1945 list of soldiers from the Clewiston camp who claimed to be citizens of nations other than Germany. In Baum's case, this was Czechoslovakia. Capt. Dwight Field, who signed the form as the commander of the camp, added at the bottom of the list of sixteen Austrians, seven Czechs, two Italians, and one Pole the following: "REMARK: No POW on the above roster has ever advanced himself as being a national other than German prior to the termination of war in Europe."[44] It is also interesting to note that only one of the four escapees from Clewiston seems to have been from the older Afrika Korps group: Anklam's co-escapee, Wilhelm Stüttgen, twenty-one, captured in Tunisia in 1943. Karl Behrens, eighteen, was captured in Cherbourg in June 1944, and Gerhard Anklam, twenty-one, was captured in Italy in September 1944. Gottfried Pernull, nineteen, was probably too young for the Afrika Korps.[45] The Clewiston escapees were in all likelihood fleeing the alienation they felt behind the wire more than they were fleeing "German-hater" Captain Fields. The Afrika Korps men had the peer group that made life bearable even in a sugarcane-cutting camp.

By September 8, 1945, the Clewiston camp was a memory. The camp closed on September 6 and its German POW contingent took up residence at Green Cove Springs on September 8.[46] The vacated Clewiston POW camp at Liberty Point was used by later sugarcane cutters—also migrant laborers but volunteers from the West Indies. The temporary housing that made up the structures of the camp eventually decayed out of existence.[47]

What remained were memories. As with most of the POW camps throughout America, the memories were generally good. American soldiers and civilians who worked or lived with the POWs saw them as humans and vice versa. Funny stories and happy memories replaced sordid details or unfortunate incidents. The Germans were remembered pleasantly by civilians in Clewiston with whom they worked and shared lunches.[48] They were also remembered by a Lutheran pastor from West Palm Beach, who drove weekly to the POW camps at Belle Glade and Clewiston in order to minister to the small group of stalwart Protestants who attended his services. He invited his German flock to write to him after their repatriation, but none ever did. He kept a 2' 6" by 1' 6" painting of a German winter scene that was given to him by one of the POWs. It was signed, "Rubner—USA—1944."[49] Pleasant memories also remained in the mind of David Forshay, the American guard from Lake Worth. He remembered joint American-German fishing excursions, teasing the "good soldier Schweik" types, and admiring the courage and skill of the German snake hunters who wanted the hides for souvenir belts.[50] Even Gerhard Anklam, the would-be escapee who recalls "the German-hater" Capt. Dwight Field, had exciting escape-attempt stories to remember and his own snake-skin belt from his Clewiston days.[51]

Other memories are not as pleasant. On February 26, 1979, I visited the Palm Beach County Court House office of Judge Hugh MacMillan, the former wartime FBI resident agent in West Palm Beach and later Palm Beach Circuit Court judge. When I arrived, the judge rose from his desk to reach for and consult a small diary he had kept while with the FBI during the war. As he brought the diary down from its upper shelf, a photograph fell at our feet. It was a shadowy exposure that had been taken on January 1, 1945. Barely recognizable in the picture was the form of a man hanging by his neck from a tree. It was a picture of eighteen-year-old Karl Behrens.[52] He had escaped the Clewiston camp in body, but not in spirit.

1. Sgt. Tom W. Malone with German POWs at Clewiston. Courtesy of Clewiston Museum.

SITE OF WORLD WAR II
PRISONER OF WAR CAMP

—•●•—

The demands of World War II created a shortage of agricultural workers here at home. To alleviate the problem, the Prisoner of War Special Projects Division of the United States Army established some 500 camps with a total capacity of 378,000 prisoners to supply laborers.

Camp Blanding, near Starke, was headquarters for the 22 Prisoner of War camps in Florida, with the Dade City camp being designated Branch Camp No. 7. Before assignments were made, U. S. officials picked out the hard core Nazi party members for placement at locations away from the rank and file prisoners. Operations began here in March 1944, and the camp housed an average of 250 men—many from Rommel's famed *Afrika Korps* - during its two-year existence.

Built by the U. S. Army Corps of Engineers, this camp had a three-tent mess hall which was also used for church services, classes and movies; a canteen attached to a small day room; a larger day room with table tennis and a piano; sleeping quarters and latrines.

(Continued on other side)

SITE OF WORLD WAR II
PRISONER OF WAR CAMP

(Continued from other side)

—•●•—

The prisoners (PWs) worked at Dade City's Pasco Packing Association, at the McDonald Mine in Brooksville where they made limestone bricks for Pasco Packing Building No. 7, and at Cummer Sons Cypress Mill in Lacoochee. They were paid local prevailing wages for their labor with the money - except for an $.80 daily allowance for personal needs-going to the U. S. Government.

Although guarded by U. S. officers, the PWs were under the command of a German officer. Religious needs were met by the minister of the Zion Lutheran Church of Tampa and priests from nearby Saint Leo Abbey.

Several who were incarcerated here have kept in touch by letter, a few have returned for nostalgic visits and many fondly recall the care they received here during this difficult time.

PLACED BY
THE PASCO BOARD OF COUNTY COMMISSIONERS
AND
THE PASCO COUNTY HISTORICAL PRESERVATION COMMITTEE
IN FLORIDA'S SESQUICENTENNIAL YEAR - 1995
CELEBRATING 150 YEARS OF STATEHOOD

2. Pasco County historical plaque at the site of the Dade City camp. Courtesy of Werner H. Burkert.

3. Horst Finke in Afrika Korps uniform, Tripoli, 1942. Courtesy of Herman Finke.

4. Horst Finke in Afrika Korps uniform. POW picture taken in Aliceville, Alabama, in 1943 for relatives in Germany. Courtesy of Herman Finke.

PRISONER OF WAR CAMP

CAMP BLANDING, FLORIDA

This **Certificate of Achievement** is awarded to:

F I N K E Horst   81G-82264

WHO HAS SUCCESSFULLY COMPLETED A COURSE IN

Geography of the U. S. A.

FOR PRISONERS OF WAR CONDUCTED AT

POW Branch Camp, Belle Glade, Florida

IN WITNESS THEREOF, THE UNDERSIGNED HAVE SET THEIR

NAMES THIS 23rd DAY OF January 1946

NAME   C. CLARK   RANK   NAME   RANK   NAME   GRADE
ASSISTANT EXECUTIVE OFFICER   CAMP COMMANDER   PW DIRECTOR OF STUDIES

5. Certificate of achievement, geography of the United States, for Horst Finke. Courtesy of Herman Finke.

PRISONER OF WAR CAMP

CAMP BLANDING, FLORIDA

This **Certificate of Achievement** is awarded to:

F I N K E Horst   81G-82264

WHO HAS SUCCESSFULLY COMPLETED A COURSE IN

The Study of the English Language

Intermediate
FOR PRISONERS OF WAR CONDUCTED AT

POW Branch Camp, Belle Glade, Florida

IN WITNESS THEREOF, THE UNDERSIGNED HAVE SET THEIR

NAMES THIS 23rd DAY OF January 1946

NAME   C. CLARK   RANK   NAME   RANK   NAME   GRADE
ASSISTANT EXECUTIVE OFFICER   CAMP COMMANDER   PW DIRECTOR OF STUDIES

6. Certificate of achievement, study of the English language, for Horst Finke. Courtesy of Herman Finke.

7. Horst Finke (with hat and back to camera), working at *déminage*, St.-Aubin-sur-Mer, France, July 1946. Courtesy of Herman Finke.

8. Gerhard Anklam *(right)* with POW comrades Walter and Kurfürst, Camp Blanding. Courtesy of Gerhard Anklam.

9. Gerhard Anklam in his air force uniform, Rovaniemi, Finland, Christmas 1941. Courtesy of Gerhard Anklam.

10. Lüdeke Herder. POW picture taken at Camp Gordon, Georgia, for relatives in Germany. Courtesy of Lüdeke Herder.

BASIC PERSONNEL RECORD
(Alien Enemy or Prisoner of War)

81 G - 125 956
D.891349

(Internment serial number)

Burkert , Werner
(Name of internee)

male

(Sex)

Height .... 6 .... ft. .... 0 .... in.

Weight 160

Eyes .... grey

Skin .... fair

Hair .... brown

Age 21

Distinguishing marks or
characteristics:

F. P. C.* ....

Reference * ....

INVENTORY OF PERSONAL EFFECTS TAKEN
FROM INTERNEE

1. ....

2. ....

3. ....

4. ....

5. ....

6. ....

7. ....

8. ....

9. ....

The above is correct:

Werner Burkert
(Signature of internee)

30 Nov 1943   Camp   Gordon

(Date and place where processed (Army enclosure, naval station, or other place))

RIGHT HAND

1. Thumb	2. Index finger	3. Middle finger	4. Ring finger	5. Little finger

LEFT HAND

6. Thumb	7. Index finger	8. Middle finger	9. Ring finger	10. Little finger

W. D., P. M. G. Form No. 2
11 June 1943

16—35679-1

Note Amputation in Proper Space

* Do not fill in.

11. Basic personnel record for Werner Burkert. Courtesy of Werner H. Burkert.

1. L/Cpl   Army
   (Grade and arm or service)

2. Army
   (Hostile unit or vessel)

3. 1./I.E.B.457 / 5674
   (Hostile serial number)

4. 1 Jan 19?2   Germany
   (Date and country of birth)

5. Berlin Wilmersdf. Landhausstr. 33-?5
   (Place of permanent residence)

6. Emma Burkert   mother
   (Name, relationship of nearest relative¹)

7. ee 5
   (Address of above)

8. none
   (Number of dependents and relationship)

9. ---
   (Address of above)

10. 13 May 1943
   (Date of capture or arrest)

11. Tunisia
   (Place of capture or arrest)

12. 8th Army
   (Unit or vessel making capture or arresting agency)

13. Student
   (Occupation)

14. Tech high Shool
   (Education)

15. Germ
   (Knowledge of languages)

16. Good
   (Physical condition at time of capture or arrest)

17. Single
   (Married or single)

18. Protestant
   (Religious preference)

ADDITIONAL DATA:

Sailor and par or Pw Ci / is

Transferred from	Date depart	Transferred to	Date received	Official signature of receiving officer	Personal effects not transferred²
POW Cp Gordon Augusta, Ga.	4/10/44	POW Cp Blanding Florida	4/11/44	W.H. Lowman Att W.H. LOWMAN, Maj.CMP	
PWC, Camp Blanding, Fla.	MAR 5 1946	Shipment 6445 X.X.XXXX C&C			
4 MAR 1947		transferred from 11 Camp to 17 Camp			WOUM 1185 PWI
2 1 MAR 1947		repat. to Berlin			17-1-47
		From 17 CAMP		AUTH WOUM/1785 PWI DATE 17 1 194.	

REMARKS:

¹ If no relative, name person to be notified in case of emergency.
² If personal effects taken from individual are not transferred, note exceptions and place of storage or depot.
16—35079-1   GPO

12. Vehicle check, motor pool, Camp Blanding, Florida. Courtesy National Archives, photo no. 208-AA-309K-9.

13. German POWs harvesting orange crop, Leesburg, Florida. Signal Corps photo. Courtesy National Archives, photo no. 208-AA-309L-3.

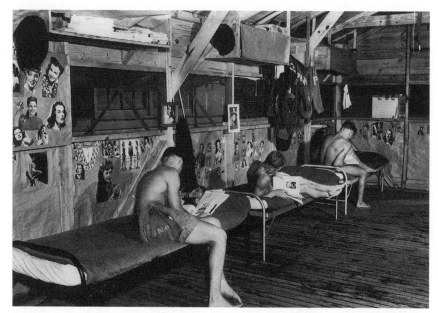

14. Interior view of German POW barracks, Camp Blanding, Florida, June 17, 1943. Courtesy National Archives, photo no. 208-AA-309S-24269.

15. POWs listening to the radio, Camp Blanding, Florida, June 17, 1943. Courtesy National Archives, photo no. 208-AA-309V-24268.

6

ESCAPEES: THE INDIVIDUALISTS, THE
THREATENED, AND THE ALIENATED

All of the German POWs who escaped from Florida camps long enough to have their escapes reported in local newspapers were returned to custody. None but Karl Behrens, who committed suicide, escaped for long; and all but two were back in custody within a week or less of their escapes.

The names and descriptions of thirty-three escapees were reported in the Florida press between May 1944 and June 1946. These press reports of escapes provide indirect testimony to the existence of problems within the camps. They also are an indication that even the casual civilian Florida newspaper reader was occasionally reminded that there were German prisoners of war in the state—in fact, that there might be an escaped German prisoner of war close by.

Nevertheless, while the POW camps in Florida multiplied and their populations swelled to almost 10,000, the army assured the public that there were few escapes nationally. Indeed, Florida had even fewer. The army claimed that during the year ending June 30, 1944, the rate of escapes nationally for POWs was 1,036 for an average population of 288,292. This the army erroneously said was a rate of 0.45 percent, but it was actually 0.36 percent.[1] The rate of escapes was less than that of maximum security federal penitentiaries. With 69 escapes for an average population of 15,691, penitentiaries had a rate of 0.44 percent. The rate of escapes in Florida between May 1944 and June 1946—33 escapes per about 10,000 POWs—was about 0.33 percent. Though these numbers are potentially misleading—rather like comparing apples and oranges because of the disparity in dates and rough statistics used for the total German POW population in the Florida sample—they are, nevertheless, indicative of the relatively small percentage of POWs who attempted escape both in Florida and throughout the United States.

The largest number of escapes from one Florida installation (eleven) occurred at the large base camp at Camp Blanding. Actually, of the eleven, eight were from Blanding's smaller naval compound. The second largest number of escapes (five) was from Dade City, with two escapes in May 1944, two in January 1945, and one in February 1945. Third in totals was Clewiston, where in December 1944 and January 1945 four escapes took place, one ending in suicide. Escapes at the other Blanding branch camps included two at Kendall in September 1944, two by the same individual at Orlando in January and July 1945, one at Winter Haven in July 1944, one at Daytona in September 1945, and one at MacDill in March 1946. Camp Gordon Johnston and its branch camps had fewer escapes: four at one time from Telogia in August 1944 and two from the main camp in September 1944.[2]

There were basically three types of would-be escapees from the Florida camps: the individualists, the threatened, and the alienated. Sometimes the same people might fit into multiple categories. This is especially true in cases such as those found in the naval compound at Camp Blanding, where some inmates were so outspoken in their condemnation of Hitler's Germany that they aroused the patriotic ire of their fellows in an anti-Nazi facility. In other cases the motivations of individual escapees cannot be assessed well enough to fit them into one of these three categories—or even to create a new one. But no matter what the categories, the escapees from the Florida camps seemed to come from all branches of the German armed forces, except the U-boat men. It was other naval personnel who did the escaping. There were also Afrika Korps men, paratroopers, and regular army men from the Italian and French campaigns. They all wore Wehrmacht uniforms, but their military units and wartime experiences, as well as prewar and ideological backgrounds, made each individual unique. Therefore, an examination of their escape stories reveals more about the variety of POWs who came to Florida than it does about their motivations for wanting to leave the camps there. Nevertheless, the categories of individualists, threatened and alienated, may give some insights into the disorder of real life in the Florida camps.

Among the individualists should be counted Gerhard Anklam, an escapee from the Clewiston sugarcane camp, and Fritz Dreschler, the "escape king of Florida," a two-time escapee from Orlando and one-time escapee from Camp Blanding.

Gerhard Anklam was one of four men who attempted to escape from the Clewiston sugarcane camp within a little over a month's time: Karl Behrens's flight and suicide were on December 30, 1944; then Gerhard Anklam and Wilhelm Stüttgen attempted escape on January 23, 1945; and finally Gottfried Pernull made his attempted flight on January 27.

A brief FBI-generated physical description of the escapees Anklam and Stüttgen appeared in the *Palm Beach Post* on Thursday morning, January 25. It did no more than note that both POWs were twenty-one years of age, blond, and would probably be found wearing regular prisoner of war uniforms.[3] The next morning the paper reported that they were captured at 1:15 A.M. on Thursday morning, not far from the camp. They were apprehended by Deputy Sheriff Lacey Raulerson of Glades County and Game Warden Silas (Barney) Snell, accompanied by Fireman Second Class Charles Keller, who was on leave from the navy. The three were hunting game-law violators when they discovered the escaped prisoners. The Germans were wearing "Nazi uniforms," and they had toilet articles and a supply of water when they were captured along the highway near Palmdale. "They told captors they planned to go to Jacksonville and stow away on a ship."[4]

An article in the local *Clewiston News* presented a few more personal details about the POWs. When the army or FBI interposed itself between the POWs and the press, personal details regarding specific prisoners were kept from public knowledge. But the *Clewiston News* reporter talked to the POWs or their captors before the army or FBI could intervene and learned the provenance of the two would-be escapees: Wilhelm Stüttgen, captured in Tunisia in 1943, was a native of Düsseldorf; and Gerhard Anklam, captured in Italy in September 1944, was from Berlin.[5]

Interviews with an older Gerhard Anklam some fifty years later reveal additional details.[6] By the time Anklam was captured in Italy on September 19, 1944, he had been in the Wehrmacht for almost four years. He had left high school in Berlin without finishing his graduation examinations and entered the German Air Force, the Luftwaffe, at age seventeen. After a poor showing at flight school in Warsaw—he later recalled not having been careful to remember to put down his landing gear—he was transferred first to Oslo, Norway, then Rovaniemi, Finland, and later to Norway's Lofoten Islands. Tired of such base duty, Anklam applied for acceptance in a Luftwaffe parachute regiment. Subsequently, he was transferred to the Fourth Parachute Division, Twelfth Regiment, stationed south of Rome. Between late January and September 1944, he and his regiment were heavily engaged in the fighting against the American advance north into Italy. During this time he sustained three minor wounds but was always able to return to action with his unit. He was captured with his comrades by American soldiers on September 19, 1944. The new POWs were taken to Livorno to be transported by Liberty ship to a camp in the United States. The transport left Livorno on October 11 and arrived in Newport News, Virginia, on November 9. From Newport News, Anklam and his fellows were taken by train to Camp Blanding. They arrived on November 11, 1944.[7]

Describing his feelings upon arrival in the Florida base camp, Gerhard Anklam exclaimed, "It was heaven on earth! No gunfire, you can eat as much as you want and so on." Still, as a prisoner he felt like a second-class person. Because of his ability to speak some English—left over from his school days in Berlin—he became a work unit leader and interpreter, employed in a Camp Blanding icehouse and later a store until January 4, 1945.

"After an accident, I had a difference with the civilian manager. In the morning, I had to start to Clewiston." It did not take the cocky ex-paratrooper long to decide that he did not want to stay at the Clewiston camp. The camp had major disadvantages: it was surrounded by swamps and sugar fields, and "Captain Dwight Field demanded more and more productivity in the sugar fields." Anklam decided the situation was not for him. On January 22, he and Wilhelm Stüttgen agreed to attempt an escape. Interestingly, Anklam had no problems with the Afrika Korps men at the Clewiston camp. In fact, Wilhelm Stüttgen was one of them. But then, the Berliner had let his Afrika Korps comrades know his experiences in Italy had been "no stroll in the park" either.[8]

On January 23, at about 9:30 P.M., during a movie night at the camp, Anklam and Stüttgen stole away under the fences and into a neighboring sugarcane field. Hearing no commotion that would indicate awareness of their departure, they proceeded with their planned escape. They made their way first through the village of Moorehaven and headed along the road in the direction of Sebring. For a little over twenty-seven hours they eluded searchers. They slept in pastures during the day and walked along Florida's deserted country roads at night. However, at about 12:30 A.M. on January 25, a car without lights suddenly appeared behind them and they heard the order to put up their hands. They were captured near Palmdale, about thirty-five miles from the Clewiston camp.[9] The police patrol car took them back. At the POW camp, on January 26, they were interviewed by the camp commander, Capt. Dwight Field, and then again by the FBI. When Anklam was asked whether he would try to escape again, the feisty Berliner replied that he would try at the very next opportunity. As a result, he was immediately handcuffed—usually considered an action in violation of the Geneva Convention.[10] On January 27, he and his fellow escapee, Stüttgen, were transferred from Clewiston back to an arrest barracks at Camp Blanding. Anklam had been at Clewiston for less than three weeks.[11]

Anklam's attitude and experiences at Clewiston can be better understood in light of the spirited and obstreperous character that he demonstrated during his time under arrest at Blanding. This sequel to the Clewiston story is important because it reveals the army's attempt to punish the POWs and the attempts by Anklam and Stüttgen to circumvent those efforts. Back at the Blanding POW base camp, the two would-be escapees stayed in arrest barracks for a month and dined on an official punishment diet of bread and water for the first two weeks.[12] The army's punishment was not to the taste of Anklam and his colleague. They had other ideas. They loosened the planks of the barracks's ceiling and climbed through to a crawl space. From there they made their way to the ceiling of an adjacent room and dropped into it. Removing boards from the floor of this room, they then arrived at the ground beneath the barracks. Working in the dark of night there was no problem for them to move through the barbed-wire fence into the regular camp and to get into the POW canteen for food and drink. Every other day they repeated the excursion. By February 10, they were officially back on normal rations, and their nocturnal excursions had still not been discovered.

On the morning of February 24, their last day of arrest, an American staff sergeant appeared unexpectedly. Striking his stick against the barracks's ceiling, he caused the loosened boards to fall into their room. Both Germans were moved to separate cells, and their requests to speak with the American commandant, Major Woodruff Lowman, were denied. On February 27, however, they spoke with the German company leader, and the next day they were dismissed from their cells. However, they were forbidden to participate in work details outside the confines of the POW camp.[13] Little was lost through their escape efforts, and Gerhard Anklam only added to his collection of interesting stories. The escape from Clewiston and the "escapes" from his detention cell at Blanding preluded the many others he made after returning to postwar Germany.

Fritz Dreschler was another individualist. A Gefreiter (private first class) of the Sixteenth SS Division, Sixteenth Field Reserve Battalion, First Company, he was—like Anklam—captured in Italy in 1944, but in July. Born on June 22, 1924, he was twenty years old at the time of his first Florida escape in January 1945.[14] On January 2, 1945, the Florida press buzzed with news of two escapes. "Nazi POW Hangs Self; Another Escapes from AFTAC," said the *Orlando Morning Sentinel.* The headline referred to Karl Behrens, who was found hanging two miles from the Clewiston camp, and to Fritz Dreschler, who the FBI had just announced as escaped from the Army Air Force base at Orlando. The FBI encouraged informants to call T. C. Allen, the FBI agent in Orlando; to contact local law enforcement officers; or to get in touch with R. G. Danner at the Miami FBI office.[15] The *Tampa Morning Tribune,* in a front-page article, "Escaped German Prisoner Hangs Himself at Clewiston," exclaimed that a second escape, this one from the Orlando army base, had occurred early in the morning the day before. Like the Orlando paper, it noted that Fritz Dreschler, twenty, was five foot eight inches tall, weighed 170 pounds, had black hair, gray eyes, and a light complexion. Readers were informed that the escapee was a former private in the German Army, spoke a little English, and wore a khaki uniform with the letters PW on the back. As Dreschler had been a mechanic by trade, the FBI informed the public that he might seek a job in that field. Garage men were particularly encouraged to be on the alert for him.[16] Even the faraway Tallahassee *Daily Democrat* reported the Dreschler escape, proclaiming "Escaped Nazi Is Sought Here."[17]

The next day, January 3, the Orlando paper ran two photographs of Dreschler with the heading "Have You Seen This Superman?"[18] On Thursday, January 4, the *Tampa Morning Tribune* published a photo of Dreschler's prisoner identification card, with a photo of the subject from front and side views. The headline read "Search for Escaped German Prisoner in Tampa Area Fails to Bring Clue." There was a separate photo of Mr. and Mrs. W. B. Barton of Tampa looking at the floor of their home on 9406 Nebraska Avenue, where Dreschler's PW uniform was found. The article noted that the house was found ransacked, two dozen eggs had been cooked, and a large bag of oranges and other food had been taken. Also missing were a watch and other jewelry that it was believed Dreschler might try to pawn. The public was informed that clothes had been taken, which Dreschler might be found wearing. These included a tan field jacket, two pair of tan trousers, two pair of blue trousers, two plain blue shirts, one blue sport shirt with red stripes, and a pair of black, plain-toed shoes. A dark blue overnight bag was also taken.[19]

A small headline on page 5 of the Saturday, January 6, *Tampa Morning Tribune* admitted: "Tips Flood FBI but Prisoners Are Not Found." The article referred to Dreschler, but also to Harry Fischer and Gunther Gabriel, who had escaped from the Dade City camp on January 5.[20] By Sunday, January 7, a new headline read "All Three Nazi War Prisoners Are Recaptured: 1 Caught Near Tampa; 2 at Jacksonville."[21] The report concerned both Fritz Dreschler, who was captured in Gibsonton, near Tampa, and the Dade City POW escapees, Fischer and Gabriel, who thought they were headed for New York and a ship back to Germany. The Dade City POWs were discovered by the FBI and railroad police in a sealed boxcar in a railroad yard in Jacksonville at about 3 P.M. on Saturday afternoon, January 6. They were found in a weakened condition because of two days without water, according to FBI agent R. G. Danner of Miami. Small mug shots of the two men accompanied the story, and it was noted that both men were corporals in the German air force. Harry Fischer, a former actor and radio singer, could speak English fluently and had been practicing popular songs in English.[22]

The *Tampa Sunday Tribune* reported that Dreschler escaped

from the Orlando army air base on December 28 and wandered in and around Tampa. Driven by hunger, he finally approached the home of H. J. Rimes, a farmer at Gibsonton. Mr. and Mrs. Rimes and their twenty-year-old daughter, Esther, opened the back door on Saturday, January 6, at about 8 A.M. to find the German sitting with his head in his hands, asleep, on their back porch. The Rimes invited the hungry Dreschler to breakfast while their daughter ran to a phone to call police. "The docile German waited by the stove until sheriff deputies Grady Sweat and Morris Goldberg arrived to take him to the [Hillsborough] county jail."[23] Pictures accompanying the story show Dreschler talking with County Jailer Rau, County Patrolman Sweat, and Deputy Sheriff Fernandez. The article stated Dreschler was "a member of Hitler's highly vaunted SS elite troops, but he was a wilted and quiet young man as he told the story of his escape and wanderings to Harry Rau, county jailer, who speaks German fluently."

Dreschler had broken into Sterling Cleaners at 5102 Florida Avenue in Tampa and taken a suit of clothes, a sweater, an overcoat, and twenty-seven dollars cash. Later he took a bicycle and used it to get to Gibsonton. He planned to head for Key West and "paddle back to Germany." During his thirteen days at large, Dreschler had only one meal; he lived on oranges picked in groves along the way from Orlando. His papers indicated that Dreschler was a veteran of the Russian campaign, had been wounded and sent back to Germany to recover, and then had been sent to Italy. It was there that he originally was captured by American forces. Of the American fighting men, "he had the highest praise he had to offer. He said, they were 'as good as the Germans.'"

The news story reported that though the sheriff's office was holding Dreschler on a charge of breaking and entering for the robbery of the Barton house and the Sterling Cleaners, there was little hope of prosecuting him. A *Tampa Morning Tribune* story on Monday, January 8, titled "Captured Nazi Prisoner Back in Camp," noted that police turned over Dreschler to military authorities for return to the Orlando army air base, but he still had two charges over his head for breaking and entering. According to Sheriff Culbreath, "Dreschler would be returned to stand trial when the case is brought to court."[24] If the case ever did come to trial, it certainly did not make headlines. Though POWs could be—and sometimes were—tried by military courts-martial for various criminal offenses and sentenced to up to several years of hard labor, escapees were often protected under Article 50 of the Geneva Convention and subject only to a month military arrest with the first two weeks on a diet of bread and water.[25]

On Wednesday, July 11, 1945, the *Orlando Morning Sentinel* informed its readers that Fritz Dreschler was loose again. "German Escapes from Local Base" was the heading, which topped the brief story. It noted that R. G. Danner of the FBI in Miami reported that Fritz Dreschler was abroad again since July 10. On Tuesday afternoon, he was reported missing from the motor pool at the Orlando air base. Readers were reminded that Dreschler spoke some English and that he had disappeared from the base once before. That time, the story recalled, the escapee had been found seven days later in a little town south of Tampa, after having stolen a bicycle and ransacked a house for food and clothing.[26]

Dreschler was recaptured again in the Tampa area. On Friday, July 13, the *Sentinel* reported that Dreschler was picked up by Charles J. Weaver, the operator of the Lone Star Service Station at Rocky Point. The German had stopped at the home of Mrs. Ethel Felders and asked for a glass of water. Weaver, who had been on the lookout for a "peeping Tom" in the neighborhood, located the German a half mile from his service station. When the German showed fight, Weaver pulled a revolver, and the POW surrendered.[27]

Never outdone when it came to sensationalism, the *Tampa Morning Tribune* ran the headline "Nazi Again Caught Here Wearing Two Pink Panties." Like the Orlando paper, the *Tribune* told the story of the service station operator's capture of Dreschler. It noted that the German had come to a woman's house and Dreschler had tried to make her give him a drink of water. She had given him a glass and told him to go to a nearby creek, but he had refused and forced his way into her kitchen. Charles J. Weaver, the operator of a filling station at Hillsborough Avenue and Memorial Drive, who had been given a tip that there was a "peeping Tom" in the area, found and recognized the German at the woman's house half a mile north on Memorial Drive. When Weaver ordered Dreschler to leave with him, the German attempted to hit him with the water glass but gave up when the Tampan "covered him with a pistol." The story noted that Dreschler was not only wearing brown tweed pants with a coat and white polo shirt he had stolen, but that he had on two pairs of women's pink panties. He also wore bedroom slippers. In his pocket was $4.11. Somehow he also had acquired a newspaper clipping telling of his escape. After questioning by the FBI, Dreschler was turned over to military authorities at the local prisoner of war camp at Drew Field.[28]

The Palm Beach Post's Associated Press story from Tampa that ran on July 13 added a few small details. It mentioned that Fritz Dreschler, twenty-one, had twice escaped from the Orlando air base and each time been captured in the Tampa area. It added that he was being held at Drew Field Army Air Base for his return to Orlando.[29]

Dreschler's third escape came on January 7, 1946. A small note on page 13 of the January 8 edition of the *Florida Times-Union* of Jacksonville announced "Blanding Prisoner Flees Third Time." The article described the escapee and noted that he was dressed in khaki trousers and shirt with the letters PW on both. As a warning and for the information of the public it was noted that "Following both of his previous escapes in December, 1944, and July 1945, the prisoner was recaptured in Tampa, the FBI said."[30]

Dreschler's freedom ended on January 14. An Associated Press report from Miami dated January 17 told the story to Jacksonville readers of the *Florida Times-Union* on Friday, January 18. J. E. Thornton, agent in charge of the FBI in Miami, reported that Fritz Dreschler was captured in Walterboro, South Carolina. Sheriff's Deputy E. F. Sineth of Walterboro picked up the German when he found him trying to keep warm by a fire built beside the Walterboro-Charleston Highway. Dreschler readily admitted to his identity and to having burglarized a house near Camp Blanding on January 9. He had taken food and the clothing found in his possession. Deputy Sineth turned Dreschler over to military authorities, who planned to return him to Blanding.[31] Thus ended the travels of Florida's POW "escape king." Fritz Dreschler, like Gerhard Anklam, was an individualist. But individualism may not have accounted for all of his escape attempts. His second and third escapes, occurring in July 1945 and January 1946, may have been motivated by increasing rumors that POWs would be handed over to the French for postwar work and then returned to the regions where they had been inducted into the service. Dreschler was from

Chemnitz, a part of Germany located in the postwar Soviet occupation zone. As an SS man who had seen action on the eastern front and been wounded fighting the Russians, he may have wished to avoid forced repatriation first to the French and then to the Russians.[32]

The motivations of Fritz Dreschler may have been mixed, but those of Bruno Balzer are much more evident. Balzer was one of the alienated and threatened of the camps. But that could not be learned from newspaper reports. The second most frequent POW escapee from Florida camps, with two attempts from the naval compound at Camp Blanding, Bruno Balzer was described by the FBI as twenty-seven-years old, five feet seven inches, 155 pounds, with gray-brown eyes and a medium complexion. He spoke German, Italian, Portuguese, and Polish.[33]

But there were things about Bruno Balzer which the FBI did not say and only a close look at his records could reveal. The detention roster of the naval compound at Camp Blanding revealed only that Bruno Balzer, 5G-5000 NA, was born on November 16, 1916, and captured on September 1, 1943, while assigned to Port Unit 61615, at Palmi, Italy.[34] His serial numbers indicated that he was processed "in the field" by the Western Defense Command (Fifth Service Command); he was German (G); he was the 5,000th prisoner so processed; and he was a naval prisoner (NA).[35]

Balzer was one of those prisoners whose views and associations led to his alienation from comrades and whose life was threatened behind the wire. Blanding authorities became aware of this almost as soon as Balzer was transferred from Fort George Meade, Maryland, to the Florida naval compound in May 1944.[36] He was part of a group of ten prisoners who were immediately ostracized and threatened by fellow prisoners because of their political opinions. Shortly after their arrival, one was severely beaten by fellow naval prisoners. Their lives were threatened because they expressed the opinion that Germany was losing the war. The German camp spokesman, U-boat Capt. Klaus Bargsten, told American authorities that he would not attempt to protect these men, and he asked, therefore, that they be removed from the naval compound.[37]

Balzer and his colleagues were then rationed and quartered separately from the regular compound, and Blanding authorities requested permission from the Fourth Service Command offices in

Atlanta for the immediate transfer of these ten prisoners from the camp.[38] In fact, permission was received to ship them to Camp McCain, Mississippi, but the transfer never happened. Blanding's officers learned that seventy-eight anti-Nazi naval prisoners from McCain were in the process of being transferred to Blanding. That, they concluded, would make the transfer of ten anti-Nazi prisoners from Blanding to McCain "neither feasible or plausible." They could only hope that the arrival of seventy-eight more anti-Nazi prisoners would equalize the anti-Nazi and Nazi elements within the Blanding naval compound and somehow restore peace in the camp.[39]

In February and again June 1945, Balzer took to his heels for a taste of freedom from the Blanding naval compound and its divided population. The report of his capture on Thursday, June 21, 1945, after his second flight from Blanding, is a wonderfully colorful description that could only appear in a newspaper with direct access to local informants and no FBI interference. The front-page story in the *Bradford County Telegraph* of Starke proclaimed, "German Prisoner Found in Hide-Out Near Alligator Creek; Treed by MPs."[40] The report noted that Balzer was one of five who escaped from Blanding the week before and that he was the last to be captured.[41] He had hidden under a large oak in some dense growth on the edge of Starke, a stone's throw from a field of yellow corn, orange and peach trees, and running water.

After having escaped on Sunday evening, June 10, his four days of freedom ended on Thursday evening, June 14. At 5 P.M. housewife Ruby Johns saw puffs of smoke coming from the woods beyond the field near her home. Remembering the island near Alligator Creek where small boys played, she worried about the fire. Having found the fire, she told the man there to put it out when he was done cooking so it would not spread. Because he reacted in a startled manner and did not reply, she became suspicious and had one of her roomers, a Blanding sergeant of German extraction, go after him. When he returned to the site, the sergeant found a German-English dictionary and called the military police. Five MPs came from the Starke City Hall office and two radio cars with ten more men came from Camp Blanding to comb the woods. Two hours later they found Balzer perched in a small oak tree near the train trestle a mile or so below Starke. Evidence indicated that he had hidden for two or three days in the spot where he had been seen by Mrs. Johns. He apparently got water from a faucet at the end of the corn field.[42]

The *Bradford County Telegraph* story illustrates not only something of the life of Bruno Balzer, but also the nature of small-town Florida and its newspaper coverage of German escapes. The Balzer article in the Starke paper got two long columns on the front page. The location and space given to his and others escapes in other newspapers indicates the relatively low priority given to stories on the German prisoners of war in Florida. There were just too many other issues of importance in Floridians' wartime lives. When Balzer and three other naval prisoners—all non–U-boat personnel—fled Blanding on June 10, the nearby Jacksonville *Florida Times-Union* of Tuesday, June 12, presented descriptions given by R. G. Danner of the Miami office of the FBI on page 11. The *Tampa Morning Tribune,* always more on the lookout for sensational news, devoted only a small note to the descriptions from the FBI, though it put them on page 1. The *Miami Herald,* on Wednesday, June 13, reported that "Floridian Captures 3 Nazi Prisoners" in a brief note on page 9. The Tallahassee *Daily Democrat* of Friday, June 15, ran the Miami AP note that "German POWs Are Retaken" on page 3.[43] When a fifth Blanding naval prisoner, eighteen-year-old Rolf Fitzner, escaped on June 12, the *Florida Times-Union* ran the notice story on page 11.[44] In short, Floridians saw the flotsam and jetsam of the world war tossed about on their shores, but the evidence was meager, and popular attention was focused elsewhere on more "important" domestic and international news.

The third category of escapee was the alienated. Alienation might occur within a POW compound, as it did in the case of Bruno Balzer, because of his defeatist comments or the defeatist attitudes of the company he kept. On the other hand, alienation might come because of the individual's other personal conduct or idiosyncrasies. It is hard to tell about Johann Klapper. Like Dreschler and Balzer, he stands out on the list of thirty-three POWs who tried to make the break in Florida. They were "escape kings" because of the frequency of their attempts. Klapper won hands down for the duration of his escape. His case is also interesting because his escape attempt occurred long after the end of the war—in March 1946. It is even more intriguing because of the strange nature of his disappearance from MacDill Field and his subsequent reappearance at the same place in June. The news stories relating the escape and capture are also illustrative of what could be written by one of Florida's most sensationalist newspapers of the era after the end of wartime censorship. The circumstances of the publication of the escape stories ensured that the public would know more about Johann Klapper than about most of the other thirty-three Florida POW escapees.

Page 5 of the March 16, 1946, *Tampa Morning Tribune* story had a mug shot of Klapper and a brief description under the title: "FBI Launches State Hunt for War Prisoner."[45] The story started in standard fashion: "FBI alerted a statewide net of state and local police yesterday in search of Johann Klapper, 49, German prisoner of war who escaped from MacDill Field Thursday"—with description of height, weight, color of hair, eyes, and complexion. It was also noted that he was believed wearing a tan shirt and pants, high-top GI shoes, and a drab olive raincoat at the time of his escape. His left index finger had been amputated. The FBI indicated that while Klapper was listed as knowing only German, he possibly could speak some English. In a postwar effort at detail, the paper was also able to inform its readers that Klapper, captured at Cherbourg, France, was an infantry man with only an eighth-grade education. As a civilian in Germany, he had been a farmer with a wife and five children.[46]

On Wednesday, June 19, three months after his escape, the *Tribune* story on page 7 proclaimed, "War Prisoner Found Hidden in Own Foxhole at MacDill." A marvelous picture of the heavily bearded and bedraggled forty-nine-year-old Klapper talking with the two MPs who had discovered him has the caption: "Foxhole prisoner caught—shown as he emerged yesterday from a 95-day stay in his foxhole beneath a MacDill Field building is Johann Klapper, left, German war prisoner who escaped last March. Center, his captor, Sgt. S.C. Berry, with S/Sgt. Richard B. Edwards, right, interpreter, who questioned Klapper."[47]

The news story elaborated on how the MPs investigating a prowler ended a ninety-five-day voluntary foxhole stay by Klapper. He had escaped from a work crew on March 14 and, while sought throughout the Southeast, had hidden under the post exchange building in a foxhole he had lined with bits of cardboard and paper. He was only discovered two months after his German comrades had been transferred from MacDill in April 1946. Post police were told that a strange bearded man was seen near the post exchange. Sergeant Berry discovered a small opening beneath one of the buildings and, crawling underneath, found the foxhole. Meanwhile Klapper was spotted as he squirmed beneath another building. When shouted to by the MPs, the long-bearded, filthy Klapper, who had worn the same clothes since his escape, came out with his hands up. He had never left MacDill Field. In fact, he did not know until told by an American interpreter that his fellow prisoners had been sent off for their return to Europe back in April. The *Tribune* story concluded with the postscript that Klapper was to be held until guards from the German POW facility at Fort Benning, Georgia, could come to take him into custody before his deportation to Germany.[48]

A Tampa AP story in the *Florida Times-Union* of Wednesday, June 19, explained to Jacksonville-area residents that at the time of Klapper's escape it was generally known that MacDill Field would soon begin returning prisoners to their homeland. "Klapper, who does not speak English and who conversed through an interpreter, did not explain why he did not want to return to Germany, or how long he had planned to hide out if he had not been detected." He did say that he had gone to the post exchange immediately after leaving his work detail and made a den underneath the building, hiding the opening with a pile of boxes. During his three-month seclusion, he had used a trickle of water seeping through the floor from an icebox to drink and to wash his hands and face. At night he stole out to nearby mess halls to forage for food. When found, he was hungry but in good health. His black hair was long, twisted, and matted; he had a heavy beard; and his clothes, the long wool underwear and PW fatigue suit he had worn for three months, were ragged and dirty. Johann Klapper, who military authorities decided had no assistance in his escape, was scheduled for no further punishment than what he had already inflicted upon himself. The long story ran discreetly on page 6.[49]

It is difficult to account for Klapper's strange behavior. Perhaps it was individual idiosyncrasy. Or, perhaps he feared that he would be turned over to the British or French for a prolonged period of internment. The fact that he was unwilling to face continued association with his comrades in the camp suggests that Klapper lacked a supportive peer group. Klapper was almost twice the age of most of the men in the POW camps—reason enough for alienation from his fellows.

Other escape attempts were made by men alienated from their prison compound peers. One occurred in July 1944, early in the Florida German Army POW experience. Twenty-nine-year-old Franz Drews escaped from the Winter Haven camp. The report of his escape on page 3 of the *Winter Haven Daily Chief* on Monday, July 10, explained that local and county officers and the FBI were joining in a search for Drews in "the first authentic escape of a POW from the local camp since it was established in the middle of March."[50] It was noted that Drews was five foot ten inches, 178 pounds, had a fair complexion, and was dressed in blue denim clothes. He had escaped from the camp on Third Street early that morning, at about 1:30 A.M. Drews was seen by guards as he scaled the fence on the west side of the enclosure and fled northward across lots and a grove near the Atlantic Coast Line railroad track. Dr. F. G. Garner, who lived within a block of the west end of the camp, reported that he heard the noise of an intruder at about that time, and authorities believed this was the fleeing German. Later in the morning, officers V. E. Loughlin, M. L. Gibson, and J. V. Barnes of the Tampa FBI office arrived to assist MPs in the search.

Drews, who the FBI described as having gray eyes and blond hair, although nearly bald, was recaptured within four days.[51] He had not gone far. On Friday, July 14, the *Winter Haven Daily Chief* reported that the escapee was recaptured in an old shack in the northeast Florence Villa section of town. He had been seen by Jesse Scott, a caretaker of the George Kunberger grove, a quarter mile northeast of First Street and Avenue T. The paper said, "The prisoner was taken by prison camp guards when they were notified by a colored man that someone was occupying [a] building which had not been used for a long time." Drews, who suffered exhaustion due to lack of food, offered no resistance and was glad to be back where he could be fed. The story concluded with the speculation that the German would likely be transferred away from the Winter Haven camp. It noted that "other POWs were averse to having him kept there."[52] Why he may have been unwelcome was unstated, but that he was alienated from his peers was obvious.

Another such case occurred at the Dade City camp in February

1945. Four other POWs had already attempted their escapes from the camp: Walter Weber and Joseph Summerer in May 1944 and Gunther Gabriel and Harry Fischer in January 1945.[53] The fifth Dade City prisoner to escape was twenty-eight-year-old Theodor Hermann Hanns. He walked out of the Pasco Packing Association plant in Dade City on February 23, 1945, sometime during the third shift between 4 and 8:15 A.M. A German artillery corporal before his capture in July 1943, he was described by the FBI as "not only unfriendly toward his captors, but . . . unfriendly to his fellow German prisoners."[54]

The *Tampa Sunday Tribune* reported that Hanns might have learned some English in lessons at the POW camp. At the time of his escape he was wearing a patch over his right eye to cover a cut, and he was in blue denims to cover a khaki uniform, though all of his clothing was marked with the letters PW. He was five foot seven inches, 155 pounds, with green eyes, blond hair, thick eyebrows, and a fair complexion. An excellent mug shot was reproduced on page 2 of the *Tribune* with the caption: "Roaming Somewhere—Theodor Hermann Hanns." He was caught on March 9 in Lakeland. Like Gabriel and Fischer, his capture was by railroad police. Hanns told police that he had lived on oranges as well as fish and game in the swamplands bordering the Withlacoochee River near Laughan. Dan Shore, an Atlantic Coast Line railroad inspector, discovered the German corporal in an empty boxcar during a routine check.[55] So ended Hanns's eighteen-day adventure, one of the longest escapes in the Florida POW experience. What had made him "not only unfriendly toward his captors, but . . . unfriendly to his fellow German prisoners" is not clear. As was often the case, an escapee was probably motivated more by alienation from his peers than by other factors.

Werner Jentsch's escape exploits rivaled those of "Florida escape king" Fritz Dreschler—if not in number of attempts, at least in distances traveled. He, like Dreschler, was a former member of the SS. His escape from the POW camp at Daytona Beach in September 1945 was a reminder to Floridians that though the war was over in Europe, dangerous Germans were still at large in America. Indeed, R. G. Danner, special agent in charge of the FBI's Miami office, informed the press and public that Jentsch, twenty-two, was "a former member of the German SS troops and may be dangerous."[56]

A report of the escape in the *Daytona Beach Evening News* described Jentsch as "an ardent Nazi."[57] And at six foot two inches, in an age when the average German POW was closer to five foot six or seven inches, Jentsch, at 174 pounds, with blue eyes and a fair complexion set off by dark hair, sounded fairly threatening. The Daytona newspaper story was quick to note, however, that Jentsch "is the first POW to escape from the compound at NAS [naval air station]."

A week later, but after a "vacation trip" that took him from Daytona to Miami Beach, Jentsch was again in captivity. He was apprehended by Miami police while sleeping in a truck. He told police that he had hitchhiked from Daytona Beach to New Smyrna Beach, then hopped a freight train to Miami. He bragged that he had spent most of his time "swimming at Miami Beach and seeking employment."[58] Perhaps the braggadocio SS man, like the escape artist Fritz Dreschler, was not just escaping boredom in a POW camp but attempting to avoid an uncertain fate in postwar Europe.

What conclusions can be drawn from a study of the POW escapes in Florida? A few generalities may be essayed. A number of the escapees were men notable less for their patriotic zeal than for their inability to get along with comrades within their own compounds. Sometimes this meant anti-Nazis or nonconformists escaping German patriots. The examples that come to mind are various escapees from the naval compound at Camp Blanding. The compound was designated as anti-Nazi by American authorities, but it contained prisoners threatened by fellow inmates because they were considered unpatriotic. Bruno Balzer, a two-time escapee from Blanding's naval compound, is an example of such a prisoner.[59]

Of the eleven escape attempts from Camp Blanding, eight were by naval prisoners, but none were U-boat men. Of the seven men involved—Balzer made two attempts himself—three men were from the merchant marine, and four were from port guard and support units.[60] All of them were interned in a naval compound of proud U-boat professionals—whether the U.S. government classified them as anti-Nazis or not. It is not difficult to imagine internal compound conflicts that would encourage attempts at escape.

Sometimes the escapee may have been more of a diehard than his camp colleagues or for some other reason just could not get along with them. Theodor Hermann Hanns, an escapee from the Dade

City camp, was described as "not only unfriendly toward his captors, but . . . unfriendly to his fellow German prisoners."[61] There was also Franz Drews, an escapee from the Winter Haven camp whose return was unlikely because his fellow prisoners were "averse to having him kept there."[62]

Finally, there were those who escaped because they were individualists protesting what they considered to be an unfair camp situation. The escape of Gerhard Anklam and Wilhelm Stüttgen from Clewiston in January 1945 is such an example. Gerhard Anklam insists fifty years later that he refused to tolerate the unfair work quotas in the sugarcane cutting camp he was sent to because of his disagreements with a work supervisor at Camp Blanding.[63]

With the possible exceptions of Fritz Dreschler, three-time Florida escape artist, and Werner Jentsch from the Daytona Beach camp, none of the escapees fled merely for the adventure involved. None besides Dreschler and the threatened Bruno Balzer attempted more than one escape while in a Florida camp. Dreschler seemed to make the practice his hobby. Fear of the FBI did not deter him from regularly stealing the clothing, jewelry, and money he felt he needed for his escapes. Interestingly, Dreschler's name is not listed among Florida's former POWs detained after the war at the military prison at Fort Leavenworth, Kansas, or at a federal penitentiary because of crimes committed during internment.[64]

While it was every German soldier's duty to attempt escape, relatively few tried.[65] Of the 2,222 Germans who attempted flight from camps within the United States between 1942 and 1946, only 33 (1.5 percent of the total) were in Florida.[66] Perhaps that is because the Florida most German prisoners saw was not tourist Florida, but swamps and woods, rural citrus and potato fields, and old-time county sheriffs and farmers with shotguns, dogs, and speech patterns that made even those Germans with some knowledge of English think they had stumbled back into the American frontier. Rural Florida in the 1940s was not the end of the world, but it must have seemed so to many Germans—as, indeed, it did to some of the American military men who guarded them.[67] Only the individualist, the threatened, or the truly alienated tried escape in such a place.

7

MACDILL MENUS AND BELLE GLADE BEANS: THE PRESS AND CODDLING CHARGES

Escape attempts revealed that all was not well within Florida's POW camps. Yet both contemporary records and memories of "alumni" prove that work and the general routine of camp life were positive experiences for most. When selective transfers of trouble-makers removed the most ardent partisans from Florida's camps, a relative calm settled. A small number of individualistic, threatened, and alienated prisoners undertook escape attempts. Riots— like those in Blanding's army compound in December 1943—occurred no more. Individual camps took on their own unique profiles; most of their inmates bent to local peer pressures and soldiered on in the American labor program. To their guards and employers they were no longer Nazis, but Uncle Sam's smiling workers. Positive stereotypes replaced negative ones among those in close contact with the POWs. But as newspaper articles concerning POW escapes reveal, the term *Nazi* remained the favored usage of the press. For those unfamiliar with the POW program, earlier stereotypes remained. Their perpetuation by the media haunted the POW program, causing misunderstanding among the uninitiated, press campaigns against "coddling" of POWs, and, finally, two congressional investigations. Incidents in Florida camps figured prominently in the press campaigns that provoked congressional inquiries: extravagant-sounding POW menus at MacDill Field and a strike among POW workers at a Belle Glade bean cannery.

For those not directly involved with the prisoners, the opportunities for misunderstanding and resentment of the U.S. government's handling of the POW program were boundless. This is because of the low public profile given to the program, the self-censorship encouraged by the government within the press corps, and the general tendency in wartime—if not at all times—of suspecting that our side is playing fair while the bad guys are not. Added to these problems was wartime rationing for the U.S. civilian population. Rationing grew tighter as the war progressed because Uncle Sam's first priority was to feed, clothe, and transport overseas warriors. Seeing to their needs required a general, though temporary, decline of living standards for the folks back home.

Complicating the issue further was the Geneva Convention of 1929, of which both the U.S. and German governments were signatories. According to Article 2, prisoners of war "must at all times be humanely treated and protected, particularly against acts of violence, insults and public curiosity." Additionally, according to Article 10 and 11, with regard to dormitories and food, "the conditions shall be the same as for the troops at base camps of the detaining Power. The food ration of prisoners of war shall be equal in quantity and quality to that of troops at base camps."[1]

Because of these three articles, the U.S. government was slow to authorize the release of public information about German POW facilities and punctilious in observance of the Geneva Convention's housing and rationing standards. This punctiliousness was due chiefly to a desire to protect American servicemen in the hands of the Germans in Europe, though the moral imperatives accepted by ratification of the Geneva Convention were also frequently cited.[2] Most of the American public neither understood these official motivations nor particularly cared. American civilians, who had neither experience with nor understanding of the lot of the prisoners of war, were irritated that "Nazis"—as all German POWs were indiscriminately called at the time—received food that seemed, and often was, of higher quality and greater quantity than that available to home-front Americans effected by rationing.

As early as June 1943 an article in the *New York Times* titled "Axis Captives Find Ease in Tennessee" described life for POWs at Camp Crossville as coddled. A *New York Times Magazine* article of November 21 elaborated on that theme, noting that POWs were better off than typical American citizens who had their food rationed. Phrases like "piles of juicy hams, plenty of butter, steaks and sausages" were bound to arouse the public.[3] On December 24, a letter appeared in the *New York Times* under the heading "Prisoner Camp Menus Criticized." Thus, complaints about POW menus were circulating as early as 1943, but there seemed to be little outcry then, or even in 1944, because food was still relatively available to the American public.[4]

However, by the summer of 1944 various veterans organizations began to issue statements and send petitions to their congressmen alleging pampering of the POWs. For example, the New York Department of the Army and Navy Union charged that prisoners were "being coddled and favored . . . supplied with the finest foodstuffs, housing and recreation facilities and social services," while Americans in the military suffered "intolerable conditions when taken prisoner of war by enemies."[5] As a result of such allegations the House Military Affairs Committee, headed by Andrew Jackson May of Kentucky, launched a quiet, but nevertheless publicized, investigation. On August 20, 1944, the *New York Times* reported on the work of the committee in an article entitled "House Group Sifts Prisoner 'Coddling'."[6]

Meanwhile, in what appeared to be two War Department–inspired articles, funneled to the national press by National Education Association and AP correspondents, the American public was informed of the POW program as the army wanted it to be seen. The first, which could be read by residents of Palm Beach County in the *Palm Beach Post-Times,* appeared on Sunday, September 24, 1944. Under the headline "Army Treats Prisoners Different Way Than Goebbels," with the byline of Peter Edson, NEA staff correspondent, Washington, were two photographs of German POWs in unnamed American camps. One photo showed two prisoners in a library; the other displayed two prisoners engaged in wood carving. The article stated that there were 243,848 prisoners in the United States, most of whom—192,846—were Germans. They were currently in 126 base camps and 400 work camps, administered by Brig. Gen. Blackshear M. Bryan, Jr., who was described as "a Louisianan, former line coach at West Point."[7]

The long and descriptive article noted that there had been much recent public criticism of the army's failure to propagandize Germans into "good liberal democrats." The writer claimed there was much misinformation and exaggeration in such criticism. His article was obviously designed to correct both problems. It stated that the government had found that the best line of education for the Germans was to let them absorb what they could see with their own eyes as they worked in American communities and soak up U.S. newspapers, books, radio programs, and movies.

This, the article suggested, they were doing. About 60 percent of the Germans were working in army camps, and 40 percent were in labor camps doing farm, factory, or forest work. The rule was "no work, no eat." Every prisoner had a ten-cent-a-day allowance to buy soap, razor blades, and other items at the post exchange, because if given free these things might be wasted. Prisoners on contract labor, however, made eighty cents a day from the army. Employers paid the U.S. Treasury the going rate for the job. This was not all profit; the army had to feed, house, transport, and guard the labor. Contracts were not made where there was no hope of the government at least breaking even. The prisoners themselves were paid in the form of coupons redeemable at POW post exchanges, or they could be saved in savings accounts.

Of course, there were other problems that the article was forced to deal with. But it did so in a way that made the news reporter sound more like an army public information officer: "It is a queer and little known segment of American life today. There have been murders—nasty ones—and suicides. The Army was worried recently by what it thought was a wave of prisoner suicides. But insurance actuaries proved the rate was lower than in a normal city of comparable population."[8]

Additionally, it was noted that over 600 German POWs had tried to escape, but no more than thirty were ever at large at one time—and, "they all get captured eventually." The article concluded: "Every prisoner is told plainly that if he tries to escape he may be shot—and some have been shot. The army then gives them a military funeral, with a volley fired over the grave, and a German chaplain's church service in German with all the other prisoners drawn up to see."[9]

Obviously the purpose of the article was to explain—clearly, dispassionately, and reassuringly—the POW program, its realities and its benefits to the Germans and to the American government. The essay conveyed a tone of firmness and fairness that the War Department maintained was the basis of its all-too-often misunderstood and assailed POW program.

A second article, published on October 8, 1944, reinforced the same message but moved from the generalities found in the first article to specifics as they were exemplified in a particular POW camp; in this case, Camp Pickett in Virginia. This article appeared—among other places—in the *Palm Beach Post-Times* under the title "Life of German Prisoner Not Easy, But He's Treated Well." The byline was Frank H. Fuller, Camp Pickett, Virginia. This article, unlike the first, named specific American camp officers, and it explained, often in their own words, their work and intentions. "'We follow the law,' says big ruddy-faced Major John R. Gleason, commanding officer." There was no coddling or fraternizing. Punishment for failing to work cut off the prisoner's pay and the opportunity that came with it to buy tobacco and two bottles of beer a day. As far as regular food was concerned, the prisoners could cook and serve their own food as they liked, but it was American food that was supplied.[10]

This reference to "American food as it was supplied" played a key part in a larger controversy concerning "coddling" that arose in Florida and on the national scene several months later. Excessive food and particularly exotic-sounding dishes available to POWs in a time of increasingly tight civilian rationing within the United States were sore points. And, it was the publication by a Tampa newspaper of the menus at the POW camp at MacDill Field in January 1945 that helped create a major bone of contention between the army and the press and public in the first six months of 1945.[11]

The House Military Affairs Committee's report of November 30, 1944, which absolved the War Department of coddling, did not reduce the flow of complaints.[12] The issue was just too provocative for newspaper men and radio commentators to leave alone. The result was major public attacks on the War Department's handling of the German POWs during the last months of the war. Edward Pluth describes the public attacks on POW policy in 1945 as consisting of "two somewhat distinct but related phases lasting from February to July, 1945." The first phase stemmed from a combination of coincidences: a spectacular escape of twenty-five prisoners from Papago Park, Arizona, on Christmas Eve, 1944; news of the Malmédy massacre during the Battle of the Bulge; and increasing food shortages in the United States. The contrasts between the apparently lax administration of prisoners of war in the United States and the murder of American prisoners during the Battle of the Bulge were striking. Furthermore, Americans, who were growing tired of rationing, were more than ready to be appalled at the suggestion that Nazi prisoners might be fed better than they were. The result was a flurry of public complaints against the War Department by American citizens and their congressmen. One of these congressmen was Robert L. F. Sikes of Florida, a member of the House Military Affairs Committee. On February 9, 1945, he commenced an attack on "elaborate" POW camp menus.

A second phase of coddling charges occurred in April and May 1945 and resulted in another congressional investigation into the prisoner of war program. This phase was prompted by the shocking revelations associated with the liberation of survivors of German concentration camps and the discovery of malnutrition and disease among former American prisoners of war who had been in German hands.[13] In this context, a strike by German POWs in Camp Blanding's, Belle Glade branch camp—a strike in protest of an absent cigarette ration—aroused national attention in April. It helped provoke a second congressional investigation.

During each of these two phases of the national outrage against coddling, incidents in Florida and the involvement of Florida's Rep. Robert Sikes were important, but they were hardly exclusive or dominant factors on the national scene. Leading critics of the War Department's prisoner of war policies included Samuel Dickstein of New York and Richard F. Harless of Arizona.[14] It was the mass escape at Papago Park, Arizona, that got the greatest national attention. Nevertheless, the popular political turmoil that arose in Florida contributed to, as well as exemplified, national trends. It thus deserves independent consideration.

MACDILL MENUS: FIRST CODDLING CHARGES

The furor associated with the first phase of coddling charges began in Florida in early January 1945 because of the zeal of a Tampa newspaper. The ire of its editor was aroused by the discovery of the content of MacDill Field's POW menus. The drama began because of the crusading, populist—if not just plainly sensationalist—editorial policies of the *Tampa Morning Tribune*. Before the *Tribune* had finished exploiting the "coddling the German POWs" theme, it aroused its central Florida readers, helped ignite a congressional investigation, and put the War Department on the defensive. Defensive action by the War Department included a national publicity campaign that continued through two phases and lasted well beyond the end of the war in Europe. It would also include a drastic—though temporary—curtailment of POW privileges and food.

The uproar started in the Tampa area with a page-one story in the *Tampa Sunday Tribune* on January 7, 1945. The piece was titled "GI Hits Pepper Stand on Nazi War Prisoners: Tampa Soldier Blasts Easy Life of Germans." The managing editor of the *Tribune* noted that he had received a letter from a Tampa GI stationed in Belgium, who stated that he had complained to Florida's Sen. Claude D. Pepper about the comfort enjoyed by German POWs in the United States "while Americans were murdered and starved in Germany." The Tampa soldier had sent the *Tribune* a copy of both his letter and Pepper's reply. Pepper's comments were that he was "not for mollycoddling, but that he did not want anything done that might endanger our prisoners in Germany." Such a view clearly satisfied neither the soldier nor the *Tribune's* managing editor. The latter quoted the GI, saying that "he was expressing the sentiments of millions of fighting Americans in kicking about the way prisoners were being 'pampered and mollycoddled,'" and he was disappointed Pepper was doing nothing about it.[15]

By Wednesday, the subject had moved to the editorial page. "War Prisoners There and Here" reported evidence of Japanese and German atrocities and concluded that "It's about time we began paying the enemy in its own coin—not of course to the extent of murder and starvation, but, at least, by treating these war prisoners as enemy prisoners, not as favored guests of the nation."[16]

On Thursday, the "As Tribune Readers See It" section of the paper commenced the anguished howl against coddling that would characterize the letters of the next few months, as well as the popular sentiments to which the managing editor of the *Tribune* was obviously appealing. Early letters included one from Mrs. R. A. Milton of Lacoochee, who was incensed that POWs rode to movies while civilians had "to beg for gas to visit a doctor." "Why not take them to Church instead of the picture show on Sunday morning?" she asked. Joining the chorus, a mother from Lake Wales stated her agreement with what the GI had written to Senator Pepper. She denounced the good treatment of German POWs in America: "If we will give them what they give our boys maybe they will be treated better."[17]

But the first-page story in the *Tribune* on Saturday morning, January 13, 1945, was the one that really unleashed Floridians, Congressman Sikes, and a national call for renewed congressional investigation. "German Prisoners Eating Better Than American Civilians" was the headline. The story was one long editorial, highlighted by a copy of the daily menu that reportedly had been served to German prisoners at the prisoner of war compound at Tampa's MacDill Field during the week of Sunday, January 7, through Saturday, January 13. Though Capt. George R. Gresham, commandant of the MacDill Field POW camp, insisted that the Germans were issued the same rations as those given to American soldiers at MacDill and explained that "this policy is in accordance with article 2, chapter 2, section 2, title 1, general provisions of the articles of the Geneva Convention," the *Tribune* writer had a field day. In his words, the menu "showed that the Germans were served rationed food that would call for four times the food stamps now allowed American civilians."[18]

In an editorial on January 16, the *Tribune* stoked public passions by a rehash of the menus story and a further denunciation of the army's handling of the German prisoners under the title "Prisoners or Guests."[19] In fairness to the editor and to his readers, it must be noted that not all of the readers' responses were in tune with the views of the editor. Pfc. W. A. Renick of Sarasota wrote, "I do not think we can sincerely ask God to help us and then in turn mistreat our prisoners." Charles W. Bressler-Pettis of Kissimmee suggested, "To all war prisoner critics: If we treat our war prisoners better as prisoners than they were treated as fighting men by their own countries, this information will soon reach their comrades who are still being forced to fight against our boys."[20] Another reader, Ruth C. Waller of MacDill Field, warned the *Tribune*, "You are publishing no more than 'divide and conquer' propaganda very similar to any of the material put out by Goebbels." Why, she asked, did the *Tribune* feel it needed to level blows against civilian and military morale by its prisoner of war stories? "What side are you on, the Allies or the Axis?" she asked.[21] The newspaper kept up its editorial ranting about German reciprocity, referring to reports that Germans were killing American prisoners so as not to have to feed them. The *Tribune* also included lots of letters from readers in places like Dunedin, Arcadia, Winter Haven, and Tampa that echoed the views of the managing editor. At least one letter suggested that perhaps escaped prisoners should be shot.[22]

After several weeks of confining the POW issue to the op-ed pages, the crusading *Tribune* triumphantly returned it to page 1 on January 30. The headline read: "MacDill Nazi Prisoner Food Probe Asked: Peterson Requests Army Check of Complaints of 'Comforts'." Appending another rehash of its own January 13 story to one by the Associated Press from Washington, the *Tribune* reminded readers that it was the *Tribune* article that initiated the current AP story. Now, much to the editor's obvious satisfaction, the AP story stated: "A full investigation was promised today by Rep. Peterson of Florida . . . of reports that German war prisoners in Florida have been receiving better food than American civilians." Congressman J. Hardin Peterson said he had referred the MacDill matter to the War Department, and "If after a full check of the facts, I think it necessary, I will refer the case to the house military affairs committee for further investigation."[23]

And, of course, the *Tribune*'s readers had their own comments that the newspaper was pleased to print in the "As *Tribune* Readers See It" columns. From Camp Blanding, a private wrote: "It may be a good idea as long as Rep. Peterson is conducting an investigation into the excellent food the Nazi war prisoners are receiving at MacDill Field to take a peep at the menu at Camp Blanding. Boy, they are really guests at this institution. While our boys cannot partake of such extras as chewing gum, those Jerries walk around with packages of it."[24]

The *Tribune* articles and the efforts of Congressman Peterson—along with similar tirades by Rep. Samuel Dickstein of New York and Sen. Ernest W. McFarland of Arizona concerning "revelations" from their own states—focused renewed attention on the POW program's problems and made reforms by the War Department necessary.[25] Both Peterson and the *Tribune* were pleased to take credit for such reforms when they were announced—naturally, failing to mention the influence of numerous other congressmen and incidents on the national level. On February 16, Peterson told the *Tribune* that the army had banned "fancy frills in foodstuffs and anything else beyond the limits of the Geneva articles." Though he said he was not at liberty to disclose the actual text of the War Department directive, he claimed that he had been given a copy of it. "All I am interested in is that we do not pamper these prisoners. Good wholesome food without frills is sufficient," the congressman was quoted as saying. The *Tribune* could not resist closing the story with a flattering reference by the congressman to its own role: "'The *Tribune* story and editorials on the prisoners of war menu together with the protests of Congressman Sikes and myself are responsible for the new army directive,' Peterson said."[26]

The army attempted to respond to past criticisms and avoid future ones by a "no frills" directive. However, Secretary of State Henry L. Stimson and Sen. Claude Pepper of Florida assured the public of the necessity of upholding the provisions of the Geneva Convention both as a matter of treaty obligation and in order to prevent the possibility of retaliation against American prisoners of war held by the enemy. On February 18, the editor of the *Tribune* quoted an excerpt from a letter from Stimson to Pepper that said just that. But the Tampa paper in its editorial section merely printed the excerpt in order to ridicule it: "Possibility of retaliation is an amusing phrase, in view of the proof we have of enemy treatment of our prisoners." The editor then elaborated on Japanese mistreatment of Americans and reminded readers of earlier revelations regarding similar acts by the Germans.[27]

Meanwhile, reverberations of the *Tribune* story about MacDill menus could be seen clearly even in a small-town weekly newspaper like the *Bradford County Telegraph*. Granted, the paper was published in Starke, the site of Camp Blanding, but it was a paper that printed not a single story about prisoners of war—at Blanding or elsewhere—during 1944. Now, however, on February 16, 1945, the editor and owner of the newspaper, E. L. Matthews, wrote an editorial that revealed the impact of the national media on the editor's thinking—as well as the influence of the *Tampa Morning Tribune*'s original MacDill menus story on the national media. Under the title "The Germans Shoot Their Prisoners; We Feed Ours Shortcake," editor Matthews revealed that he read both *Life* magazine and Drew Pearson's syndicated column, "Washington Merry-Go-Round." From *Life* magazine of February 5 he took excerpts of the Malmédy massacre story and contrasted them with information from Drew Pearson's column of February 4 that revealed to a national audience the "scandal" of the POW menus at MacDill Field. Matthews's bottom line: He felt that because the

Germans and Japanese obviously did not abide by the Geneva Convention, "we shouldn't kill them with kindness." [28]

The response of the public relations officer at nearby Camp Blanding to the *Bradford County Telegraph*'s editorial was almost immediate. It got first page treatment, though not the most prominent headline. The March 9 article was titled "Treatment of POWs Discussed at Club by Capt. Theil." Capt. Leon S. Theil, public relations officer of Camp Blanding, explained to the Starke Rotary Club that U.S. treatment of POWs was based on the "twin policies of protecting Americans in German hands and easing our man power shortage under the Geneva Convention." Theil also emphasized that "Our Treasury has realized $25,000,000 from the labor of German prisoners. . . . This represents the difference between the 80 cents a day paid the prisoners in canteen checks, under the law, and the amount paid for their labor at prevailing labor wage scales." The article also noted that Theil quoted a previously published news release that "in Florida alone $777,058.81 was realized by the government for prisoner of war contract labor over a four month period ending December 31, 1944."[29] It was obvious that while the *Tampa Morning Tribune,* Drew Pearson's "Washington Merry-Go-Round," and even the *Bradford County Telegraph* were arousing the American citizens against the War Department's handling of the POW program, the army was attempting on both the national and local level to win adherents to its more positive perspective.

But War Department concessions to the public outcry seemed necessary, and so they were initiated. On March 14, the *Tribune* was given another chance to preen and crow about its influence in bringing about these concessions. Two stories appeared on its front page: "Army to Feed Prisoners on Oleo, No Butter: Ban All Frills, As Reported by the Tribune" and "Tribune First to Print Story." The first article had a Washington, March 13, AP dateline. It stated that "Prisoners of war, like civilians, will eat substitutes for butter, meat, chicken, and other foods that are scarce." Lt. Gen. Brehon Somervell, chief of the Army Service Forces, directed commanders of prison camps to "make every effort" to put on POW menus such foods as salted fish, eggs, spaghetti, macaroni, beans, and cold meat cuts as replacements for beef, pork, ham, lamb, bacon, chicken, and "other meats virtually unobtainable at markets." "Fancy names on prisoner menus, as well as for soldiers, will be dropped. Boiled potatoes will be simply that instead of parsley potatoes and ground meat served in gravy or sauce will no longer carry the title 'à la king'."[30]

The *Tribune* had an additional opportunity to brag in a related story on the same page: "Tribune First to Print Story." It trumpeted that it was in reaction to the *Tribune*'s first MacDill menu story of January 13 that Congressmen Peterson and Sikes demanded a congressional investigation. Then, nationally known columnist Drew Pearson reprinted the MacDill menus, which he took from the *Tribune*.[31] The Tampa newspaper proclaimed it suspected that the army's new policy was the result of all of these initiatives: the current announcement making official the reforms that Congressman Peterson had revealed in the *Tribune*'s February 17 article, reforms that had been denied initially by Secretary of War Stimson.[32]

BELLE GLADE BEANS AND SECOND CODDLING CHARGES

The turmoil aroused in part by the MacDill menus was not over. International news kept it alive. The *Tampa Morning Tribune*, unwilling to lose its readers' attention or its own crusading reputation, continued to preen and scream. The liberation of the first concentration camps and prisoner of war camps in Germany—their substantial differences often confused or deliberately overlooked in press reports—set the scene for a second phase in the Florida and national outcry against coddling German POWs in the United States.

"Nazis Starve Wounded U.S. Prisoners: Hospital Found To Be Slow Death Factory for Yanks" was the headline of one story from Germany that came over the UP wire service from its correspondent, Malcolm Muir, Jr., in Heppenheim, Germany, on March 28.[33] Then came the first graphic pictures and stories from the recently liberated concentration camps like that at Ohrdruf, near Gotha.[34] Just as coverage of the discovery and liberation of German concentration camps and prisoner of war camps hit the headlines, reports from Belle Glade provided an unfortunate contrast. "U.S. Accuses Germany of Cruelty to Prisoners," said the *Palm Beach Post* headline of April 13. The Associated Press story proclaimed, "America, where one group of Nazi prisoners of war went on strike recently because cigarets were late, formally accused Germany Thursday of shockingly inhuman treatment of American prisoners."[35]

Suggesting that German prisoners in the United States were going to lose some privileges, the article took the Belle Glade camp as an example of how German POWs in America were coddled: "From Belle Glade., Fla., came the story of 250 German prisoners working at a bean cannery who went on strike for two days when their cigaret ration was late. Camp officials said they promptly put the prisoners on bread and water—also that cigarets are now coming through."[36]

It is remarkable that the Belle Glade episode made national news: the camp had barely opened, there had been other strikes by German POWs in other states, and the camp was in existence only from February through December 1945.[37] Yet the Belle Glade story that made the headlines has a background that helps elucidate the German POW experience in Florida and in America as a whole.

The POW camp at Belle Glade was originally planned as a means by which to supply some 250 to 500 Germans for work on Palm Beach County farms. In January 1945, M. V. Mounts, the county agricultural agent, called a meeting of about 100 farmers at the town hall in Belle Glade to explain the POW work system. However, he could not persuade sufficient numbers of farmers of the value of POW labor to warrant a large German presence. Thus, only one German labor company of 250 men were sent in March to help at the Belle Glade Canning Plant and to assist the U.S. Corps of Engineers on the Okeechobee dike.[38]

The western Palm Beach County residence of the Germans, surrounded by a fence and small guard towers, was located about two-and-a-half miles east of Belle Glade, next to the Everglades Agricultural Experiment Station. It was there that the Germans arrived in mid-March 1945, fresh from picking oranges near Orlando, Leesburg, and Gotha.[39] They were guarded by a small detachment of American guards under 1st Lt. Horace C. Smith, Jr., from Tennessee. Not atypical of his men was an eighteen-year-old draftee from Tulsa named Charles M. Blackard. Blackard had arrived for infantry replacement training at Camp Blanding in September 1944. At the end of his training in December, he was assigned to the 1440 SCD (Service Command Detachment), which guarded German POWs at Camp Blanding. In March 1945, Blackard joined the guards at the newly created Blanding branch camp at Belle Glade. He traveled to West Palm Beach, where he was met and taken west to the camp.[40]

There had been other stops along life's way for the POWs who came to Belle Glade. A POW who remembers Belle Glade, the strike, and its impact on his own life is New York resident Herman Finke, formerly Horst Hermann Finke of the Afrika Korps, First Artillery Regiment.[41]

Finke, from Neustettin, east of the Oder in Pomerania—after 1945 part of Poland—had been in the Wehrmacht for nearly six years when he arrived at Belle Glade. For two of the last years, since his capture in North Africa in May 1943, he had been a prisoner of war. The story of Finke's pre-POW days help place the events at Belle Glade into a larger context and remind us that the Wehrmacht experience in Florida was only part of an odyssey that was transpiring on the world scene.

Before the war in Europe, which began with the German invasion of Poland in September 1939, Finke had spent four semesters in an agricultural school and performed compulsory paramilitary service with the RAD, the Reichsarbeitsdienst (Imperial Labor Service). Then in August 1939, in preparation for the war with Poland, Horst Finke was transferred to an army replacement unit. Originally mobilized between August 26 and December 9, with an armband signifying temporary Wehrmacht replacement status, Finke was not formally inducted into a regular Wehrmacht unit until January 8, 1940. Then followed three months of basic training, and—because Finke was "too big for marching," as he later said—he was transferred to a heavy artillery unit. He spent the following two years employed in a training unit at an artillery school at Jüterbog about seventy kilometers (or forty-four miles) south of Berlin. The school sent brigades by train to the Russian front.

In January 1942 Finke was transferred to a special light gun company near Naples, Italy, and on May 13, 1942, he joined Rommel's Afrika Korps as a member of a communications platoon attached to the First Artillery Regiment. It was his feeling then, and it has remained some fifty years later, that the Afrika Korps was a "special unit," one whose men could trust and depend on one another. Conflicts within the prisoner of war camps in the United States between Afrika Korps men and the "young ones," draftees in units captured by the Allies later in the war in Italy and France, arose from this self-professed feeling of Afrika Korps uniqueness and superiority.

The collapse of the German armies in North Africa in May 1943 meant the beginning of captivity for Finke and the men of the Afrika Korps. They surrendered as a unit to English troops on May 13. Then, after being turned over to the Americans on June 23, Finke and many of his friends were shipped to the United States. The convoy that took them from Casablanca to Norfolk between September 8 and September 24 consisted of ninety-six ships. After Finke's arrival in Norfolk, his first POW camp of residence was at Aliceville, Alabama, where he arrived by train on September 27.

It was the decision of the American government to use German prisoners of war for civilian labor that gave Finke and his fellow prisoners their opportunity to get a closer look at the countryside and eventually to visit Florida. His first American work experience was lumbering in the Alabama forests while at Aliceville. The Germans worked in three-man teams, two with a saw and one with an ax, in order to cut timber in ten-, twelve-, and fourteen-foot lengths. American civilians supervised and kept axes and saws filed to appropriate sharpness. Finke enjoyed the outdoor activity. He was reassigned in September 1944 to Camp McCain, Mississippi, where he was on a detail that prepared jeeps and trucks for shipment overseas. His first real stop as a "migrant laborer," however, was at Camp Drew in Mississippi, a side camp of Camp McCain, where he was sent on July 1, 1944.

At Camp Drew, Finke and his comrades were initiated into the fine art of cotton picking and labor strikes. The Germans found that they were quite capable of picking their daily quota of 100 pounds per man. If each man worked without a break for one hour, they could pick up to twenty-one pounds apiece; they could easily achieve their overall quota at little effort if they shared the work and the rest breaks. But that led to trouble. The farmer for whom Finke and his gang of twenty-one POWs were working accused them of not working hard enough and taking too many breaks. They, in turn, claimed that they alternated work breaks throughout the crew and that no one took more breaks than he should. They were fulfilling their quotas and angered at the farmer's accusations, so they staged a strike. They stopped work and demanded that their civilian employer call the army captain in charge of POW labor. When he found that the Germans were picking the cotton cleaner than American blacks were doing in a neighboring field, he promised that they would no longer be harassed by the outspoken farmer. But that did not satisfy the POWs. They told the American officer that they would rather face the guard house than work for that particular farmer again. They did not. Finke and his crew were shifted to another farmer, a Mr. Wilson, for whom they enjoyed working. He appreciated their talents and did them the favor of allowing each of the Germans to count cotton picked over the daily hundred pound limit as part of the quota for the next day.[42]

Finke's travels as a migrant laborer eventually led him to Camp Wheeler in Macon, Georgia, at the end of January 1945 and down to Camp Blanding in early February. After about three days at the base camp, he was sent to Leesburg—from early February until mid-March—and then down to Belle Glade by March 19. The Leesburg experience, which lasted only about a month, was one of conflict. Not atypical of developments after the Allied invasion of Normandy in June 1944, Finke and his Afrika Korps colleagues found themselves billeted with soldiers captured in France—from German units of lesser pedigree than that of the Afrika Korps. At Leesburg, the Afrika Korps men, a company of 200, found themselves in a camp with another company of 200 "young guys," members of units captured in France. Deemed by the Afrika Korps men to be "black marketeers" and otherwise untrustworthy, these later captives and the earlier "Africans," like Finke, did not get along.[43]

Then it was off to Belle Glade, where Finke and his buddies made the national news with their bean cannery strike. The strike occurred in the recently opened branch camp just as the American population was reeling from news stories of the horrors of freshly liberated concentration camps in Europe. According to Finke, faced with an empty post exchange and following a suggestion of their guards, whose own beer and cigarettes came from the same post exchange that served the Germans, the POW cannery workers staged a two-day strike on Wednesday and Thursday, April 4 and 5, 1945, which made the national news.[44] In order to get production back on schedule, the owner of the canning company offered to supply the Germans with cigarettes, but Lt. Horace C. Smith, Jr., the American officer in charge of the camp, refused to give in to the Germans. He immediately placed the strikers on a bread and water diet. He also had the guards stand the recalcitrant prisoners out in the sun of the stockade to encourage them to change their minds.[45]

However, on the second day of the strike, Smith did agree to send a truck to Camp Blanding for cigarettes and other supplies. Its return to camp with provisions for the post exchange ended the strike, though not the national stir to which it contributed. Lieutenant Smith explained to the press that his German POWs had been transferred two weeks earlier from camps in the northern part of the state, where there had been a plentiful supply of cigarettes. The change to the new camp, which had not yet received cigarettes, had provoked the Germans. Smith, however, was chagrined because "some of those who refused to work had cigarettes stored away in their quarters."[46]

In addition to the bad publicity for the American POW program, the strike brought workday losses: 239 man days lost because POWs refused to work and 124 man days lost due to disciplinary action.[47] Nor were local farmers happy when, as a result of the POW strike, 5,000 hampers of beans were temporarily left on a loading platform and a number of farmers had to call off picking crews.[48] An unhappy Lieutenant Smith transferred thirty-nine of the leading troublemakers to Camp Blanding on April 7.[49]

But that did not prevent the repercussions that the strike was to have on the national scene. The Belle Glade strike contributed to a growing public uproar against what was perceived as army coddling of German prisoners within the United States. In an attempt to diminish the impact of those accusations, the army, in turn, initiated stern measures and restrictions of POW privileges nationally. All of this brought the Germans at Belle Glade close to the center of a storm that raged around the army's handling of POWs in America in the spring of 1945. The canning plant strike of the German POWs at Belle Glade contributed to the storm, and the POWs in the Glades, like their comrades throughout the United States, became "victims" of the turmoil that their actions helped foster.

The role the Belle Glade strike played in all of this was modest, but hardly inconsequential. While it was reports of coddling at camps in Arizona that particularly made the headlines, the Belle Glade strike became part of the evidence in an anticoddling campaign waged by the press.[50] An AP article dated April 12 and titled "U.S. Vows to Punish Nazis for Cruelty to Prisoners" mentioned that "America, where one group of prisoners of war went on strike recently when cigarettes were late, formally accused Germany today of shockingly inhuman treatment of American prisoners." It went on to retell the Belle Glade strike story and to suggest that "it is apparent that German prisoners here are going to lose some privileges—though eye-for-eye retaliation for Nazi neglect, indifference and cruelty is not contemplated." It was noted that, while the War Department did not officially say so, a general tightening up was underway at various POW camps around the country.[51]

Several of America's well-known and popular political commentators, especially Drew Pearson and Walter Winchell, jumped on the coddling issue. Pearson, in his syndicated column, "Washington Merry-Go-Round," was especially influential.[52] His column, which appeared on Sunday, April 15, ran under the title "Congressmen Demand End of Coddling Prisoners." In it, he asserted that resentment over U.S. coddling of German prisoners was reaching a fevered pitch on Capitol Hill because of the publication of news stories and pictures of starved American prisoners and German concentration camp victims. Pearson noted that the chairman of the House Military Affairs Committee, Andrew Jackson May of Kentucky, showed pictures to his committee and that Representative Sikes of Florida demanded to know, "When are we going to do something about our own coddling of German prisoners here?"[53]

Florida, through Congressman Robert Sikes, was again in the forefront of a coddling investigation. On April 24, 1945, the *Tampa Tribune*'s headline was "Congress to Probe Florida Nazi Camps." Again the Tampa paper, ever ready to take credit for its role as populist crusader, nearly broke its arm patting itself on the back: "As a result of the *Tribune*'s stories last January concerning the fancy food frills being fed to German prisoners of war in this country, the military affairs committee of the House of Representatives is sending a special investigator to Florida to look into conditions in war prisoner depots at Florida army bases." In fact, the paper announced, Representative Peterson informed the *Tribune* that the investigator was coming within a day or two.[54] The *Tribune* and Representative Peterson, joined again by Congressman Sikes of the House Military Affairs Committee, were determined that Americans would know the truth about their government's undue generosity and the abuse of that generosity by foreign adversaries.

As a round of the investigations by the House Military Affairs Committee was set to open on April 25, the army began its own defensive action.[55] A five-page press release was prepared explaining the various phases of the POW program, including explanations of the Geneva Convention, the Nazi problem within the American camps, and the positive effect of good POW treatment on German soldiers' willingness to surrender. Additionally, Gen. Archer L. Lerch, the provost marshal general, wrote a lengthy article in defense of the army's policies. It was published in the May issue of *American Mercury* that appeared on the newsstands as the committee hearings opened. One historian, Edward Pluth, called it "the most candid public explanation of the prisoner of war program ever made by the War Department."[56]

But the War Department also went beyond explanations. It took action as well. Just prior to the opening of the House committee's discussions, the army abolished the Nazi salute in its prison camps and announced that the prisoners would be forced to view films of the liberated concentration camps. Additionally, the army sought to avoid coddling charges by introducing the policy of seeking veterans and former American prisoners of war as guards for the Germans in the United States.[57] More changes, including menu and canteen restrictions, were to come after V-E Day.

Meanwhile, the House Military Affairs Committee hearings began on April 26. And, while the final official report did not appear until June 12, the press carried accounts of testimony before the committee throughout the late spring of 1945. In essence the committee was responding to reports of "brutal and inexcusable treatment of prisoners overseas" and alleged coddling of prisoners in the United States. The issues considered were the army's policy and practice of handling prisoners of war; the nature and extent to which the United States and other countries, particularly the Germans, observed the Geneva Convention; and the degree to which noncompliance with the Geneva Convention released other nations from their obligations.[58]

The army's position in the hearings was direct and persuasive: the Geneva Convention was part of the "supreme law of the land," and adherence to the convention was necessary in order to prevent German retaliation against American soldiers in German hands.[59] It was a position that the army elaborated on, stuck to, and eventually won acceptance for in the House committee's final report.

During the hearings, the House committee heard plenty of criticism from representatives like Robert Sikes of Florida. In the opening hearings, at the end of April, Sikes confronted the military with letters from Floridians and clippings from Florida newspapers that registered popular anger at what appeared to be coddling of the Germans. There were, he asserted, examples of POWs "catcalling" at American girls near Miami, Germans working side by side with American women in a laundry in Orlando, and prisoners receiving special hot lunches at a canning plant in Lake Wales.[60]

But such specific complaints seemed to the committee to be outweighed by the overall persuasiveness of the army's arguments that caution in observance of the Geneva Convention and avoidance of harsh reactions to specific incidents paid dividends. Gen. Blackshear M. Bryan, assistant provost marshal general, in his appearance before the committee on April 30, cited a report from Gen. Dwight Eisenhower's European headquarters that stressed that good treatment given German prisoners had both undermined German willingness to resist surrender and favorably affected the treatment of American POWs in German hands.[61]

Testimony given by Maurice Pate, the director of Prisoner of War Relief of the American Red Cross, confirmed the military's testimony about the benefits of adherence to the Geneva Convention. Pate affirmed that U.S. treatment of German prisoners had assisted the American Red Cross in carrying out its work of providing aid to American prisoners held by the Germans. "Some have lightly called the policy of our army 'mollycoddling.' The truth is that the army has maintained the highest discipline in handling enemy prisoners. It treats these men strictly but fairly."[62] "The United States Army, in faithfully carrying out the Treaty of Geneva toward Axis war prisoners, has rendered a great service in enabling us to demand many things in hard-pressed, blockaded enemy countries which we might not otherwise have been able to obtain for our prisoners."[63]

The conclusions presented in the committee's report to Congress on June 12 indicated the persuasiveness of the army's witnesses. The committee's report noted that the hearings had been called for and taken place simultaneously with the disintegration of Germany. It was at this turbulent and confusing time that news reports focused public attention on the liberation of "prison camps." Because of such vague wording, confusion existed in the minds of

Americans who were suddenly confronted with reports of German atrocities to "prisoners" and at "prison camps." Such reports did not make clear that the bulk of the "prisoners" referred to were actually German civilians and other civilian "slaves," not American prisoners of war.[64]

The committee noted affirmatively that the keystone of War Department policy toward prisoners of war was the Geneva Convention, an international treaty, which, under the U.S. Constitution, had become part of the supreme law of the land. The State Department had also assured the committee that the army had succeeded in "adhering very closely to the Geneva Convention." Ultimately, the committee was convinced by the statements of the provost marshal general that "We do not coddle prisoners of war, but we treat them fairly and firmly."

Thus, the committee concluded: "For us to treat with undue harshness the Germans in our hands would be to adopt the Nazi principle of hostages." Furthermore, the policy followed by the army had already, in the committee's opinion, "paid large dividends," as attested to by the Red Cross and American commanders abroad. "Had promises [of fair treatment] not been true, and believed, victory would have been slower and harder, and a far greater number of Americans killed."

While the report of the House Military Affairs Committee did not end stories of coddling or occasional additional protests by congressmen, the storm was largely over. For the prisoners at Belle Glade and throughout the nation, the impact of the coddling charges, combined with the defeat of their homeland, had repercussions lasting through the summer and early fall of 1945. The charges and the defeat influenced their working conditions, diets, and general treatment by the victorious and initially vindictive Americans.

Following V-E Day, the War Department bowed to public criticisms by issuing regulations that reduced the amount and quality of food for German POWs. While it was announced that the cuts were due to food shortages and food requirements overseas, the press, POWs, and American personnel at the camps were sure that the cuts came in response to public pressure. Herman Finke recalls the reduced meat ration at the Belle Glade camp and the forced viewing of the concentration camp films by the prisoners.[65] The cuts in caloric intake by the prisoners were noted in the press, by the prisoners, their guards, and the International Red Cross.[66] Complaints made to the army from numerous sources—POWs, the International Red Cross, and American work supervisors—during June and July led to an easing of restrictions by the military through the distribution of a revised menu guide on August 4.[67] By the fall of 1945, conditions were eased and Germans, some of whom had lost between ten and thirty pounds from diet reductions and extended work hours, began to return to the halcyon days before the coddling charges of the winter and spring of 1945.[68]

Misunderstanding of the POW program by the press, the general public, and Congress, in conjunction with revelations of the horrors of the Nazi concentration camp system, had a direct and dramatic effect on the lives of the German POWs throughout the United States. Though that effect was temporary—good sense on the part of American authorities replacing vindictiveness by the fall of 1945—it left lasting memories among the POWs in American hands. It demonstrated the powerful impact of negative stereotypes. It showed that Americans were not above being manipulated by the kind of hate for national groups of which they accused their German prisoners. That made the reeducation of their German captives during 1945 even more difficult. American actions spoke louder than words to German POWs, who, though they might be shamed by revelations of the conduct of their own government, were not impressed by the "holier than thou" attitudes of their captors.

8

ON THE THRESHOLD: REEDUCATION EFFORTS IN THE BLANDING AND GORDON JOHNSTON CAMPS

In April 1945, just prior to the opening of the second series of hearings by the House Military Affairs Committee on the army's handling of POWs in America, a member of that committee, Congressman Robert Sikes of Florida, declared that "the present policy of 'voluntary indoctrination' in democracy for prisoners who wanted it was ineffective. German war prisoners should be thoroughly indoctrinated into the workings of democracy. . . . Although forcible indoctrination is prohibited by the Geneva Convention, force should be used, if necessary, because the United States is the only country to observe the convention."[1]

Congressman Sikes's concerns were not unique. News reports of Nazi terrorism in Europe, POW escapes within the United States, and prisoner work strikes aroused the American public. There were those who thought German soldiers incorrigible. There were others, however, who felt they might be "reeducated" so that they would not perpetuate Nazism in a postwar Europe.[2] What Sikes and other Americans did not realize was that since March 1944 the army had been secretly developing and introducing a subtle—perhaps too subtle—system of reeducation.[3]

Behind the scenes, the army had been discussing the possibilities of a reeducation program since March 1943. However, the idea was shelved. One of the major opponents of reeducation was the provost marshal general, Maj. Gen. Allen W. Gullion. He felt that such a program, which could be construed as contrary to the Geneva Convention, might legitimize a counterpart program in Germany. He also noted the potentially high price of such a reeducation program, both in terms of American personnel and in German labor lost through time in classrooms. Finally, he felt reeducation efforts would be useless: "Enemy prisoners of war are, for the most part, not children. . . . Those who have sufficient intellectual capacity to be of value to a post-war world have already built the philosophical frameworks of their respective lives. Those whose minds are sufficiently plastic to be affected by the program, are probably not worth the effort."[4]

The difficulties involved and the potential danger to the army's reputation for discipline if it moved into the social and political education business seemed too great. The idea was put on the back burner. There were more important things that concerned the PMGO at the time. During these early army discussions of a possible reeducation program, the number of German POWs in the United States jumped enormously: from 2,755 in March 1943 to 80,558 in July. The press of purely administrative business occasioned by these massive arrivals helped delay the development of a reeducation program.[5]

The idea of an organized attempt to reeducate or reorient the German POWs reemerged in the spring of the next year, when the private and personal intervention of Eleanor Roosevelt led a newly appointed provost marshal general, Maj. Gen. Archer L. Lerch, to dust off the earlier unimplemented plans.[6] It was decided that while Article 17 of the Geneva Convention might prohibit forced propaganda, its encouragement of "intellectual diversion and sports organized by the prisoners" provided an opportunity for intervention.[7] The goal of the program would be to give the German POWs an understanding of American institutions and ideals.

Secretary of War Henry Stimson insisted, however, that "it is essential to the success of such a program that it shall be carried through without publicity" so as to avoid a confrontation either with Nazi Germany or the protecting powers, who might see the program as contravening the Geneva Convention.[8] Reeducation was also to be voluntary and take only tertiary priority, behind POW labor and security. On April 18, 1944, the Interdepartmental Board on Prisoners of War—made up of representatives of the Departments of War, Navy, State, and Justice—agreed that the reorientation program would be based on three important principles: its control would be strictly military; the program would be voluntary; and the first priority would still be work—the second, security; and the third, reeducation.[9]

Despite these agreed-upon reservations, the goal of the program was incredibly idealistic and optimistic. It was nothing less than to provide objective facts through literature, motion pictures, music, art, and educational courses so that German POWs "might understand and believe historical and ethical truth as generally conceived by Western civilization, might come to respect the American people and their ideological values, and upon repatriation to Germany might form the nucleus of a new German ideology which will reject militarism and totalitarian controls and will advocate a democratic system of government."[10]

For purposes of the program, assistant executive officers (AEOs) were assigned to all POW base camps and a national biweekly newspaper/magazine, *Der Ruf* (The call), was to be written for POWs and edited by specially selected cooperative prisoners of "liberal and democratic leanings." These POWs were housed at Fort Kearney, a camp in Rhode Island, and the national publication was initiated in March 1945.[11] It was also the responsibility of the cooperative German prisoners at Kearney to monitor existing camp newspapers. The job of the American AEO at each POW base camp was to gain the confidence of prisoners through his work as an interpreter and assistant to the chaplain. He was to help organize recreational programs, secure books and magazines, select movies, and set up special interest courses. That meant, among other things, an attempt to show fewer gangster and "wild West" films. More films that highlighted heroism and the achievements of democratic peoples (film versions of the lives of Alexander Graham Bell, Mark Twain, and Louis Pasteur, for example), or those showing the capacity for goodness of the German people, such as "The Seventh Cross," were to be selected. It also meant, beginning in June 1945, the showing of newsreels of German concentration camps. Meanwhile, it entailed banning some German-language newspapers from camps because of their chauvinistic or Nazi leanings, and stocking post exchanges with copies of the *New York Staats-Zeitung, Time, Newsweek, Saturday Evening Post, Christian Science Monitor,* and the *New York Times.*[12]

Because of Article 17 of the Geneva Convention—"belligerents shall encourage intellectual diversions and sports organized by the prisoners of war"—POW self-generated "intellectual diversion" programs had been in existence since the arrival of the Germans in the American camps. They were aided, supported, and encouraged by the International Red Cross and YMCA. It was these programs that the AEOs sought to take charge of and redirect for their own ends at the beginning of 1945.

Because of the AEOs' need to redirect existing POW educational and leisure activity programs, it is useful to consider what "diversions" existed in the camps before the arrival of the AEOs. Base POW camps, like that at Camp Blanding and Camp Gordon Johnston were where diversions—intellectual and athletic—were most available. Smaller work camps, with their limited American personnel and labor-weary Germans, offered fewer opportunities. It is, therefore, with Florida's base camps that any survey of the changes that took place in the camps should begin.

The first diversions in Florida were initiated by the German Navy prisoners, the first military prisoners housed at Camp Blanding. One of the early articles that appeared in the American press regarding POWs in America was an article in the *Jacksonville Journal* of June 30, 1943. It was headed by a photo captioned: "Self-organized classes in English are held by Nazi prisoners of war at camp Blanding's internment camp. Here a former German officer is shown teaching rudimentary English to a group of his fellow prisoners. Reading, letter-writing, and study, all conducted by themselves, helps while away hours of confinement." The article noted that the English class, which met daily, was instructed by "a German officer—a captain—who speaks English fluently and is looked upon by the prisoners as their commander, since he is at present the highest ranking German officer."[13]

Besides having their own self-organized classes in English, by the summer of 1943 the mere handful of German naval prisoners at Blanding had few other remarkable diversions. According to the *Jacksonville Journal* report, they were "provided with one newspaper each day and weekly copies of two magazines." Which ones were not stated. The article also noted the existence of "a small library of German books." The *Journal* explained that "No effort is made to censor their reading matter."[14] Later, when the American reeducation program was under way, the AEOs worked harder at screening prisoner libraries and ensuring POW access to American publications like the *New York Times, Time, Life,* and the *Saturday Evening Post.*[15]

Leisure time was about all the German naval prisoners at Blanding had during their first year of captivity: "The Blanding concentration camp functions as a reception center for captive Germans. It is not, at least for the present, a work camp. Prisoners are held here only temporarily, and are transferred to work camps as needed." One POW pastime was the beautification of their wooden barracks. And, according to a visiting reporter, in those efforts, the Germans were "going about the job with the customary German thoroughness."[16] They also planted vegetable gardens, cut their own firewood, and carved jewel boxes and built ship models. Of course, they enjoyed sports. They built and played on their own tennis court, enjoyed Ping-Pong, and got further exercise through calisthenics, high and broad jumping, and workouts on the horizontal bar. Several times a week the prisoners were allowed to march down to Kingsley Lake for a swim under the watchful eyes of their American guards. The Germans also enjoyed get-togethers on Saturday nights for songfests accompanied by their own musical instruments—an accordion, a mandolin, and a guitar.[17]

The arrival of large numbers of Afrika Korps men from Aliceville and Opelika in November 1943 initiated a new phase of the POW program at Camp Blanding and the need for additional diversions. Because the naval compound was officially designated as an anti-Nazi compound, the regular army compound had to have its own separate facilities and programs. However, because of the turmoil among the new army arrivals, as well as because of the rapid expansion of the camp, little immediate effort was made regarding recreational diversions for the rambunctious German Army internees.

As of December 1943, there was no motion picture entertainment provided. Games and sport and recreation kits supplied by the Provost Marshal General's Office had arrived but had not been turned over to the prisoners because of the unrest in the camp. However, the prisoners themselves had brought along from earlier camps a limited number of soccer balls and Ping-Pong sets. There were no prisoner orchestras or theatricals. Nor had musical instruments been obtained for the army compound. As for a library, there was no appreciable supply of books, but some small shipments had arrived.[18]

An army inspector's report on his late 1943 visit to Camp Blanding and on the issue of POW camp newspapers is interesting as an indication of American concerns, not only in upholding the Geneva Convention but also in preventing its misuse by subversive German elements. POW camp newspapers were encouraged as a diversion called for in Article 17 of the Geneva Convention, but the content of such newspapers could be a source of trouble. The inspector reported that the American camp commander at Blanding had shown him a copy of a camp newspaper from the prisoner of war camp in Trinidad, Colorado, and asked if he should distribute copies to the Blanding prisoners if any such papers arrived in the future. "No" was penciled on the inspector's report—obviously added by someone in Washington or elsewhere along the chain of command who suspected the potentially Nazi content of the Trinidad camp paper.[19]

By early April 1944, when Blanding was visited by delegates from the International Red Cross, the Swiss Legation, and a member of the U.S. Department of State, pre-AEO recreational facilities and intellectual diversions among the prisoners had begun to make progress. Under the direction of Capt. G. R. Gresham, the camp welfare officer, assisted by Chaplain Edwin R. Carter, the POWs organized athletic contests, theatricals, and other entertainment. Athletic supplies were furnished almost entirely by the Red Cross, the YMCA, and the Catholic Athletic Aid Society. While theatricals were not yet well organized, a sixteen-piece band had been formed, the instruments having been donated or purchased from canteen profits. The camp library had accumulated about a thousand volumes, mostly supplied by the International Red Cross. However, the Red Cross visitor was displeased by the relative lack of books on hand and by the fact that new prisoners had not been permitted to bring books with them from earlier camps—books that had been supplied in large numbers by his organization. On the other hand, prisoners seemed not to respond to an offer that they might subscribe to German papers that appeared on a list submitted to them. Prisoner-initiated schooling had as yet received little attention, but preparations were being made for studies in advanced English, German, engineering, and other technical subjects. As for religious activities, Chaplain Carter made arrangements for Sunday services for both Protestants and Catholics, but the response had not been encouraging. Attendance was reported to be very small.[20]

The report of Dr. Marc Peter of the International Red Cross complements the State Department report. It noted the IRC man's concern that the recent establishment of branch camps at Leesburg and Winter Haven meant there would be a problem in supplying books, musical instruments, and games and sports equipment to those men who had arrived in the Blanding branch camps, bringing nothing with them from their earlier camps.[21]

The Red Cross man had been informed by Sgt. Maj. Karl Gerner, the German camp spokesmen at Camp Blanding's army compound, that an educational program had been initiated at the camp by the prisoners as early as January 5, 1944. Seventeen Germans instructed their fellows in subjects such as English, chemistry, biology, history, geology, stenography, accounting, elementary and higher mathematics, electricity, agriculture, and motor vehicles. Instruction was given every day from 7:30 P.M. until 10:30 P.M. The majority of the teachers were university students and graduates of secondary schools because there were no professional teachers. The German spokesman requested that appropriate German educational advisers be transferred from other camps.[22]

A battalion library held 300 recreational books (novels, stories, travel books, plays); 15 classics (such as Schiller, Goethe, Lessing, and Shakespeare); 15 textbooks (subjects like physics, chemistry, history of art, history of literature, languages, and political economy); 14 copies of *Meyer's Blitzlexikon;* and 350 *Soldatenbriefe,* paperback military manuals dealing with diverse subjects. There were also 200 textbooks in English and 30 recreational books in English. The library was open two days a week.[23]

Choral singing had made good progress since the arrival of songbooks, and the camp had a chorus of about thirty-five men. Additionally, a camp orchestra—working with four violins, two accordions, two saxophones, two guitars, a jazz trumpet, a jazz clarinet, a slide trombone, a set of drums, and a piano—practiced three times a week and presented four concerts between the acquisition of its instruments in January 1944 and the beginning of April. The camp also entertained itself with soccer and Faustball, both in organized competition between the four companies and informally within companies.[24]

Though the decision to undertake a national program for the re-educating of German POWs was made in April 1944, its implementation was slow and laborious. Not much was done in Florida or elsewhere until early 1945. There was too much planning, staffing, and logistical work to be completed first. It was only in early 1945 that the program and its AEOs could be put in place and their initial work evaluated. Field service reports of visits by an agent from the Special Projects Division (SPD) to Camp Blanding and several of its branch camps in early February 1945 indicate the early activities and problems faced by the Special Projects Division and its AEOs in Florida as elsewhere. The agent who visited Florida was Capt. Robert L. Kunzig. Kunzig was one of Col. Edward Davison's early recruits to the Prisoner of War Special Projects Division, the branch of the PMGO in charge of the reeducation program. He was an attorney and instructor at Gen. Frederick Osborn's Information and Education School at Washington and Lee University, and he later became the executive officer of the SPD.[25]

One of the problems Kunzig reported from Florida was that while the new AEO at Camp Blanding, 1st Lt. Alfred F. Corwin, was doing an excellent job, his responsibilities included the eleven—soon to be fourteen—Blanding branch camps, some of which were at great distances from the base camp. Kunzig recommended, therefore, that serious consideration be given to the assignment of extra officers in situations such as the Camp Blanding extended branch camp system. Also, the new branch camps had insufficient money in canteen profits to purchase audiovisual equipment. Kunzig recommended that a special request be sent to the Central Prisoner of War Fund for a grant to cover expenditures for projectors, noting that Camp Blanding had turned over $29,000 to the Central Prisoner of War Fund and "hasn't seen one penny to purchase projectors at present."[26]

The good news was that Kunzig had found the Camp Blanding post commander, Col. Edward Rose, his executive officer, Col. Harry Johnston, and the commanding officer of the POW camp, Maj. W. H. Lowman, interested and supportive of the work of the new Special Projects Division. Major Lowman considered Lieutenant Corwin, the AEO, "one of the finest officers on his staff." The spokesman at the German army camp had told Lowman that Lieutenant Corwin was "firm, fair, and possessed an understanding of the problems of the prisoners, [and] was the finest example of a real American officer." The program was "well underway at this post."[27] The Blanding German Army compound, with its 848 prisoners, had excellent dayrooms, a large theater, fine library, classrooms, and motion pictures twice a week. A new POW newspaper—*Zeitspiegel* (News mirror)—sponsored by Lieutenant Corwin, had evoked great interest among the prisoners, and the German Army camp spokesman requested the AEO to give lectures on America.[28]

Kunzig did note, however, that there were some complications due to the existence of the 848-man army compound and the separate 216-man navy compound, especially since the army compound was a normal prisoner of war camp and the navy compound was a strictly anti-Nazi camp. He recommended that the facilities be more equally divided between the navy and army camps: "The anti-Nazis must have equally as good facilities as the Nazis."[29]

While in Florida, Kunzig visited several of Blanding's branch camps and identified special problems and possibilities. At Leesburg, the 250 POWs who were in camp buildings formerly part of an Army Air Force installation had excellent facilities. There was a large hall for the motion pictures ordered by Blanding's Lieutenant Corwin. The camp, however, had no German director of studies and an attempt was to be made to transfer prisoners with adequate abilities and background from other branch camps. Among his other recommendations, Kunzig suggested that more sports equipment be ordered, correspondence and home study courses instigated, camp library books rotated from camp to camp, periodicals placed on sale in the canteen, and a chorus started. Happily, he found Capt. Benjamin Painter, the commanding officer of the Leesburg POW camp, very interested in and supportive of the Intellectual Diversion Program.[30] As his other Florida camp visits would indicate, that was not always the case.

When Captain Kunzig reviewed the program with the Orlando POW camp's commanding officer, the visitor was not encouraged. "Captain [E. D.] Smith[, Jr.,] is somewhat dubious but is, of course, willing to go along as ordered."[31] The large 650-man camp at Orlando was centrally located to Blanding's eleven branch camps and had become for that reason the base of operations for Camp Blanding's camp chaplain. Major Lowman, the commanding officer at the Blanding POW camp, also contemplated having his AEO, Lieutenant Corwin, permanently stationed in Orlando to facilitate his intellectual diversion duties throughout all of the Blanding branch camps. The problem in February 1945 was that "The camp as yet, has no educational program, and very few books. . . . There is an excellent canteen but no magazines or newspapers. . . . All in all, the program needs much emphasis at this point. Lieutenant Corwin is working to this end."[32]

Captain Kunzig's route of inspection in Florida included trips to Drew Field in Tampa, Dade City, and South Miami (Kendall). Each had unique, but also familiar-sounding, problems in regard to the reorientation program. All the branch camps needed encouragement to start courses and classes. They also all needed more access to library books, magazines, films, and sports equipment. One problem was cost and another was lack of interest on the part of the Americans or their prisoners. At Drew Field, for instance, a new camp that was started from scratch, the commanding officer, Capt. L. A. Drewery, "who expressed great interest in cooperating, said that he had insufficient money to organize all of the various media and purchase items necessary for the program."[33] At Dade City, a tent camp, there were neither sufficient facilities for a library and classes nor much interest on the part of the American officers in their availability. "The Camp Commander, First Lieutenant [John B.] Pike was cordial but obviously not interested in anything but the amount of work he could get out of the prisoners."[34] In situations such as those at Dade City, correspondence and self-study courses were more appropriate, and they were recommended by Captain Kunzig. He also recommended that the commanding officer watch for ardent Nazis and be alert for segregation problems.[35]

Despite its 300-mile distance from Camp Blanding, the camp at South Miami (Kendall) was particularly blessed with regard to its reorientation potential. In Captain Kunzig's eyes, that potential rested not with classes, books, and films, but in the camp's very setting: "This South Miami camp is a beautiful compound of plain but sturdy looking barracks surrounded by palm trees and flowers grown by the prisoners. It is just a few miles from Tropical Park. Prisoners work in ordnance plants and also as mess assistants in the big Florida hotels now taken over by the Army on Miami Beach. Thus reorientation of at least one type is well under way as the prisoners see the playground of America absolutely untouched by war, and at the same time realize what is going on at home."[36]

Kunzig noted that while no general study program had yet been initiated at the camp, English courses were getting started and the *New York Times* and *Miami Daily News* were sold in the POW canteen. "Great interest was expressed by the American officers in the future national prisoner of war camp magazine." They felt that the prisoners would receive it eagerly.[37] They also noted that the Germans were very interested in receiving books and that news of "the new 25¢ copies of books in German created interest." These were the books of the *Bücherreihe Neue Welt* (New world series), twenty-four volumes, mostly by exiles from Hitler's Germany like Leonhard Frank, Franz Werfel, Arnold Zweig, Carl Zuckmayer, and Thomas Mann. They represented a "Great Books" effort by the Special Projects Division, which nationally proved popular in sales.[38]

Official reports of visits to Florida POW camps in late February 1945 by Edouard Patte, the regional field secretary of the International YMCA, indicated the degree to which progress in the reorientation program was visible to someone as yet unaware of its existence. Patte, like all YMCA representatives, was interested in "intellectual diversion," and he began to see an increased interest on the part of American authorities, even if the cause for the interest was not immediately apparent. After a visit to Camp Blanding, Patte noted, "Movies: Twice a week, a new program being now arranged by the Executive." That reference and Patte's listing of a Lieutenant Corwin, AEO, as a member of the U.S. staff, are the only hints in the YMCA visitor's reports that an AEO was in place and beginning the work of reeducation. While they included English, classes at Camp Blanding at the time still showed the influence of internee choice: mathematics, physics, architecture, technical drawing, and French. And the classes still attracted only about 200 students—out of the 846 that Kunzig had reported living in the army compound and the 216 in the navy compound. The YMCA visitor commented favorably on the beginnings of a theatrical group, active athletic competitions, and the publication of a monthly camp newspaper.[39]

Patte's visits to Blanding's branch camps confirmed Kunzig's earlier findings: very moderate to no active education programs, depending on work circumstances, POW leadership attitudes, and relative newness of the camps. Yet the side camp at MacDill actually had more internees enrolled in classes than did Blanding itself. MacDill had 272, compared with Blanding's 200 students. Ten teachers taught such courses as English, math, history, geography, German, drawing, and French. On the other hand, the camp at Venice Field was just being organized and, despite good leadership and cooperation, had not yet introduced an educational or sports program. However, movies were being sent from the base camp. Drew Field's educational program was handicapped by the lack of a large room for classes and the negative attitude of the German camp spokesman. At Homestead, "as the men are engaged in heavy work, they have not much inclination at night for anything but a shower and a rest." Their modest activities program included movies twice a week and an occasional game of ball.[40]

Continuing his visits into northwest Florida, to Camp Gordon Johnston and its branch camps at Telogia, Dale Mabry Field, and Eglin Field, the visiting YMCA field secretary found that interest in intellectual diversion varied by camp as it did in the Blanding branch camps. He did note the presence of an executive officer, Lt. William B. Neil, at the POW base camp at Camp Gordon Johnston and another assistant executive officer, Lt. C. C. Guetschaw, at the distant Eglin Field branch camp. Nevertheless, Patte's comments regarding Camp Gordon Johnston noted, "The education and recreational activities are still underdeveloped. There does not seem to be a real deep desire [on the part of the prisoners] to take advantage of the captivity for further education." There were classes in English, German, electricity, architecture, geography, and mathematics that attracted attendance of only seventy-five men. At Telogia, lack of a large room seemed to contribute to keeping the camp's intellectual and recreational activities limited, except for interest in soccer. Nor was there much initiative for activities at Dale Mabry. Only about seventeen men attended classes in English and Russian. At Eglin Field, with its own AEO, there were classes, or at least irregular lectures, in such things as English, mathematics, history, physics, music, literature, shorthand, automobile engineering, public speaking, and natural science. Patte noted that steps were being taken by Lieutenant Guetschaw, the AEO, to procure a piano, gramophone, and radio.[41]

A report of March 2 from the AEO at Gordon Johnston, 2d Lt. William B. Neil, to the special projects officer of the Fourth Service Command in Atlanta gives a bit more background to the situation in the northwest Florida camps. The report consisted of a list of the types of classes given at the various camps, attendance, and number of class hours a week. More interestingly, it gave his evaluation of the political and educational background of the existing—pre-AEO intervention—German personnel involved in intellectual diversion efforts: the director of studies, the camp spokesman, and POW chaplain at each of the camps. It suggests the problems that an American reorientation program confronted in Florida, as elsewhere, when it sought to influence existing "intellectual diversion programs." For instance, at Camp Gordon Johnston the director of studies was described as "a moderate Nazi" but amenable to proper guidance. One of the chaplains seemed opposed to Nazi philosophy, while the other professed to be a minister, but intelligence reports indicated that he was a strong Nazi and his claims of being a pastor were unsubstantiated by credentials. Another handicap was the existence of situations in which German spokesmen were professional soldiers with limited education and only average intelligence, and directors of studies were either of "average intelligence" or "moderate" to "fairly strong Nazis" who were well educated and all too capable.[42]

A report of a visit to the POW camp at Camp Gordon Johnston on March 7–8, 1945, by Capt. Walter H. Rapp of the Field Service Branch of the Special Projects Division confirmed and elaborated on the AEO reports. Lieutenant Neil, the AEO at Gordon Johnston, was praised for all of his efforts. Elements of progress initiated by the AEO included classes organized in some ten to twelve different subjects taught by qualified prisoner of war teachers; Catholic and Protestant services and Bible study classes with increasing weekly attendance; sale of appropriate books, newspapers, and magazines; increased availability to individual prisoners of instructional and entertaining books through the camp canteen; purchase of two 16 mm projectors so that now three were available; purchase of two radios and five record players; purchase out of prisoner of war funds of additional musical instruments; and publication of a camp newspaper anticipated within a few days.[43]

Meanwhile, Field Service Officer Rapp undertook several actions and initiated recommendations of his own. These included the recommendation to the post executive officer for the construction of an attractive day and reading room and the improvement of the appearance of the camp canteen. Additionally, he recommended to the AEO the fostering of a theater group and the organization of collective wood carving and painting classes. More importantly, perhaps, he recommended that the camp authorities contact the Fourth Service Command with the request to issue orders for the immediate transfer of twenty-seven nonworking, noncooperative German noncommissioned officers out of the camp—obstacles to reorientation efforts. Finally, Rapp suggested that the Prisoner of War Special Projects Division contact the Florida State College for Women at Tallahassee to secure it as the sponsoring university for the educational programs at Camp Gordon Johnston POW camp.[44]

Even before the public was made aware of the army's incipient Special Projects Division reeducation program, the program had become so obvious that it had to be explained to some of the official international visitors to the POW camps. The secret reeducation program that was instituted by the PMGO in December 1944 had gradually led to increasing misunderstandings and criticisms by YMCA representatives. Unaware of the program, they did not understand a new censorship that was imposed first on the reading materials and then on the films that they made available for the POW camps. As early as January and February 1945, the special projects people in charge of the program found it awkward to explain a new censorship over and above that of the district postal censor. It became necessary, without divulging the whole story, for Col. Edward Davison, the head of the Special Projects Division, to talk with officials of the War Prisoners Aid of the Young Men's Christian Associations in the United States. The next problem came in March when a Special Projects Division circular to the camps provided that only approved films could be shown and that an admission charge of fifteen cents would be charged for each prisoner. That practically stopped the YMCA's own film efforts and required Maj. Maxwell McKnight, Davison's assistant director of the special projects program, to have additional discussions with disappointed YMCA officials.[45]

As the reeducation program became more known to the YMCA people, they felt that their activities would be increased rather than curtailed. Their perspective was also fundamentally different from what they perceived as that of the army. They felt that the approach to reeducation should be through spiritual development rather than through the use of censorship or propaganda. In discussions between Major McKnight and Mr. E. T. Colton, the executive director of the YMCA's New York office, these opposing viewpoints were expressed. McKnight insisted that it was the army's job to reorient the prisoners. The YMCA countered that it was "not up to them to destroy any political distinction between the prisoners but to preserve morale of all prisoners." Tempers heated in the late spring as the army received reports of some YMCA representatives on camp visits becoming "quite critical of certain camp commanders and administrative measures. I believe General Bryan and Colonel Rogers mentioned to Mr. Colton on more than one occasion that the job of the YMCA was to administer to the spiritual needs of the prisoners and not to criticize or interfere with administrative measures of the camp officials."[46]

The final result, after an exchange of letters between the secretary of state and the secretary of war, was that the YMCA was informed that modifications had to be made in their prisoners' aid program. Chief among these changes was that henceforth a representative from the Department of State was to accompany YMCA field secretaries on their visits to the camps—as they did with IRC representatives—and they were no longer allowed to interview POWs alone. The YMCA reluctantly accepted these changes, though at first they felt their whole program would be devastated: "Your letter of July 24 brought grave concern to those of us who enjoyed such splendid collaboration with the War Department over three years. Our feeling at first was that it contained a directive which made it extremely difficult for the World's Committee of the Y.M.C.A. to continue its services without denying its basic purposes to serve all prisoners of war irrespective of their nationality, race, or creed and to bear witness to its faith in the deeper spiritual values expressed in the commandment 'To love God and our neighbor'. Our conversations with you and members of the State Department, while making it clear that a world Christian organization could not wholly identify itself with a national educational program for German prisoners, convinced us, however, that it was highly desirable and possible to work out satisfactory agreements within the bounds imposed by military necessities and national policies."[47]

In the end, the YMCA agreed to the changes in their program. They consented to welcome representatives of the State Department on their visits. However, they proposed that if such representatives were not available, YMCA field secretaries would tour camps accompanied by officers appointed by the camp commanders. They would then return to Washington after each three-month tour to report to the State Department. The YMCA also proposed that in the future only seven field secretaries, rather than ten, would conduct three-month tours of the camps in their respective regions. Edouard Patte of Aiken, South Carolina, the well-loved visitor to the Blanding and Gordon Johnston camps, was to be the field secretary for Virginia, West Virginia, North Carolina, South Carolina, Georgia, Florida, Alabama, and Tennessee. The War Prisoners Aid also planned to "continue to supplement the recreational, educational, and cultural programs of both base and branch camps" by purchasing, publishing, or reprinting books for general reading, subject to clearance through camp officers and prior approval of the Special Projects Division; increase the distribution in branch camps of the YMCA's "concert and theatrical kit service"; furnish supplies and materials for recreational usage; and, finally, though discontinuing its film service in the secular field, provide religious films, as approved by the Special Projects Division.[48]

On May 28, 1945, nearly three weeks after V-E Day, the existence of the army's POW reeducation program was finally revealed to the public. In a seven-page statement, Brig. Gen. Blackshear M. Bryan, the assistant provost marshal general, explained, "We are taking some 350,000 German prisoners of war—men meandering in a morass of myths—and conducting a well-calculated, thorough and pointed program of exposition."[49] Surprisingly, the American press and public, aroused earlier by what seemed the absence of a program of reeducation, now seemed relatively disinterested.[50]

A lengthy article appeared in the *Palm Beach Post* on July 13, with the byline of Peter Edson, NEA staff correspondent, Washington. It was titled "Army Gives German POWs Large Doses of Nazi-Purging News and Literature" and presented Floridians with a very detailed overview of the army's special education program. It explained how in early 1945 the army began the publication of *Der Ruf*, the biweekly newspaper/magazine for POWs. The article proclaimed that the prisoners were now able to buy twenty-five-cent reprints of books previously banned by Hitler: Erich Maria Remarque's *All Quiet on the Western Front*, Thomas Mann's *Magic Mountain*, and Heinrich Heine's poetry. Likewise, whereas Hitler encouraged gangster and high society scandal films to show American decadence, the POWs could now—for a mere fifteen-cent admission price—see *Abe Lincoln of Illinois, Union Pacific*, and *Cimarron*. The article also mentioned the more academic educational program available in the camps through sponsorship of nearby colleges, correspondence courses from distant colleges, and Armed Forces Institute correspondence courses conducted by the University of Wisconsin. The article's author concluded that perhaps 15 to 20 percent of the prisoners might be considered incorrigibles, and he speculated that they would probably be the last to be repatriated: "An entirely unofficial view on which there is no U.S. government or War Department policy is that these irreconcilables will make good material for repatriation labor battalions. The mere possibility of such a development is said to be having a salutary effect on discipline in the PW camps today. The idea of having to go to work to rebuild what they have destroyed in France or Russia they don't like at all."[51]

The writer was correct in one assumption: the POWs did worry about being turned over to the French and Russians. It would be a major source of concern during their last months in the American camps. Ultimately, he would be proved wrong about incorrigibles being turned over to their former European enemies. Being cooperative did not help much, either. POWs considered citizens of the Soviet Union were subjected to forced repatriation to their homeland.[52] Other German prisoners would be turned over in large numbers to the British and French in order to fulfill work quotas previously agreed upon.[53]

Another long article, also printed in the *Palm Beach Post* on July 13, presented more specifics regarding the army's special projects program. It quoted Maj. Gen. Archer L. Lerch, the provost marshal general, as saying that up until now the army had been damned for not doing anything in that line, while in fact it had. It just had not been able to talk about it, because "First and foremost, it didn't want the German prisoners to know that they were being re-oriented on some of their Nazi ideas. Now that Germany is defeated, that doesn't make any difference." Second, it was feared that "a few loudmouthed elements in the United States" would misunderstand what was being done and claim that the "Nazi prisoners were being mollycoddled." Also, the army feared German retaliation.[54] The article went on to say that the job of reorienting the POWs was handed to Lt. Col. Edward Davison, who was head of a Prisoner of War Special Projects Division in the Provost Marshal General's Office: "The name sounds innocent enough, but hidden behind that nameplate is a fascinating story of intelligence work which has until now never been told." It went on to tell of the program efforts to "reorient Nazi thinking" through books, newspapers, magazines, camp papers, and schools.[55] The secrets were revealed to the American public, as well as to German POWs who might, thanks to the reeducation program, have access to American newspapers.

The program was not ending, but rather just beginning to reach high gear with the end of the war in Europe. Field service reports of visits by Special Projects Division officers to Camp Blanding and Camp Gordon Johnston in early September 1945 showed the nature of the changes in the reorientation effort that had taken place since the end of the war. Foremost was the recommendation that classes in U.S. history, civics, and geography be established and accelerated at base and branch camps as provided for in a Prisoner of War Special Projects letter of June 28, 1945. Established classes in biology, architecture, electrical engineering, world geography, and mathematics in the base camp were to be discontinued.[56] Career and general education programs were out, and the reeducation and Americanization of the POWs were the focus of the Special Projects Division's efforts.

Further indication of the progress of the reorientation program in the Florida camps can be gained by a look at the camp newspapers that began to appear regularly in the spring and summer of 1945 under the guidance of Special Projects AEOs. The most regular—appearing biweekly on Sunday, after several initial months of being merely a monthly publication—was the *POW-Zeitspiegel* (POW times mirror) at Camp Blanding. MacDill Field had a monthly titled *Was bei uns los ist* (What's going on here), and Eglin Field had the biweekly *An der Schwelle* (On the threshold).[57] These papers, in addition to serving as sources of information and literary diversion, became vehicles for democratic propaganda—or at least for a reconsideration of former beliefs and habits.

The summer 1945 issues of the *POW-Zeitspiegel* are perfect examples. The July 15 issue had within its brief ten pages stories, jokes, and word puzzles, as well as a medical article on the sex organs and an article on the physics of the atom. But it also had a two-page article that recommended the learning of the English language while in American captivity. In anticipation of a divided Germany, a western portion under American control, the POW author emphasized the usefulness of learning this foreign tongue.[58] A longer article in the August 12 issue was titled "Prisoner of War As Helper in the Rebuilding of His Homeland." It was accompanied by a three-page article "Concerning Democracy."[59] On a more immediately practical level—and an exercise in democracy—another article explained "Why Representatives."[60] It discussed current camp elections to select six representatives from each company—three for meetings with the camp spokesman and three for meetings with company leaders. The author expressed the hope that the branch camps would follow suit with the experiment.

The POW newspapers not only ran articles on democracy and American history but encouraged attendance at courses offered at the camps. The MacDill Field paper of June/July 1945 remarked that the greatest enemies of the POW had been distrust and boredom, but since the end of the war in May, depression was the new enemy. It had to be overcome through activity. The author recommended that a good exercise would be to enroll in a course.[61] The August issue said that few had attended such courses during July, but that by August about 60 percent of the camp was involved in one course or the other. It was noted that the English course was the best attended.[62]

An der Schwelle, Eglin Field's paper, announced in November 1945 that new courses had begun at the base camp at Camp Gordon Johnston in September. They featured English, American history, and geography. Apparently attendance at these classes was up from the previous winter. The paper heralded the fact that during October 1945 every man at the base camp attended about three and a half hours of classes. At the Gordon Johnston's branch camps, it was another story. The paper explained that because of hard work at woodcutting and peanut harvesting, the men of the branch camps attended an average of a mere 0.64–0.88 hours during that month.[63] Things were different at the Camp Blanding base camp. The POW paper there noted on October 14, 1945, that the new classes were popular and that six English classes were under way.[64]

Meanwhile, AEOs saw to it that the prisoners viewed newsreels of German concentration camps as they were found by the liberating American and British armies. These films were shown at the POW branch camps as well as at the base camps. Horst Finke and his comrades at Belle Glade had to view the films and sign a list indicating their attendance.[65] At Camp Blanding, the reaction of some of the prisoners led to the collection of funds to be sent to the dependents and survivors of the concentration camps. The POW spokesman at Blanding explained:

> the whole company had the occasion on 10 June 1945 to convince itself through a moving picture how the German government, during the past years, has mistreated and tortured to death citizens, foreigners, and prisoners of war in the concentration camps and POW camps. Voluntarily, the company decided to forward the amount of $411.00 to the German Red Cross, to be used for women, children, and men, regardless of religion, who have suffered the most during the years of the German [Nazi] government. . . . We hope that all those criminals, regardless of class, religion, party, organization or military unit, will suffer just punishment.[66]

On September 16, the Blanding *POW-Zeitspiegel* announced that recent collections amounting to $836.68 had arrived to supplement the funds already collected and that they totaled $5,917.73. The most recent funds came from the branch camps: $167 from Kendall, $59 from Leesburg, $300 from Belle Glade, and $310 from Drew Field.[67]

Unfortunately, such collections did not reflect the attitude of all of the prisoners—or all their guards. Horst Finke, for whom the concentration camp horror films were the first revelation of the Holocaust, recalls that when the films were to be shown at Belle Glade, some of the older American guards—themselves recent returnees from overseas duty—said "don't believe that baloney."[68]

Nor could all of the Germans tolerate the rather heavy-handed and all too self-righteous efforts by their captors to "Americanize" them—supposedly making them into better human beings. At Drew Field a group of Nazis antagonized an American army chaplain who tried to win them for democracy. They drove him raging from their midst by embarrassing him with the American race problem.[69]

Nevertheless, the efforts to democratize the German prisoners of war in Florida, as throughout the United States, continued with vigor. Visiting Camp Blanding and its branch camps in October 1945, Edouard Patte of the YMCA reported: "There is a profound desire of the Assistant Executive Officer and the German director of studies to teach first of all the English language to the prisoners of war. Both men feel that with a thorough knowledge of English the prisoners will be able to get their information about democracy, about freedom, about civics, directly from the sources—newspapers, books and magazines—therefore, the main effort is applied to the school of English language at the base and all the branch camps."[70]

Herman (Horst) Finke still has one of his elementary English books from the classes at the Belle Glade branch camp. They were taught by a fellow German POW, "a regular hillbilly, but a man who could hear an English word once and then know it." The little English manual is titled *Englisch Wie Man's Spricht: Spoken English, Basic Course, Units 7–12*. It was War Department Technical Manual, German, TM30–1506A, produced in July 1945 and published by the U.S. Government Printing Office, Washington. Lesson 10 has a subject and phrases that can be taken as representative of the American effort to have the German POWs pick up both useful colloquial English and a feel for America at the same time. The lesson is titled "Blick auf New York" (A look at New York). It presents German sentences, their English translation written phonetically, and finally the English translation as it is written in American English. What attracts one's attention are the sentences themselves. Several examples will suffice:

Well, Max, you said you wanted to see New York. Where do you want to go first?

New York is so big and so different from any place I've ever been. I'd like to see everything.[71]

Edouard Patte, the YMCA visitor to the Blanding camps in October 1945, also noted the existence of courses in civics, American history, and geography. Based on conversations with the men of the various units, he felt that real progress had been made.[72] Horst Finke, for one, received a certificate of achievement on November 20, 1945, because he "successfully completed a course in American civics for prisoners of war conducted at Belle Glade, Florida." The certificate was signed by Alfred F. Corwin, captain, assistant executive officer; Horace C. Smith, Jr., first lieutenant, camp commander; and Josef Huber, POW director of studies. Finke obtained additional certificates of achievement while at Belle Glade: American history, December 4, 1945; geography of the United States, January 23, 1946; and the study of the English language, intermediate, January 1946.[73]

The YMCA visitor to the Florida camps expressed special pleasure at the organized programs called "Question Hours," during which prisoners were able to ask and discuss current questions.[74] In one such *Aussprachabend* (Speak out evening) on October 3, for instance, Captain Corwin, Blanding's AEO, tried to answer questions that most concerned the prisoners: Germany's future; when the prisoners would be going home; and the current situation in America.[75] Patte also noted that "an effort to interpret democracy in German terms was successfully attempted by a German pastor who lectured several times before large groups of men on 'The Sense of a Free Life' and 'Toward an Understanding of Liberty'."[76] The YMCA man's concluding remarks regarding the Daytona Beach branch camp indicated his awareness of the limitations of the army's reeducation program. One of its major problems by the fall of 1945 was that the prisoners' thoughts turned increasingly toward home. "In this little camp men seemed to be particularly quiet—almost passive—men have only one idea—to go home as soon as possible."[77]

Life in the camps dragged on. Repatriation seemed endlessly delayed, and rumors—increasingly believable—of forced labor in France before return to Germany dampened POW interest in education. In the September 30, 1945, Camp Blanding POW paper, a letter that was written by two Belle Glade internees expressed the growing fears of many of the POWs. They reported seeing an article in the September 5, 1945, *New York Times,* which suggested that as many as 300,000 German POWs held in America would be turned over to the French at the rate of 50,000 a month beginning in December. They expressed horror at such a "slave trade" and said that the idea of the "collective guilt of a race or people is the creation of fascist-totalitarian ideas" repudiated by Roosevelt and Churchill. The writers wanted to know the answer to one question: "Is the deportation of German prisoners of war from the United States to France really intended?"[78]

Rumors, quite justified as it would later turn out, were rampant that many of the German POWs in American camps would be turned over to the vindictive French. Worries led to the development of physical symptoms of distress as well. Reports from the Bell Haven camp made this clear. "The German doctor here states that he finds too much stomach trouble both here and at Kendall, although the sick rate is quite low. He attributes this to nervousness over the possibility of being transferred to French control."[79]

By November, some of the POWs knew that there was little that they could do to determine their postwar fate, whether they were active in the army's reorientation program or not. Along with other "star pupils" of the reorientation program, some Florida prisoners had been chosen to be participants in a special program that was to prepare them to return to Germany early to assist the work of the Allied military governments. The program was started experimentally with sixty prisoners at a special sixty-day crash course at Fort Kearney, Rhode Island, in May. Ultimately two other special schools were established in Rhode Island, on Narragansett Bay, across from Fort Kearney: an administrative school at Fort Getty and a police school at Fort Wetherill. To get to these schools, selected POWs were screened at their own camps and then at Fort Devens, Massachusetts. A total of 17,833 men were screened, but only 816 were accepted for the Fort Getty program and 2,895 for the Fort Wetherill program.[80] However, lack of clarity and coordination between various military authorities led to the transfer of some of these men into the hands of administrators in Europe who knew little and cared less about the POWs' special training in America.

Much to their disappointment, some of the Germans found themselves in normal European POW work camps. A State Department representative who visited the POW branch camp at Welch General Hospital in Daytona Beach on November 26 noted the impact of news of such developments back in that POW camp: "morale now seems not to be quite so good." The reason was a letter from a former prisoner to his friends in the Florida camp. He reported that he was currently spending an unhappy time in a camp in Belgium. The letter writer had been considered by his comrades to be a "star pupil in the Reorientation Program and to be going home for work in the Allied Military Government." The disillusionment that was aroused at the camp after the arrival of the letter was obvious.[81]

Sometimes the lengthening postwar stay in America led to high jinks by prisoners during the reeducation efforts that worried individual American officers, while hardly ruffling the feathers of other official observers. Reporting on his visit to Banana River Naval Air Station on November 27, while accompanying an IRC representative, J. L. Toohey of the State Department made this comment regarding discipline and morale at the POW compound: "Although I discovered no indications of anything being amiss in this direction, the Base Camp is suspicious of the prisoners here since Lieutenant [Warren S.] Olin [Banana River executive officer] discovered that the education program was being slyly sabotaged by the three best teachers. The discovery was made as the result of an investigation after he found a picture of Hitler (painted by one of the teachers from Red Cross materials) hidden inside a double blackboard in the messhall."[82] Not everyone was taking the army's reeducation program as seriously as the American authorities desired.

Visiting Camp Blanding at the end of January 1946, Edouard Patte reported, "The huge camp seems now almost deserted, and the POW compounds may be vacated within a few weeks. Already the Navy compound is empty; alone the large compound on the hill remains activated."[83] As to new programs: "None. The base camp is in the mood of 'folding up'; and the branch camps follow suit. . . . General Impression: A little dull, inactive, disappointing. We feel definitely that the POWs in these camps are tired of this long captivity and do not have enough 'pep' left in them to undertake any new program. I tried to instill, particularly, with the leaders and ministers, a will to act with more energy and hope for the future."

But in his conferences with leaders, Patte was "constantly asked three questions which seem to be predominant in the mind of every man interned: '1. Why don't we have any mail from Germany? 2. Where are we going to be sent, to France or home? 3. When do we leave?'"[84]

The reorientation program was ending; its teachers and students were being returned—if not to Germany, at least to Europe. *Der Ruf*, the national POW newspaper/magazine, designed as the model for but never quite as popular as local camp papers, ceased publication on April 1, 1946.[85] Reorientation at the national level, as at the local level, was at an end.

What good did it do? There is extensive literature that debates the impact and degree of the success of the national program.[86] While the Special Projects Division personnel and their commanding officers in the Prisoner of War Operations Division of the Office of the Provost Marshal General liked to think that their efforts had a moderate degree of success, their conclusions were based on a mixture of anecdote and modest statistical study.[87] The results of questionnaires given over a six-week period to about 25,000 POWs before their repatriation did seem to indicate some attitudinal shifts. The survey showed 74 percent left America with "an appreciation of the value of democracy and a friendly attitude toward their captors"; 33 percent "anti-Nazi and pro-democratic"; but 10 percent were still "militantly Nazi," and a further 15 percent, "while not strictly Nazi, still . . . not favorably disposed toward America or democracy." American intelligence had roughly estimated that prior to the inception of the reeducation program POW political attitudes could be divided into three categories: 13 percent Nazi; 13 percent anti-Nazi; and 74 percent neutral.[88] Thus, while there seemed to be an increase in those in the anti-Nazi and democratic category, there had been little change in the Nazi numbers. The bottom line seems best summed up in a German study of the POW experience in America, which suggests that the impact of the program had neither width nor depth, but that a number of the participants had "certainly experienced assistance in coming to terms (bei der inneren Auseinandersetzung) with National Socialism."[89]

About the prisoners in the Florida camps, there is too little information to make a judgment. Because the English, history, and civics classes sponsored by the Special Projects Division were voluntary, Gerhard Anklam, the feisty escapee from Clewiston and sometime Camp Blanding resident, did not attend.[90] As has been noted above, Horst Finke attended classes and received certificates in English, American history, and American civics. He later returned to America in 1952 to become a U.S. citizen. Certainly there were many factors involved for this native of Pomerania, who returned to Germany to find his mother living in the Russian sector of Berlin and his hometown part of Poland.[91] But the reeducation program had not hurt.

What did hurt the reeducation program, as well as the reliability of the surveys that were designed to test its effectiveness, was the combination of rumor and fact regarding the return of the POWs to their homeland by way of work camps in France and Britain.[92] Rumors and uncertainty led to disillusionment with the high ideals of America propagated in the Special Projects courses. The fact that 178,000 of the 378,000 POWs in America would, indeed, face a year or more of confinement in Europe before repatriation to Germany gave many Germans time to think about the contrasts between the rhetoric and reality of American ideals during their long way home.

9

THE LONG WAY HOME: REPATRIATION

Repatriations began while the war still raged in Europe. Based on provisions of the Geneva Convention that called for the amelioration of the fate of the sick and wounded, the International Red Cross Committee and the Swiss Legation arranged agreements for exchanges. Mixed medical commissions composed of one American and two Swiss doctors began their work in the United States in November 1943.[1] By April 1945 they had examined 7,941 German POWs and recommended 1,015 for direct repatriation and 359 for care in a neutral country. To this number were added 1,166 German prisoners of war who were already in hospitals.[2] In five different exchanges between September 1943 and January 1945 a total of 2,181 POWs, along with 102 German medical corpsmen and doctors were returned to Germany. They were exchanged for 886 Americans. These included 809 sick and wounded American soldiers who were exchanged between October 1943 and January 1945 and a special exchange of 77 American corpsmen and doctors in March 1945.[3] The Germans were shipped under Red Cross or neutral flags by way of Göteborg, in southwestern Sweden, and then to Germany or through Barcelona, in neutral Spain, and then to German-occupied Marseille and home to Germany. An earlier chapter reviewed the reports made to the Wehrmacht by four former Blanding captives who were part of the February 1944 exchange. That particular group of 132 Germans sailed with the SS *Gripsholm*, bound from New York to Lisbon, Portugal.[4]

These medical repatriations involved individuals rather than specific types of soldiers, and individual cases were often denied. There remain in the archives requests from three of Camp Blanding's German medics, who in April 1944 asked to be repatriated along with exchanged sick and wounded. They based their pleas on an alleged agreement between the United States and Germany to exchange six protected personnel (doctors, medics, or chaplains) with every thousand POWs repatriated. With a cover letter of support for their case to the provost marshal general from the German spokesman at Camp Blanding, Sgt. Karl Gerner, medical lance corporals Bruno Kitow, Siegfried Fuchs, and Helmut Hoefling made their individual cases. Each claimed a medical disability of his own; each documented that problem with a cover note from one of Blanding's German POW doctors; and each mentioned that on April 6, 1944, the Germans had been told by a visiting representative of the protecting power, Switzerland, that an exchange of medical personnel was to be arranged.[5]

On April 6, Dr. Edward A. Feer of the Swiss Legation visited the base camp at Camp Blanding in the company of Dr. Marc Peter, a delegate of the International Red Cross Committee, and Charles C. Eberhardt of the Department of State. However, no mention of such a specific comment by Dr. Feer about medical personnel and repatriation exchanges occurred in the reports of either Dr. Peter or Mr. Eberhardt.[6] The response from the PMGO to the Blanding corpsmen's request was that "No agreement exists between this country and Germany providing for the exchange of protected personnel to accompany repatriated prisoners of war."[7] The German corpsmen stayed at Camp Blanding.

General repatriation of the Germans had to await the conclusion of peace. Article 75 of the Geneva Convention provided that "repatriation of prisoners shall be effected with the least possible delay after the conclusion of peace."[8] Therein, however, lay the rub. Hostilities between the United States and Germany were concluded through the capitulation of the Wehrmacht on May 8, 1945, but no peace treaty was signed. This became an excuse to delay the repatriation of prisoners to Germany.[9] More important in causing the delay in repatriation was the need for postwar labor for reconstruction in Europe. President Franklin Roosevelt had inserted into the final protocol of the Yalta Conference of February 1945 mention of the use of German labor for the rehabilitation of war-devastated Europe.[10]

There were other considerations as well. The American government had entered into wartime agreements with both Britain and France regarding the future of German POWs in American hands.

As early as January 1943, American Secretary of State Sumner Welles and the British ambassador in Washington, Lord Halifax, agreed that the United States would furnish accommodation for 150,000 "British-owned" prisoners of war. Though that number was later modified downward, the British insisted on regaining at least 130,000 American-housed German POWs. Eventually about 123,000 Germans held in America were turned over to Britain for postwar labor rather than for direct repatriation to Germany.[11] The French also desired a considerable number of German POWs for agricultural labor and for the rebuilding of their war-damaged territories. The provisional French government sent such a request to General Eisenhower's allied military headquarters in September 1944, and an agreement in that regard was signed on December 23, 1944, between the Supreme Headquarters, Allied Expeditionary Force (SHAEF) and the French government. A further agreement on May 26, 1945, provided that a total of 1,750,000 German prisoners under American control were to be turned over to the French. Most of them were to come from the captives still held by the Americans in Europe. However, because of the precipitous and summary release of large numbers of these prisoners in the early weeks after the Wehrmacht capitulation, it was decided to supplement the POWs in Europe with additional prisoners held in America. About 55,000 POWs from America made up this supplement.[12] Thus, of the 378,000 German POWs in America only about 200,000 went directly back to Germany. That was about 53 percent of the POWs in America. The remaining 47 percent took the long way home—by way of labor camps in Britain or France for another year or more.[13]

A slow stream of POWs began their return directly to Germany in the summer of 1945. In June the first group of repatriated Germans numbered 2,800. Those departing early for direct repatriation included members of groups especially necessary for the rehabilitation of their homeland, such as miners and technicians with the postal telegraph and telephone communication services. Monthly repatriations remained limited: 4,000 in July; 12,000 in September; 4,000 in October; up to 26,000 in November; and then back to 11,000 in December. Most of these men were returned to Germany by way of Camp Bolbec near Le Havre, France. From there they were sent to discharge centers in the American zone—such as Babenhausen, near Darmstadt; Bad Aibling, near Munich; or Münster, in the British zone.[14]

Meanwhile rumors of the transfer of American-held POWs to dreaded French custody began to worry those who remained in the States. The fact that the army's reeducation program encouraged the POWs to read American newspapers helped fan the rumors, which would ultimately prove at least partially true, even if the numbers involved were not as great as initially cited. The letter from Belle Glade prisoners Wolfgang Speer and Karl Bartsch printed in the September 30, 1945, issue of Blanding's *POW-Zeitspiegel* has already been mentioned. They said that POWs in America had been startled as by "a stroke of lightning" by the story in the *New York Times* of September 5. It suggested that as many as 300,000 of the POWs in the United States might be turned over to the French at the rate of 50,000 men a month beginning in December.[15] The numbers were exaggerated, but some truth was there. The American authorities, while telling the POWs not to believe the rumors, were vague at best—and intentionally misleading at worst—regarding what the future might hold.[16]

The slow repatriation process merely fueled the rumors and made many POWs edgy. By November 20, 1945, only 73,178 German prisoners had been repatriated. The government announced that all remaining POWs in the United States "will be entirely out of private contract work, including agriculture, by the end of February, and will be withdrawn from military work by the end of March, 1946." However, upon the protests of American farmers, on January 25, 1946, President Truman announced a sixty-day delay on the repatriation of POWs involved in critical segments of the economy.[17] The end of repatriation of all POWs to Europe was set for June 1946. Monthly shipments to Europe of POW laborers considered unessential to American agriculture continued. In January alone 38,000 were returned. February, with 73,000 POWs on the way, was the month in which the largest single number of departures took place. There followed 68,000 in March; 56,000 in April; and 47,000 in May.[18] By May 15, 1946, there were still 46,739 German POWs in the United States. Florida camps, however, had only about 242 left: 120 at Telogia, whose base camp was now Fort Benning, Georgia, rather than Camp Gordon Johnston; and 122 at Welch Hospital in Daytona Beach, whose base camp was also Fort

Benning, rather than Camp Blanding.[19] The Camp Blanding and Camp Gordon Johnston base camps and their numerous branch camps had been closed.

When 37,000 German POWs departed the United States in June, the POW program in America was effectively over. The army announced the departure of the "last" German POWs on July 22, 1946. This was the last large group of Germans, 1,388 officers and enlisted men, to depart. With the exception of 134 men in hospitals or psychiatric wards, 25 escapees still at large, and 141 men serving prison terms, that was the end. The 141 in criminal detention had been condemned to various periods of time in penal institutions for crimes committed during their stay in America.[20] Two of these men were former prisoners at Camp Gordon Johnston: Pfc. Hans Krings and Pfc. Walter Schultz. On February 16, 1945, they had been sentenced by a military court to eight and seven years of hard labor, respectively, and sent to serve their time at the U.S. Disciplinary Barracks at Fort Leavenworth, Kansas. The sentences came as a result of their assault on a fellow POW at Camp Gordon Johnston on December 12, 1944.[21]

Both Gerhard Anklam, of Clewiston escape fame, and Horst Finke, who spent most of his time in Florida at the Belle Glade camp, were part of the large repatriation movement of February 1946. Both left America by way of Camp Shanks, New York; both were shipped to Le Havre, France; and both arrived at the reception center at nearby Camp Bolbec on February 25, 1946. But medical examinations of the men led one to an early return to Germany and one to two years of labor in France. The story of these men is typical of the divergent fates of many thousands more who were returned to Germany through camps in France.

Gerhard Anklam, failed Luftwaffe pilot, later paratrooper captured by the Americans in Italy, and escapee from the sugarcane-cutting camp at Clewiston, won the race back to Germany and to his hometown, Berlin. After his failed escape from Clewiston and subsequent adventures in an arrest barracks at Camp Blanding, the native Berliner was transferred to various POW camps in Pennsylvania: Gettysburg, Indiantown Gap, and the Letterkenny Ordinance Depot on the outskirts of Chambersburg. His path toward home began on January 18, 1946, when he was sent to Fort Eustis, Virginia. After a brief stay there, he left on the afternoon of February 11, arriving at Camp Shanks, New York, the next morning at 5 A.M. On the morning of February 15, he and his traveling companions were loaded on board the *Waycross Victory* for their nine-day voyage to Europe.[22]

The ship arrived on February 24 at the French port, Le Havre, and the POWs were taken to the nearby camp at Bolbec. Between February and May 1946 it was from this camp that healthy and work-fit POWs were turned over to the French. It was here that about 55,000 of the "Americans" (as the German POWs who had been held in America were called) began French tours of duty that lasted for some through 1947 and into 1948.[23] Indeed, as Horst Finke was to discover, for those who were employed in *déminage* (the clearing of explosive mines) one false step might mean a grave in France forever.[24]

But Gerhard Anklam was both intrepid and fortunate. While waiting to be examined by a mixed medical commission that was to determine his fate, the feisty Berliner acted to ensure himself a smooth passage home. Briefly in possession of his personnel and medical documents, he found and furtively discarded a sheet that described him as an "escaper." His luck continued. Because of a wound acquired in Italy that left him with a scar on his left shoulder, the medical commission at Bolbec disqualified him from labor service in France. He was to be sent back to Germany. [25]

After a month in a special holding compound at Bolbec, Anklam was sent to an American zone discharge camp at Marburg. There on March 27, 1946, he received his official military discharge papers.[26] Equipped with mustering-out pay of forty reichsmarks, the Berliner was headed to Berlin—he hoped. His train crossed into the Russian zone at Bebra at 4 A.M. in the morning of March 28, and he arrived in Eisenach at 1 P.M., where he was registered and again given a medical exam—this time by the Russians. The next day the same process occurred in Erfurt.[27] When his shipment of returning POWs left Erfurt by rail on the afternoon of March 30, none of the men were sure of their destination. Anklam had heard that it was not to be Berlin. When at 6 A.M. on the last day of March 1946, the train arrived in Magdeburg, the Clewiston escapee did a repeat performance. He hopped off the train and concealed himself in the cathedral. Later in the day, he climbed on a freight train headed for Berlin-Wannsee, a western suburb of the former German capital.

After waiting at the Red Cross Station in Berlin-Wannsee, he caught the first Stadtbahn at 7 A.M. on April 1 and arrived at 9 A.M. in the destroyed central city, praying that his mother was still alive. She was, though living in a partially bombed out building.[28]

The similarities and differences between the Gerhard Anklam and Horst Finke stories are significant. Each story displays the role played by health, chance, and ingenuity in each man's repatriation experience. Finke, who also wound up in Berlin—but only in September 1948—was found fit during the Bolbec medical examination and spent two years in France.

The Belle Glade bean canning experience and work for the Clewiston engineers ended for Horst Finke and his comrades with the closing of the Belle Glade camp in early December 1945. The closing of the camp also meant the dissolution of Camp Blanding's Eighteenth POW Company and the transfer of that POW company out of Florida. On December 10, Horst Finke and his Belle Glade comrades became Company No. 5 at Camp Forrest, Tennessee. It was at Camp Forrest that Finke was separated from his friend Gottlob Hasel, his companion since Aliceville camp days. Hasel, an older veteran whose wounds in Russia had sent him as a tailor to the Afrika Korps, was slated for early repatriation to Germany. A mailman in civilian life, he had been a member of the Nazi party, a fact that aroused the suspicions of American intelligence officers. Hasel was redlined for early repatriation to Germany as part of the American denazification process. Once in Germany, he was quickly released. On the lookout for bigger game, major players, and possible war criminals, the Americans let Hasel go when it was clear he had joined the Nazi party merely to ensure his post office job.[29]

It was at Camp Forrest that Finke and his comrades had to surrender their German uniforms and American work khakis and receive the black apparel they were to wear for their return to Europe.[30] The PMGO was informed by the commanding general of U.S. forces in the European theater that military authorities there wanted POWs repatriated from the continental United States to be transferred wearing and in possession of clothing that was dyed black. On November 20, 1945, an ASF circular ordered that beginning December 1 all outer clothing issued to POWs returning to the European theater would be dyed black, instead of olive drab, and clearly marked with the letters PW. As several movements of prisoners took place after the deadline, with prisoners still wearing undyed uniforms, a February 21, 1946, circular required the dying of all national uniforms as well as work clothes.[31]

Finke and his fellow returnees were sent to Camp Shanks, New York, on February 1, 1946, and shipped out on the troopship *Albany* on February 13. A strike at the oil companies that provided fuel for the ship required that it go first to Boston to refuel. Finke recalls how on this first leg of the journey he suffered from his own cleverness. Seeing the five-tiered bunks on the ship, he and a friend stayed close to a passageway where there would be more air. However, the same fuel shortage that necessitated the stop at Boston meant that there was little heat on the ship between New York and Boston, and even less in the exposed location that Finke had chosen to make his berth.[32]

Finke also recalls that the Germans on the *Albany* had been told that they were going to England, not Germany. However, in the middle of the ocean it was announced that their destination was France. Whether the change in announced destinations was subterfuge or altered orders is unclear. Between March and August 1946 about 123,000 German POWs who had been held in America were bound for Liverpool, or Antwerp and thence back to England, for work there into 1947 and 1948.[33]

Finke just turned out to be on a ship bound for France. He arrived at Le Havre on February 25 and was taken—as was Gerhard Anklam—to the camp at Bolbec. His first experiences in a French camp were remembered—and perhaps experienced—differently than were Anklam's. Anklam remembered having to fend off a French guard who tried to help himself to the cigarette ration that the German brought back from America. Finke says that at the Bolbec compound into which he came, it was former members of the Wehrmacht—fellow Germans—who caused the trouble. Acting as the unarmed guards in the watchtowers and as the inquisitive inspectors of luggage of new arrivals, these long-term inmates of the French camp relieved the later "American" arrivals of "the goodies" they had thought to bring back from America. Cigarettes and clothing disappeared and even extra army blankets issued by the Americans were taken and replaced with dirty, old blankets that had already seen long service. Such memories still leave a negative impression on Finke, the former Afrika Korps man. It confirmed his view that German soldiers who had been stationed in France had become used to making a fine life for themselves at the expense of others.[34]

But even Finke was ready to work the system in order to supplement the meager food ration of the French camps. While at a camp in Cherbourg, he took advantage of the offer of double rations that was made to those Germans willing to join the French Foreign Legion. He and several of his buddies expressed their interest in enrollment and more than willingly enjoyed the extra helpings of victuals that rewarded their decision. Afterward, however, when a French captain made a speech to all the potential legionnaires and indicated that he knew that many of the Germans were more interested in extra rations than in joining the legion, Finke and his friends took up the offer to step out of the ranks and be returned to their former camp.[35]

Finke was chosen to work at the dangerous task of *déminage* at St.-Aubin-sur-Mer, clearing the mines on the Normandy coast where the Americans had landed in 1944. There he was housed with several other prisoners in an abandoned two-family house surrounded by barbed wire. During the day, Finke worked with other Germans, who—in teams of three—carefully searched for, defused, and removed explosive remnants of a war, which for them was not quite over. Saltwater corroded the mechanism of anti-tank mines, and when Finke arrived he was told of an accident in which three POWs had been killed, their bodies blown into nearby trees.[36]

On weekends, Finke and his fellow prisoners were allowed to earn spending money by working on local farms and in town. The Germans sometimes helped find and defuse bombs in farmers' fields. Finke also found work in a local restaurant. He chuckles at the memory of one of his jobs there. It was to put labels on wine bottles. The task entailed putting six different labels on various bottles of wine—bottles that were filled from a single wine cask. Finke enjoyed being asked to eat in the restaurant by the French girls who worked there—extra food was a major incentive for him taking the restaurant job. One Sunday he was invited by several older French restaurant customers to join them in dominos. He claims that, because of his ability to count in French and the fact that the games were played with little talking, it was not until the third Sunday of his participation that his French partners realized he was a German POW.[37]

After a year of clearing mines in and around in St.-Aubin-sur-Mer in Normandy, Finke's group was moved south to La Rochelle. There the Germans were to find and remove unexploded 500-pound bombs that had been dropped by the Americans. These so-called duds were still potentially dangerous. Finke had had enough. He took advantage of a new international development to preserve the hands and feet that had so far survived the war unscathed. When the Americans pressured the French to end POW usage and secure labor through offers of free worker contracts to German POWs with forestry, agricultural, or industrial experience, the Pomeranian artillery man jumped at the chance. Better to sign up immediately for a year as a contract worker with a French farmer than to spend one more day as a short-term POW bomb disposal team member whose luck might run out before he was sent back to Germany.[38]

Between June 17, 1947, and September 28, 1948, Finke worked on a French farm near St.-Georges-du-Bois. He got along well with the farmer and his older parents because his agricultural background made him a good employee. He also used his contractually agreed upon four-week unpaid vacation at Christmas of 1947 to find and renew his acquaintance with his longtime sweetheart, Hilde, from his home area in Pomerania. She, along with several of his close relatives, had moved to Berlin, and he caught up with them there. His sister lived in Schöneberg in the American sector and his mother lived in Friedrichsfelde in the Russian sector. And, it was to Berlin—more specifically Friedrichsfelde, with his mother—that Horst Finke moved to live when his French free-worker contract ended on September 28, 1948. He was released by the French with authorization papers to live with his sister in the American sector. But without either work or a ration card, he had to beg French officials in Berlin to modify his papers so that he might live with his mother in the Russian sector. After ten years of camp living as a member of the Reichsarbeitsdienst (Imperial Labor Service), the Wehrmacht (Armed Forces), and as a POW in America and France, rather than find housing in a refugee camp, Finke joined his mother in a winterized hut that formerly had been used only as a summer garden retreat along a Berlin railroad line.[39] Like Gerhard Anklam, who had returned to his home in Russian-occupied Berlin in 1946, Horst Finke began his new life as a German civilian in Russia-occupied Berlin.

Lüdeke Herder and Werner Burkert of the Dade City camp were two of the 123,000 "American" POWs who traveled back to Germany by way of England. Herder, a native of Wiesbaden, and Burkert, from Berlin, had been captured in North Africa by the British on May 12 and May 13, 1943, respectively, about the same time as Horst Finke had ended his Wehrmacht career there. Herder and Burkert, like most of the Afrika Korps, were turned over to the Americans. Herder was shipped from Oran to Newport News, Virginia, and then sent to Camp Gordon, in Augusta, Georgia, on October 28, 1943. Burkert also arrived at Camp Gordon, Georgia, but by way of New York. On March 5, 1944, Herder and Burkert were sent to Company No. 7 of the Camp Blanding base camp, the new branch camp at Dade City. They worked for the Pasco Packing Association, as did many of the POWs at the camp in the citrus country of Florida. Because of their ability with English, both Herder and Burkert served not only as laborers, but also as interpreters.[40] In Herder's case, intelligence evaluations at the Dade City camp also reveal that he was "considered anti-Nazi," had no particular political beliefs that could be determined, was a "good worker and very cooperative," and was "active in athletics."[41]

None of that would keep either Burkert or Herder from taking the long way home. When the camp closed in March 1946, they both, with a group of between 80 and 100 inmates from the Dade City camp, were sent by train to Camp Shanks for repatriation to Europe. At the debarkation camp, the prisoners were further divided for continuing transport, and Herder and Burkert found themselves on a ship bound for Europe and, they hoped, Germany. It turned out to be Liverpool, England. For Herder that meant about nine more months of POW labor for the British, mostly agricultural work and ditch digging for pipes while stationed at a POW camp at Worfield, Shropshire.[42] For Burkert there would be farmwork among the English while stationed at a camp in Kent, near Sittingburne, until March 1947.[43]

It would not take Herder or Burkert as long to return to their homes in Germany from Britain as it did Horst Finke to return to his from France. On January 21, 1947, after vetting by British intelligence, Lüdeke Herder was given an "A" security clearance. It meant that "approval [had] been given by Public Safety Branch for the provisional employment of the holder without prior examination by a German De-Nazification Panel."[44] He was sent for release back in Germany through the American reception and discharge headquarters at Dachau. There he was officially discharged on February 6, 1947. His British certificate of security clearance led him to receive a similar certificate from the American theater provost marshal. It noted that "these certificates have been issued to special 'white' prisoners of war discharged by the British after screening in England. . . . These British-discharged 'white' prisoners are considered to be in the same category as the special prisoners indoctrinated by the Americans at Ft. Getty, Ft. Wetherill, and Ft. Eustis in the United States."[45] Herder also was given a military payment order for his accumulated earnings while in American captivity. It amounted to $71.20. He cashed it in his hometown, Wiesbaden, on March 2, 1947.[46]

Werner Burkert would be back in Berlin by the end of March 1947. But his experiences in England are worthy of note because they reveal his amorous side in a setting a bit different than Dade City, Florida. "In England we were handled correctly and well, but the life of abundance was at an end." Nevertheless, there was a 9 A.M. "teatime" break daily, during which a country girl brought the German POW farmworkers a large jug of milk. On one occasion, Burkert lit a cigarette during this break and the British farm girl blew out his match. "Thereupon, I said to her that she must, according to German usage, give me a kiss. On the next morning, when she brought the milk she said to me, I better give you what I owe you." Before his comrades knew what had been said, Burkert and the girl disappeared to a neighboring room to receive what was promised. The upshot of this budding relationship was that one day Burkert and his English girlfriend agreed to spend the night together in a country barn. Burkert duly reported to the leadership of the German compound that he would be absent the next evening. As planned, he "missed" the truck that took the POW workers back to camp and headed for the barn to wait for his beloved, who was not to get off work till later in the evening. Full of expectation, he kept walking around the barn as he waited. His girl did not show. Gravely disappointed and upset, around 8 P.M. he turned himself in to the village police as a POW who had missed his transport back to his camp. He was driven the ten kilometers back to the camp in a jeep by a friendly English policeman. The next day his girlfriend told him that she had gotten off early and gone to wait for him in the barn, but she had become frightened when she heard someone repeatedly walking around the barn.[47]

In January and February 1947, Werner Burkert and his comrades in the camp were interrogated about their political pasts and divided into groups A, B, and C based on their captors' view that they were active anti-Nazis, "normal cases," or members of the Nazi party. Members of the first group were shipped back to Germany first and then a week later Burkert and others in Group B were sent home. They were shipped from Hull by way of Bremen and then taken to a release center near Lüneburg. There, too, they received their accumulated American and English pay in German marks. From England, Burkert also brought along eight kilograms of coffee and cocoa, which was worth a fortune on the German black market at the time. After his release from Lüneburg, Burkert found himself assigned, like other freshly repatriated POWs, to one of the many transport units that were sent off to the various regions of Germany from which their members had been recruited. At the end of March 1947, after six years of military and POW service, Werner Burkert was back in Berlin.[48]

Many of the returnees from American camps who took the long way home through France or Britain experienced feelings of betrayal when their fears of delayed repatriation were realized. At camps in England, as in France, guards and fellow prisoners had often made short work of the cigarettes, handkerchiefs, shirts, socks, and other extras the returnees brought with them from America. Gifts and necessities for friends and family in the Fatherland, bought with money worked for and saved in America, were lost in short order. The memories of good times and good treatment in America became shaded with feelings of disappointment about Americans who had taught them about freedom only to become part of a betrayal of that freedom.[49]

Yet America retained its glamour and mystique. One thinks of former Florida POWs like Horst Finke, the Belle Glade veteran who eventually returned to America to live, or Lüdeke Herder, who between 1946 and 1989 returned three times to visit Florida and old friends, including the former civilian foreman he worked for at the Dade City camp.[50] Werner Burkert, too, became an avid fan of America and of the citizens of Dade City, Florida. He first returned to the location of his former POW camp in 1960. He was the guest of T. D. Barfield, the wartime personnel manager of Pasco Packing Association, under whom he had worked during his stay in Dade City. Burkert, by 1960 an engineer and a resident of Switzerland, had been representing his firm at a machinery, machine tool, and production engineering show in Chicago when he met Dade City's industrial coordinator, A. Hanford Eckman. After talking with Eckman and describing Dade City as "the greatest spot on earth and the finest people," Burkert decided to visit before returning to Switzerland.[51]

These "alumni" of Florida's POW camps are not alone in their positive feelings toward America and Americans. This is seen in Hermann Jung's final assessment of the German POW experience in America, included in a volume he wrote for a series published by the German Scientific Commission for German Prisoner of War History (Wissenschaftliche Kommission für deutschen Kriegsgefangenengeschichte). Jung concludes his study by quoting a POW's diary entry, made on the day he sailed for Europe: "Stop, pay attention, this is your last step on American soil. Perhaps for ever—perhaps. What was it like on my soil, stranger? 'Oh, you know, it was nice and perhaps someday I will notice that I learned a lot here—and perhaps someday I will even be homesick for you—perhaps. But you know, now I am going home. Farewell and thanks—farewell'."[52]

10

EPILOGUE: GRAVES, ALUMNI, AND MEMORIES

GRAVES

On Friday, December 8, 1989, there was a ceremony at Camp Blanding. According to the *Middleburg Press,* it was "long and solemn, but impressive in its mixture of the German and English languages." Soldiers of a West German brigade training at the camp were commemorating comrades who had died on a foreign soil— "tradition being an important part of their training and upbringing." They had worked long and hard to clear and landscape a cemetery "located near the old POW barracks in a remote area of the sprawling [Blanding] facility and received praise from Camp Blanding officials for the quality of their work." They had cleared and landscaped the site of the German POW cemetery that existed at the Blanding POW base camp between July 7, 1944, and April 25, 1946. That cemetery, which was to have been the final resting place of Germans who died while at the Blanding base camp and its branch camps, was "located on the Main Post, east of the airfield in a section of land between Dade and Tower Roads."[1]

But that little piece of foreign soil that was to have been forever German became all but a forgotten memory after April 25, 1946. It was on that date that the seven German POWs who were interred at the Blanding cemetery were disinterred. With the end of the war, Camp Blanding ceased to be a federal military installation and returned to its status as a Florida National Guard camp. To ensure compliance with Article 76 of the Geneva Convention—that "prisoners of war dying in captivity are honorably buried and that the graves bear all due information, are respected and properly maintained"—the remains of the German POWs were removed and reinterred at the Fort Benning, Georgia, army post cemetery.[2] The German chaplain and the members of the German training brigade who participated in the ceremony at the old POW cemetery site were recalling a time, a place, and a company of warriors who were now footnotes in the story of a past struggle. Their memory was being recalled in 1989 for the political purposes of another era. The West German brigade was reconstructing the sacrifices of warriors who, though German, represented a very different Germany than their own. The West Germans were creating a revised military tradition: a tradition of honor, self-sacrifice, and national unity that was not the same as the traditions served by Hitler's soldiers when they came to the Sunshine State. The West German servicemen of 1989 were engaged, as most people have always been, in reconstructing the past in the image desired by the present.

Who were the warriors commemorated at the old Blanding cemetery site—the men who had died for German honor on foreign soil? There were seven of them. They ranged in age from eighteen to forty-four. Vitus Erler, twenty-one, and Rudolf Stamicar, thirty-three, had been captured in Tunisia: Erler on May 8 and Stamicar sometime in April or May 1943. Georg Moos, twenty, was captured in Italy on June 25, 1944. The other four were captured in France in the summer and fall of 1944: Heinrich Baumgartner, thirty-three, in Normandy on June 9; Karl Behrens, eighteen, at Cherbourg on June 27; Franz Klose, thirty-six, in Paris on August 27; and Wendelin Sturm, forty-four, in Epinal on September 28.[3]

These soldiers' Germanness had to do with their ethnicity, their service in the Wehrmacht, and their homes and families located in parts of the larger Germany that existed during the Third Reich. Of the seven deceased, three were "Austrians"—if their home address had been the determining factor before the Anschluss (union) with Germany in March 1938. Heinrich Baumgartner was from Upper Austria; Vitus Erler from the Tirol; and Rudolf Stamicar from Styria. A fourth, Franz Klose, came from Silesia—a part of Prussia since the eighteenth century but given to post–World War II Poland. The remaining three were Germans of the smaller Germany that existed as the original Federal Republic of Germany (West Germany) until 1990. There was Karl Behrens from a small town near Bremen in the north; Georg Moos from Speyer in the Rhineland; and Wendelin Sturm from Baden in the German southwest.

The men from Bremen, Speyer, and Baden were Protestants; those from Silesia and Austria appear to have been Catholics.[4]

Only two actually died while the war was going on in Europe. They were Vitus Erler, who died on July 7, 1944, and Karl Behrens, who died on December 30, 1944. Wendelin Sturm died on May 9, 1945, the day after the German capitulation. The other deaths occurred in September and October 1945 and in early January 1946. Heinrich Baumgartner died on September 7; Franz Klose on October 20; Georg Moos on October 26; and Rudolf Stamicar on January 10, 1946.

All but two died as a result of accidents.[5] Vitus Erler, who died while stationed at Camp Blanding on July 7, 1944, drowned while swimming in Lake Palestine near Cliftonville;[6] Heinrich Baumgartner drowned on September 7, 1945, while interned at the Belle Glade camp and swimming from a barge at a work site near Clewiston;[7] and Rudolf Stamicar drowned in Banana River while on a work detail at the camp there on January 10, 1946.[8] Wendelin Sturm died at MacDill Field on May 9, 1945, after he had been run over by a truck on April 20.[9] Georg Moos died on October 26, 1945, in the Army Air Force Regional Station Hospital in Orlando; he had been hit by a falling tree while on a forestry detail thirty miles south of Orlando.[10] The two nonaccidental deaths were hardly more war related than the others. Franz Klose died on October 20, 1945, at the Army Service Forces Regional Hospital at Camp Blanding from bacterial endocarditis, a heart disease;[11] and Karl Behrens died on December 30, 1944, as the only one of the deceased Florida POWs to make Florida newspaper headlines by his escape from the Clewiston camp and subsequent suicide.[12]

Some national numbers are useful for comparative purposes. The supplement to the Prisoner of War Operations Division's historical monograph presented national POW death statistics through December 1945. Though this left out several months in 1946, in which other deaths occurred—including Rudolf Stamicar's in Florida, the numbers and categories given for German POW deaths during their captivity in America put into national perspective the seven deaths at the Blanding camps. Nationally there were a total of 735 deaths. Of these, 72 were suicides, 4 murders, 3 homicides, 40 shootings, and 126 accidental deaths. These first five categories of deaths accounted for a total of 245 deaths. Additionally, there were 490 deaths "from natural causes," which included deaths from wounds received in action outside the continental United States. "A large percentage of deaths occurring among the early shipments of prisoners to the United States were of this type."[13]

Of the seven men interred in the Blanding POW cemetery, only one—Franz Klose, who died of bacterial endocarditis—could be classified under the large number of "natural causes" deaths. Karl Behrens was the only suicide, joining seventy-one others nationally. Blanding and its branches had no murders, homicides, or deaths by shootings. Deaths fell chiefly into four other categories the government listed as accidental: falling trees, motor vehicle accidents, drownings, and miscellaneous. Georg Moos's death from a falling tree put him in a category with twenty-two others nationally. Wendelin Sturm, who died from a motor vehicle accident, joined fifty-seven others for a national total of fifty-eight. The drownings of Vitus Erler, Heinrich Baumgartner, and Rudolf Stamicar, along with twelve others nationally, brought that total up to fifteen, though Stamicar's death—occurring on January 10, 1946—was not counted in the army's statistics because his death occurred after the end of 1945. There were no "miscellaneous" deaths—"various industrial and agricultural accidents"—at the Blanding camps.

Prisoner of War Circular, No. 1, distributed by the War Department on September 24, 1943, provided that

> All persons who die while interned will be honorably buried.
>
> Prisoners will be buried in the nearest available permanent cemetery. A record of location, plot and grave number or description will be forwarded to the Prisoner of War Information Bureau.
>
> The desires of prisoners concerning funeral services may be followed, if practicable, when services are held at a camp. A small group of prisoners may be permitted by the camp commander to accompany the body to the grave if the cemetery is in the vicinity of the camp.[14]

Military honors could be extended to deceased prisoners if that was desired by their fellow prisoners. These honors included draping the German national flag, if it was available and desired by the prisoners; three volleys fired over the open grave by a squad of American military police escort guards; and the sounding of taps. Such honors were rendered at the burial of Georg Moos, the prisoner who died of fractures of the fourth, fifth, and sixth cervical vertebrae and compression of the spinal cord caused by a tree-felling accident: "The deceased was buried with military honors, 28 October 1945, in the Camp Prisoner of War burial plot, Prisoner of War camp, Camp Blanding, Florida, preceded by services for him in the Post Chapel. Interment services were officiated over by an American military chaplain assisted by a prisoner of war chaplain. Sixty-five of the deceased's fellow prisoners were present at the burial ceremonies."[15]

After Moos's burial in October 1945, only one more German joined him at the Camp Blanding POW cemetery: Rudolf Stamicar, who died on January 10, 1946, at the Banana River camp. For Stamicar, from Graz, Austria, imprisonment ended just as the Florida camps were entering their last stages and the Germans were all to be shipped back to Europe. Stamicar's own journey from Camp Blanding was shorter. He joined his six earlier deceased Blanding system comrades for the trip to the Fort Benning National Cemetery in Columbus, Georgia. With them, he was interred on April 25, 1946, in section A-2 of the army post cemetery. His address became grave 188. It is near to that of Karl Behrens in grave 189, and Heinrich Baumgartner in grave 190. The other Blanding Germans are not far away: Franz Klose in grave 91, Vitus Erler in grave 92, Georg Moos in grave 93, and Wendelin Sturm in grave 94.[16]

ALUMNI

In the sense that POW camps were "schools of life" that left deep and lasting impressions on their internees, former Florida POWs are alumni of the Blanding and Gordon Johnston camps. Among those alumni who have returned to visit the sites of their "old schools" are Herman Finke and Karl Held of the Belle Glade camp and Lüdeke Herder and Werner Burkert of the Dade City camp. Gerhard Anklam of the Clewiston camp has not returned, but he too cherishes the memories in his Blanding diary. The postwar stories of these men are an important part of the epilogue of the Florida POW story.

Anklam, the Berliner, former paratrooper, Clewiston escapee, and absconder from a troop train in the Russian zone, continued to influence the outcome of his own fate. When he jumped off the train in Magdeburg and made his way back to his mother in Berlin on April 1, 1946, he found his beloved native city devastated and divided between the four victorious Allied powers. Anklam's first postwar civilian job, which he obtained on May 17, 1946, was in the district administration in Pankow in the Russian sector. Problems soon came to Gerhard Anklam, whose feistiness had not been decreased by his Florida experiences. Being sent to harvest sugarcane in Clewiston because of his outspokenness at his job at Camp Blanding had not taught him discretion. In Pankow he again triggered a life-changing experience because of his ready tongue and willingness to speak out. At an assembly of laborers from the district administration, Anklam heard praise for the treatment of German POWs held in Russian camps. His incautious response was to remind his comrades to look at the POWs who had returned home from Russia: They were hungry and ragged. Several days later, the outspoken Anklam was ordered to see Colonel Tulpanow, the Russian district commander. Anklam recalls, "I know 'it is the way of no return.' I took my map, entered the next tram to come to the western sectors."[17]

So it was that Anklam again took his fate into his own hands. Because this was before the building of the Berlin Wall in 1961, he was able to slip easily out of the Russian sector. In the West, in 1950, he took a job with the British army as a member of the GSO, the German Service Organization. This was a security service made up of native Germans and used by the British to secure and protect access to their military facilities in Berlin. From being a German paratrooper, Anklam had become a worker with the Russian sector administration and then a guard for the installations of the occupying British Army. He, like many returning POWs, learned that if there was a will to make a living and a life, there was a way to do it. He married in 1953, had a son, and by 1961 quit his GSO job to work as a driving instructor. Two years later, Anklam, the entrepreneur, opened his own driving school and taxi service. He retired in 1988.[18]

Horst Finke, formerly of the Belle Glade camp, finished his year as a "free worker" in France on September 28, 1948, and returned to

Berlin as Anklam did. But Lümzow, Pomerania, not Berlin, was Finke's native home. By 1948 Lümzow had become Lomzowa. It was administered by a Polish government under the watchful eye of the USSR. Finke, therefore, joined his family in Berlin, where they had taken refuge. He lived with his mother in the Russian sector. Unable to find regular work, Finke, like Anklam before him, wound up working for the Russians. He joined the newly reorganized Soviet-controlled East German police. Without any special training, he found himself with a police unit that guarded East Berlin's major electrical power station. The Russians feared that the West might try to blow it up. When Finke discovered that the Russians planned to turn his police unit into a new East German army unit, he decided it was time to quit. He planned to be married to Hilde, his hometown sweetheart, who had survived the war and its early aftermath in Berlin. It was while in a police hospital—a stay necessitated by a severe kidney stone—that Finke discovered a solution to his police/military problem. One of the nurses was a fellow Pomeranian, and Finke persuaded her to have a doctor friend certify Horst Finke as unfit for future police work.[19]

After his marriage to Hilde in 1950, the Finkes gained permission to move out of the Russian sector. His wife's aunt knew someone who for twenty West German marks arranged for a "paper" *Kopftausch*—an exchange of two people from the West to move East and two from the East to move West. But, of course, as Finke says, no one really was going to move to the East. The exchange was a fictitious one—but it worked. Horst and Hilde Finke officially moved to West Berlin.

After gaining permission to move to the West, the Finkes lived briefly in an apartment in Schöneberg, and they began their application for immigration to the United States. Again, a relative was helpful. An aunt of Hilde's, who lived in New York City, was willing to sponsor the young couple for the five-year period required by law. Though American officials in Berlin implied that the visa would be forthcoming almost immediately, the Finkes waited two years for the paperwork to come through. Finke still wonders if somehow his participation in the POW strike at Belle Glade back in April 1945 may have delayed the processing.[20] Finally, however, the couple was able to leave for New York aboard the SS *America*. They departed from Bremerhaven on November 24, 1952, and arrived in New York City on December 2. Almost immediately, Herman Finke—Horst sounding a bit too German for a would-be American citizen—was able to find work operating machinery in a large American bakery. He was happy to hold that job until his retirement in the 1980s. The Finkes and their adult son still live in the New York City area.

No doubt numerous former POWs have returned to Florida for visits since their original stay there. It is hard to tell how many.[21] As a vacationland, the Sunshine State attracts many tourists. Herman Finke has made many trips with German friends to the state of his former wartime incarceration. While visiting, he has driven by the old Belle Glade POW camp location and found that there is little there to remind him of his original stay. In fact, things have changed so much that it is easy for former prisoners to confuse themselves and others as to where they were during their stay in Florida.

One example is that of Dr. Karl Held of Munich. The *Clewiston News* of December 31, 1986, displayed a picture of the sixty-year-old Held and his daughter, Kathrin, taken during their visit at the Clewiston Museum on December 26. The headline of the accompanying story reads, "WWII POW returns to see campsite." The article notes: "On hand to show Held the old campsite at Liberty Point was Mary Krewson, whose husband at the time was a camp guard. Sgt. Tom W. Malone, now deceased, was a career military man stationed at the camp when Held was brought in. 'When our first baby was born, the POWs made a crib out of scrap lumber and gave it to us,' Krewson recalled."[22]

The return of Karl Held to Clewiston made for a pleasant exchange between people who had been in Florida during the time that Hitler's soldiers came to the Sunshine State. However, though it is probable that the nineteen-year-old Held worked at Clewiston with the Army Corps of Engineers in 1945, it is unlikely that he was ever in the Liberty Point (Clewiston) camp or had anything to do with Sergeant Malone. Karl Held, POW serial number 31G-51802, born April 19, 1926, was serving with a RAD (Reichsarbeitsdienst) unit when captured. He was listed—along with Horst Finke—on the Belle Glade camp detention roster in the fall of 1945.[23] The Clewiston camp closed on September 6, 1945, and its sugarcane-working POWs were transferred up to a new camp at the naval air base at Green Cove Springs.[24] The Belle Glade camp, with internees Finke and Held, stayed on to work at the Belle Glade bean cannery and for the Army Corps of Engineers at Clewiston until December 8. Then, the Belle Glade camp closed and its internees were transferred to Camp Forrest, Tennessee, in preparation for their return to Europe.[25]

In a telephone conversation in June 1993, Dr. Karl Held, who at age sixty-seven was still practicing medicine in Munich, did not correct the author's misperception—based on the *Clewiston News* article—that he had been at the Clewiston camp. Perhaps he did not actually remember. He noted that he had been captured at Cherbourg, spent a short time in England and then some six months at a larger POW camp in the United States. Held said that he was then taken by bus to Clewiston, where he worked with sugarcane and with bean canning at Belle Glade. He recalled that he was at the camp for nine months and that the whole camp had been moved during a hurricane. All of this fits the Belle Glade camp experience better than the Clewiston one, because the Belle Glade camp existed for nine months between April and December 1945, and in September the whole camp was moved briefly during a hurricane. Held thought he remembered that he left Clewiston in February 1946 and was returned to Germany in April 1946.[26]

Since the Clewiston camp was closed in September and the Belle Glade camp closed in December, Held must have gotten his locations and dates confused. It is more likely that he, like Finke, left Camp Forrest in February 1946. Unlike Finke, Held was sent back to Germany rather than to further internment in France. Held, just twenty years old in April 1946, returned to university studies and a career in medicine. One possible reason for his early return to Germany was that Held had aroused the interest of American authorities because of suspected Nazi affiliation. They noted on the Belle Glade detention roster that he had membership in the SA (Sturmabteilung—Storm Troopers, a Nazi paramilitary organization).[27] With such a designation, the young Belle Glade POW would have gotten back to Germany earlier than some of his other comrades. He would have been segregated and readied for early return to Germany for investigation and potentially prolonged detention. Once he got back to Germany, the Americans probably decided that Held was too little involved in the Nazi movement to be worth denazification sentencing.[28] Karl Held quickly returned to German civilian life, education, a career in medicine, and—eventually—a sentimental postwar visit to Clewiston. He may not have found the exact location of his earlier POW camp, but he did find local citizens who, like him, wished to revive common memories of long ago when German POWs were seen as Uncle Sam's smiling workers.

Lüdeke Herder, formerly of the Dade City camp, reinforces that stereotype. The young man from Wiesbaden, captured in North Africa, interned at Camp Gordon, Georgia, and then an interpreter/laborer at Dade City before postwar labor in England, returned to Germany in February 1947. He met his wife that year and they were married in 1950. Their son was born in 1955. Before his retirement, Herder traveled "all over the world" as an expert with a commercial air-conditioning firm. But his experience at the Dade City camp left long and positive memories. He made three return trips to Dade City between 1946 and 1989. He particularly enjoyed visiting with his wartime American civilian foreman, Bill Cox, who could fill him in on details about the camp that the former POW had forgotten.[29]

Because of these visits, contacts, and his ability to speak English, Herder was asked by local teacher Martha Knapp to correspond with her students as part of a project to help them learn about wartime Florida and the POWs of the Dade City camp. In 1991 and 1992, he carried on an exchange of letters with the students of the Florida school. Writing in short, readable English paragraphs, he answered the questions sent to him by members of Mrs. Knapp's class. Each student questioner was addressed by name and each question individually answered. What exactly did you do in the POW camp? Could you write home? Did you try to escape? Were you religious? What was your homeland like after the war? Herder also wrote to the students about how he took his wife to see the location of his former campground. "She said to me, Lü, you can be happy that you survived the war in a POW camp. Now I understand that you love this country and his peoples, for I told her a lot about this time."[30]

One of the stories that Herder told Mrs. Knapp's students was designed to illustrate how well the Germans and their American guards got along at the Dade City camp. The story concerned an

American master sergeant. Herder had been reading in the American newspapers about British and American air raids on the area around Wiesbaden where his parents lived. Worried about how they were, he was elated when he received mail from home confirming that they were well. In celebration, he used some of his hard-earned coupons to buy beer at the POW camp post exchange, and he ended up drinking too much. He could not get up for roll call the next morning. But his tent mates had a plan. They wrapped a wet towel around Herder's foot and told the American master sergeant that their comrade had hurt himself playing soccer the night before. When the American came to check and Herder told him the tale, the sergeant just looked at the German and said, "I smell it." As Herder explained, "Days later he said to me, next time you call me earlier and I help you with this football play."[31]

Werner Burkert's stories of the good times that he and his comrades had at the Dade City camp have been recounted earlier. So, too, has his first return trip to Dade City in 1960. His love affair with America, Florida, and the people of Dade City goes on. Despite ill health, Werner Burkert continues to share his stories and love of America while making plans for a reunion in Dade City with townspeople and fellow prisoners sometime in 1999.[32]

MEMORIES

Local newspaper people have revived memories of Florida's German POWs over the years. Bill Bond of the *Orlando Sentinel* has published at least two articles about the Leesburg POW camp that have included fascinating quotations from local residents who remembered the POWs.[33] In one of the articles that appeared in 1994, Bond also reported the research of Professor Pete Kehde of Lake-Sumter Community College, who studied the Leesburg camp as part of the story of the property upon which the community college now stands. On the grounds, Professor Kehde found several artifacts that date back to the POW era: two German ten-pfennig coins dated 1938 and 1940, along with U.S. Army buttons, belt buckles, and M1 rounds. In his column Bond also published a picture of an inscription the German POWs left in the Leesburg area during their stay. Etched on the wall of Howard Barkdoll's Lady Lake Texaco Auto Repair at Guava Street and U.S. Highway 27/441 is "Prisoner of War German 1944."[34] It had been scratched on the fresh concrete as it was drying fifty years before.

Most evidence of the presence of Hitler's soldiers in the Sunshine State has not been as permanent as the inscription on the Leesburg wall. There are some photographs. One of them from the Clewiston Museum shows 1st Sgt. Tom W. Malone getting a light from a German prisoner of war. The Malone picture was printed in an article by Lori Rozsa of the *Miami Herald*, which told of the Belle Glade and Clewiston camps. The photo also appeared in Eliot Kleinberg's article in the *Palm Beach Post* that recalled the fiftieth anniversary of the Clewiston escape and suicide of Karl Behrens.[35]

The photo conveys many insights into the German POW experience in Florida. Close observation reveals American Sergeant Malone standing with six POWs at the steps of a wood-framed building with a screen door. Sergeant Malone, wearing army khakis with shirt sleeves casually rolled to the forearms, is leaning to receive a light for his cigar from a POW standing one step up from the American. A POW behind the German lighting the American's cigar is already smoking his own cigarette. At first glance, none of the six Germans in the picture looks foreign. They appear to be informally dressed American troops. Four of the Germans are wearing tropical sun helmets, and the soldier with the matches holds his own sun helmet in his right hand. Three of the Germans are shirtless; two wear sleeveless undershirts. Four of them are in shorts. One of the Germans sits smiling on the bottom step, his hand loosely controlling a small dog. Only one of the Germans, the man on the left behind Malone, is wearing a dark uniform with long trousers and a shirt with sleeves jauntily rolled. His wide belt, with large belt buckle decorated with the insignia of the Wehrmacht, and the PW marked on his pant legs are about the only clues that the American sergeant was standing with captive German POWs. The informality of attire on both sides is striking, as is the relaxed familiarity of the scene. Sergeant Malone appears, because of his warrant officer's cap and cigar, to be the man in charge. But his prisoners look more like familiar employees than enemy internees. That was the situation at the Clewiston camp. The relaxed atmosphere, the heat-induced casual appearances, the mutual tobacco smoking, and the smiling faces of several of the prisoners express most vividly and quintessentially the relationships between Germans and Americans at most of the POW camps in Florida. Members of both groups—captives and captors—came to the realization that, indeed, enemies *are* human.

There are forgotten photographs that reveal less pleasant stories. One is the photo of eighteen-year-old Karl Behrens that fell from a former FBI man's 1945 diary while being interviewed about a Clewiston POW escape and suicide. The poor quality of the print revealed the bad lighting conditions in the late afternoon of January 1, 1945, when FBI agents Brouillard and MacMillan found the body of the escaped POW.[36] The sad fate of Karl Behrens was an exception in the Florida camps, but it is a reminder of the dangerous role that peer pressure and divisiveness could play within individual camps. Those who were not members of established peer groups were outsiders: forgotten, shunned, alienated, sometimes threatened.

Individual camps functioned most smoothly when the prisoners themselves got along: when individuals did not feel alienated because they were different from their peers. Such alienation did not always fit the neat categories selected by American intelligence. It was difficult for Americans to understand or deal with situations that did not conform to their stereotypes. What was to be done about prisoners in a Blanding anti-Nazi naval compound who, because of their denunciation of Germany and their fellows, were threatened by fellow anti-Nazis? What about the pressures of alienation in places like the Clewiston camp, where even the American guards followed the lead of the Afrika Korps in calling arrivals from the French campaign "young punks"?

These were not the only divisive categories. Herman Finke commented negatively that a German strike leader at the Belle Glade camp was one of the paratroopers. According to Finke, since their time together in North Africa, Rommel's Afrika Korps men and the feisty paratroopers had never gotten along.[37] Within the Florida camps, as within the wider U.S. camp system, German POWs identified and divided themselves along cleavages formed by unit experience as well as ideology.

Finally, all of the "Americans," as the POWs returning from captivity in the United States were called, experienced alienation from comrades who had been captured in Europe and were held in British and French camps. It was the fate of many of the "Americans" to be robbed of the prized possessions that they had brought back from the States. The robbers were often fellow POWs who had long been in the European camps. The remnants of Wehrmacht uniforms that POWs in Florida and elsewhere carried into prolonged captivity in America and then Europe were sometimes the only things that the inmates of a camp had in common. But, cloth uniforms did not make for uniformity.

In the small world of a POW compound, peer groups could make life tolerable or deadly. Individuals who were alienated from their peers—whether because they were perceived as Nazis, anti-Nazis, traitors, young punks, paratroopers, or Americans—could find life difficult. These men became likely candidates for escape attempts or even suicide. Those who were fortunate enough to get along with their peers did well. Most did. These men could confront captivity and labor in Florida orange groves, sugarcane fields, or bean canning factories—and even prolonged postwar detention in Britain or France—with equanimity. Then, years later, they could look back with pleasure at their days in captivity. For most of the alumni of the Florida camps, pleasant memories overshadowed distasteful ones. To the memories of comradeship on the battlefront were added those of comradeship with fellow prisoners, American guards, and civilian employers on the American home front between 1942 and 1946.

In April 1945, Blanding's *Zeitspiegel* published an article by Hans Bremer, the assistant POW spokesman at the base camp. He wrote about an unforgettable Florida tour that he took between February 21 and 27, 1945, in the company of Dr. Edouard Patte, the likeable regional YMCA secretary visitor who was visiting the Blanding branch camps. As the narrative, like the tour, came to an end, Bremer presented the highlight of the experience: "The car stops suddenly! The sharp eyes of Dr. P, who is an attentive observer of nature, spies something. We look around us, the car slowly backs up. On the edge of the highway something is slithering: a splendid diamond back! It becomes our prey. The 'snake master' in Orlando is able to remove the skin with several masterful tugs. That crowned the end of our journey. The precious snakeskin will someday find a worthy place in the trophy shelves in a comfortable living room, kept as a lasting memory of a wonderful journey in a serious time."[38]

Even Gerhard Anklam, the would-be escapee who stayed only three weeks in the Clewiston camp, returned to Germany with his own prized Florida snakeskin, a souvenir from the unforgettable Sunshine State.[39]

APPENDIX: 1,250 MILES
THROUGH FLORIDA

Hans Bremer, POW Serial Number 31G-51500, was an NCO and the assistant POW spokesman at the Camp Blanding base camp.[1] The number 31 in his POW identification number indicates he was captured in Europe, thus he was not one of Blanding's early Afrika Korps internees. That fact alone may not be significant, but often late arrivals to the camps—rather than the clannish and hard-core Afrika Korps men—tended to be less military, and occasionally more literary, in their interests.

Such was the case of Hans Bremer, who was allowed to visit Blanding's side camps throughout the state from February 21 to 27, 1945. He made these visits in the company of Dr. Edouard Patte, a representative and POW camp visitor for the International YMCA. Bremer reported his experiences in the third issue of Blanding's newly organized newspaper, *Zeitspiegel*, published April 1, 1945. His article, titled "1,250 Miles through Florida: The Report of an Experience," captures the uniqueness of the German POW experience in Florida.[2]

The environment of the prisoner of war is naturally very limited. The possibilities to learn more about the land, in which for a certain span of his life he finds himself, are very slight. The camp itself, the way to the work place, the occasional meeting with civilian workers, an accidental conversation with one of the guards, with that the experiential sources are exhausted from which he might get an impression, a mere hint, of what is for him a new world. For those with language abilities films, newspapers, and radio open further aids, but even for such a one his realm of vision can hardly be significantly widened. The question frequently asked of us, "How do you like Florida?" can thus only be answered with a polite shrugging of the shoulders. We all know only little of Florida, and from our school days there is little left or Florida took up only a modest space in our general geography concerning America.

One should therefore not be surprised at what inexpressible joy I experienced when I received permission from the camp commandant to accompany a representative of the Young Men's Christian Association, Dr. Patte, on a trip through all of the side camps. That was finally an opportunity, and indeed the first, to personally view America—Florida—and the American situation. The preparations for this excursion were quickly made: the soldier is always ready for such undertakings. So the trip began on 21 February with a five seat Hudson. With the best weather and with great speed we distanced ourselves from our home base. In a few hours journey over the flat land we reached our first destination in early afternoon: the camp at Leesburg. The 1st Company recently took up new residence. We saw a work detail busily setting up the new location. There was clearing, building, carpentry, and construction. The Landser [German colloquial term equivalent to GIs] have gotten good at such work. Our stop was to be only a short one. We continued south, passing by splendid orange groves, from which a lovely aroma filled the air. Still during the afternoon we reached Dade City, the camp taking part in the orange harvests of this land. After a long time one feels again like a free human being and enjoys in particular the joys of a hearty hospitality. Shortly after our arrival a midday meal was prepared for us. Joy was on all faces and questions of all kinds were directed at us. Again that bond of Kameradschaft [camaraderie] was rewoven, which from our days at the front was not yet rent asunder, and which is always reknotted when German soldiers are together. The camp is not particularly as spacious as others, but the internal furnishings of the tents show superlative detail work. We admire this fresh, lively spirit! Our stay is only too short, a hearty departure, our car rolls further to the next destinations. After a good day's accomplishment (about 200 miles) we arrive in the evening in Tampa, that city which in Florida and throughout America enjoys an important reputation. In MacDill Field, the accommodations of the 13th Company, we take our quarters for the night. A day full of new impressions, a holiday in the life of a prisoner of war, thus found its end. Tired, we lay down and after only a brief period of reflection, a deep sleep took us.

A sunny morning woke us. The recent side camp at MacDill Field makes an extraordinarily good impression on us. Outwardly spacious and airy, in the short time since its founding a great deal has been done. Still they have many concerns and troubles, these "Pioniere der Arbeit" [work pioneers], but a good spirit exists in the camp. They know how to get things going and are developing good ideas for the future development of the camp. Much is missing, but one begins with what one has. The construction of a stage, any entertainment program at all, is what these Comrades want most. Today I can report that since then—on 24 February—the first entertainment evening was carried out with good success. How much nicer it is when things do not fall into your lap, when one must make an honest effort, and when finally after much effort and work success is achieved! Something so achieved becomes a part of one's character.

The morning was dedicated to a visit of Tampa and a short visit at the camp at Drew Field. Our host, Dr. Patte, knows the fine art of introducing us to things, joining for us that which is necessary and that which is beautiful. He is an experienced specialist in the area of prisoner of war welfare and can empathize with our thoughts and feelings and guess our wishes. Tampa, a city of about 100,000 inhabitants, lying on beautiful Tampa Bay, shows in its inner city lively business activity. Great hotels and restaurants indicate the active tourist industry; it has throughout the character of a big city. We saw long rows of stores and shops, vehicles of all kinds; streetcars cruise the streets. A traffic light forces us to a halt. We felt the necessity of observing the colorful picture around us.

Tampa is at the same time the most important port on the west coast, which directs its shipping to all the world. The freight that passes through the port runs to the worth of $86,000,000. It owes its special reputation to the cigar industry. Founded in 1866, it reached its height shortly before the World War. Still today Tampa leads the world with high class hand-made Havana cigars. Oil, expensive woods (cedar, mahogany), phosphate, resin are along with the fruit of this land important goods of trade. Florida, formerly a Spanish possession, shows this influence in many ways. This shows itself especially in the area of architecture. The wonderful building of the

University of Tampa is an example of that. The wide promenade along the Bay conveyed to us a mighty impression of the beauty of the buildings, the grand terraces and gardens, which are produced by the opulent riches of the tropical plant world. Alongside these elegant buildings we find in the inner city simple framed houses, small low dwelling places, the home of the tobacco workers. Overall the layout of the streets and houses show the gradual development of the city. The segregated Negro settlement, about 21,000 Negroes, and the spick-and-span "Latin" settlement (Ybor City, the larger, 29,000 inhabitants) which in language and culture lead their own existence, are further remarkable points about Tampa and give this city a special character.

In the early afternoon on 22 February we leave Tampa, following the coastal road through Sarasota (Spanish name), to make our visit to Camp Venice. Venice is one of the most recent camps of our community; there is still much sand to be moved before the place can be fixed up to be used for necessary recreation and refreshment after work. Work is nevertheless in full progress, there is enough room available so that we are convinced that the businesslike and concerned company leader will succeed to give form to the establishment.

On the morning of the 23rd our travels took us through Punta Gorda (Span.) another beautiful view on the Bay, to Fort Myers. Underway we had the opportunity to see a lot of native animals in a reptile show. Crocodiles, snakes and wild cats are not new for us, we have seen them often at zoos, and still one feels somehow oddly moved to learn that these animals were caught in the local area. The pent-up wrath of a gigantic alligator, which devoured an entire pig for breakfast, did not awaken a wish for a second meeting. Among the snakes the ones that attracted our attention the most were the most poisonous—moccasin, diamond back—and among them the most beautiful specimen of the most dangerous coral snake. Expensive products from tortoise shell, snakeskin and alligator hide, which were on sale in connection with the show, found appreciation among the women visitors.

Fort Myers, at the time of our visit was occupied by only an advance party of 25 men. After the conclusion of the organizational work they expect the Company; Comrade Flamm, an accomplished painter, portrayed the reception in a manner full of fantasy on an extensive canvas. That the so hotly desired women are not missing goes without saying.—But we were able to take only a brief rest, a long way still lay before us today. The southern climate of this area, so very much influenced by the Gulf Stream, makes itself more and more noticeable. We turned to the southwest [must be southeast], following the Tamiami Trail, and enter into the fabled area of the Everglades.

The name Tamiami Trail stems from the cities at its opposite ends, Tampa and Miami. The highway binds the Atlantic with the Gulf of Mexico, as it crosses in a straight line the immense lowlands of the Everglades, an ancient swamp. The plans and measurements for this highway were completed by 1916, but lack of workers during the World War and difficulties of another kind—work in the swamp—still put the whole project in 1923. After repeated retesting in April 1923 by a specially created expedition that more than once was believed lost, this mighty highway building project was turned over to traffic in 1928. The costs amounted to no less than $13,000,000. The connection was thus made, and the trip from east to west, for which earlier a journey of more than two days was necessary, can now be made in a good two hours. This area, most of which lies under water all year, and which until 1842 remained mysterious, puzzling, and unexplored, attracted the Seminoles, an Indian tribe retreating from the pressing whites, to found an independent state. The times in which battles took place here belong to history and bespeak the fables and not the truth that on the peninsula there are still Indian tribes today that are still at war with the United States. The truth is, however, that the Tamiami Trail contributed to the ending of hostilities. There sprang up along this highway settlements and villages, the inhabitants of the swamp suddenly gave up their hiding places, hoisted flags, and offered handmade products for sale. An armistice treaty between the Seminoles and the government of the United States was signed in 1934, the proclamation announced that therewith the longest war in history had come to an end; a second such treaty was signed in 1937.

Near Ochopee we took the opportunity to visit a settlement. A young, good-looking woman with high-combed black hair, a long dress reaching to her heels, led us into her dwelling. In her demeanor there was a certain pride, a certain honor, which also manifested itself particularly in her upright stride. After our entrance, quickly a pair of children were around us, a three year old carrying a one year old child in its arms. In wonder they looked at us without speaking. These Indians speak a language other than English and understand only a few useful words of the language. The "home" of this family is really primitive. It consists of four straw huts. One of them serves as a sleeping area; on a somewhat raised wooden floor lie the bedclothes, furniture is entirely lacking. In a homemade hammock slept the smallest child. A second hut is set up as a living and work room. We see a woman squatting on the wooden floor busy with the making of a multicolored piece of clothing; she uses a hand-driven sewing machine. The so-called kitchen is in a tent. The cooking utensils are made up of rather primitive things, for cooking dinner a row of tin cans were used. A fourth room apparently serves for the storing of all possible materials and utensils, which in part have lost their original purpose. The livelihood of these people is gained through hunting and fishing; additionally wild fruits are raised for their own use. The making of wooden objects, spoons, toys, and dolls insures them a further income in the area of tourist business. We were able to convince ourselves of the business-like abilities of a five-year-old girl as we took a photograph of the group. The shutter had hardly closed, when the word "money" drew some change from our pockets.— Nourishment depends chiefly on the catch from the hunt: turkey, heron, ducks, venison as well as cereal grains. Fruit, fruit juice and syrup from homegrown sugarcane expand the menu. There are no fixed mealtimes; the daily main dish is a cereal mush mixed with meat and vegetables, which is always on the fire, and so each member of the family has the opportunity to eat when they please.—In this manner the old traditions are continued.

The Everglades allowed us to experience a piece of the romanticism, legends and history of Florida. As lonely and deserted as this area may seem, nevertheless it has an attractiveness of its own. A particularly idyllic and little touched by civilization section is the Tamiami canal, which runs parallel to the highway and finally leads directly to Miami.

Here amid the stillness and isolation there is an active life played out between cypresses, pasture grasses, palmetto and swamp grass. Birds and reptiles of all kinds bustle about in this landscape so dear to them; no human being disturbs their isolation. From time to time we see shooting arrow-quick through the water's surface fish snapping for insects. A heron, a crane, a pair of ducks go their way! They all fit into their landscape so well in their feather-dress, that one discovers them only in the last moment and only with careful observation. It is a true natural paradise!

The highway is under constant surveillance by buzzards and other birds of prey. They find rich booty here. We constantly find the smashed bodies of snakes and other animals that during the night sought the warm highway for sleep or in crossing the street found themselves before headlights and became traffic victims.

Late in the evening we reached Miami (about 125,000 inhabitants), one of the most beautiful and important locations on the peninsula. In less than a quarter century the most magnificent residences of the most diverse types and construction styles and the most splendid hotels have arisen here on rock, swamp, and sand dunes. Surrounded by luscious tropical plants and majestic palms—among them the royal palm is particularly attractive—these environs project a rather fairy-tale and fantastic feeling. In only a few places in the world could one see so much wealth and natural beauty side-by-side. Again and again we turned off the main street for a look at the blue mirror of the ocean or to admire the beautiful buildings and terraces as we drove slowly by.

Miami attracts every year, especially in winter, a stream of travelers from all over the United States in search of recreation and relaxation. The number of visitors yearly is given at 2,000,000. The leading industry thus rests substantially on used and luxury goods for the tourists. Some shipping lines travel to the West Indies; the harbor is winning importance as a home port for heavy military forces.

Fishing is one of the most pursued sports of the visitors. Everywhere where there is an opportunity, one sees young and old practicing this contemplative pursuit. Many also go out to sea. In the hundred days of the winter season alone $500,000 is spent on boat rentals.

Miami is however not only for the richest people. There is another means to come to these attractions. The comfortable travel trailer is part of the city picture on the peninsula. We drive by whole colonies of trailers. I can imagine that these tourists can rent a parking place for a certain price and, perhaps even providing their own food, spend their vacation here on this beautiful beach. On the other hand it may be difficult, in such a special location, to find quarters during the season.

For us it is no problem! After spending the night in Kendall (south of Miami) and taking a refreshing swim on Sunday morning in a nearby lake, we resumed our trip. Sunday is again devoted to Miami and its surroundings. We follow the roadway over the bay to Miami Beach and enjoy from here a free field of vision over the many artificial islands, each of which is connected with the roadway, and over the ocean. Thousands fill the expansive beach. There is so much to see, one cannot take it all in at once. A flight of hummingbirds fly over the roadway. On the water a couple of float planes bob quietly up and down; they are privately owned, another indication for the affluence of the residents of this city. Miami is probably one of the most expensive places in the world. Supposedly there are Americans who save all their lives so that later they can secure property in the south of the peninsula.

There is not sufficient time for a trip to Key West, the island group that lies south of the peninsula. But we experienced a Sunday that was the most wonderful of the whole trip. Once again we take up the hospitality at Kendall, in order on Monday morning to make our visit to the southernmost camp, Homestead. It is rather warm down here, and we can imagine that the work in the potato harvest is very demanding. Beyond that they are in a camp that still must do without amenities. A couple of locally acquired recreational games give them much pleasure. We were assured that this camp was only created for a limited time span. The two experienced and resourceful company leaders will assuredly master their task.

Only with difficulty were we able to leave the coastal highway that allowed us to see the billowing ocean in such a beautiful green and blue. The wind arose and wave after wave struck the shore, an eternal to and fro, which one can watch for hours. So our host decided to choose the coastal road up to Palm Beach. For us the theatricality of Miami Beach was repeated, which is nearly rivaled by Palm Beach. Finally with a sharp bend to the west we leave the ocean. Without success we are on the lookout for Lake Okeechobee, which should come into view (700 square miles in size). Years ago a heavy storm drove the water out of the lake and put the whole area around it under water; humans and animals fell victim to the flood. Since then this lake has been surrounded by a gigantic dam, which since then has prevented similar catastrophes. The dam cuts off our view. Slender Australian pines, which grow on both sides of the highway, are a further foil for storms and hurricanes.

The heavy, dark soil is reserved for the wide sugarcane fields. The sugarcane harvest begins in November and continues through April. The stalks reach a height that averages 15 feet. Viewed from above these sugarcane plantations look like a great chess board, whose fields are created through canals and transport lanes. Here lies the job site of our 10th Company, Clewiston. In the last year they have learned every activity from planting through harvest. Just now they are harvesting. We are engulfed in the smoke of burning fields. The sugarcane is burnt so that it can then be carried away in small trucks. Our men return dirty and tired in the evenings to their huts, and then dedicate a portion of their free time to fishing. We have the impression here of a 100 percent work camp and feel particularly obliged to these comrades.

Past splendid lakes and magnificent orange groves the lightly arched landscape goes up and down. Winter Haven lies in the middle of a group of lakes, these 30,000 lakes of Florida, and is the center for citrus cultivation (inclusive term for all orange and lemon types). Our 6th Company is hearty and dedicates much free time to gardening. Soccer, played with seven-man teams in limited space, is at a high level!

After a short rest our path carries us in a northeasterly direction to Orlando, our largest side camp. We still find many opportunities for natural science observations while underway. Lackadaisically a turtle crosses the highway. A young hare rubs its nose happily! The car stops suddenly! The sharp eyes of Dr. P, who is an attentive observer of nature, spies something. We look around us, the car slowly backs up. On the edge of the highway something is slithering: a splendid diamond back! It becomes our prey. The "snake master" in Orlando is able to remove the skin with several masterful tugs. That crowned the end of our journey. The precious snakeskin will someday find a worthy place in the trophy shelves in a comfortable living room, kept as a lasting memory of a wonderful journey in a serious time.

The mood barometer sinks rapidly as the car comes closer and closer to the base. We experienced seven days full of experience and new impressions. On the afternoon of 27 February we again reach Camp Blanding. The Sunshine State of Florida will remain unforgettable.

It may be a task for another day to deal more thoroughly with the geography of Florida. In this essay many points could only be touched upon because its purpose was to arouse general interest, expand on the report and make it richer.

HANS BREMER
(Resource: "Florida. A Guide to the Southernmost State.")

NOTES

INTRODUCTION

1. Robin, *The Barbed-Wire College*, 6, gives these figures based on the War Department's final tabulations as printed in the *New York Times*, August 8, 1947, 19: 378,898 Germans, 51,455 Italians, and 5,435 Japanese.

2. Pluth, "Administration and Operation," 237–44.

3. Article 2 of the Convention of July 27, 1929, Relative to the Treatment of Prisoners of War, printed in Bevans, *Treaties*, 2:938.

4. Pluth, "Administration and Operation," 242–43.

5. Pluth's "Administration and Operation" focuses on the government administration of the program and makes good use of congressional, State Department, and military records; records from the last two groups were just in the process of being declassified at the time the dissertation was written. See also Spidle, "Axis Prisoners."

6. Wissenschaftliche Kommission für deutsche Kriegsgefangenengeschichte. Erich Maschke, ed., *Zur Geschichte der deutschen Kriegsgefangenen des Zweiten Weltkrieges*, 22 vols. (Bielefeld: Gieseking Verlag, 1962–74). See particularly vol. 10, pt. 1, Jung, *Kriegsgefangenen*.

7. Krammer, *Nazi Prisoners*.

8. Gansberg, *Stalag: U.S.A.*

9. Fickle and Ellis, "POWs in the Piney Woods."

10. Billinger, "Wehrmacht in Florida."

11. Koop, *Stark Decency*; Powell, *Splinters of a Nation*.

12. Robin, *Barbed-Wire College*.

13. Carlson, *Each Other's Prisoners*.

14. For the Papago Park mass escape, see Moore, *Faustball Tunnel*.

15. For the story of murders, courts-martial, and hangings of POWs by American military authorities, see Green, *Extreme Justice*.

16. For the story of Georg Gaertner, the escapee from Camp Deming, New Mexico, in 1945, who turned himself in in 1985, see Gaertner, *Hitler's Last Soldier*.

17. Moore, *Faustball Tunnel*, 67–68.

18. One exploration of this situation has appeared in my article "Other Side Now." It grew out of a discovery in the German Military Archives in Freiburg of the testimony of four German Army POWs from Blanding who

were repatriated to Germany in February 1944 in the second exchange of sick and wounded POWs. They left depositions with the Wehrmacht regarding their treatment in captivity and, especially, about the presence of "traitors" among the POWs at Camp Blanding. Lewis H. Carlson of Western Michigan University, author of *We Were Each Other's Prisoners*, has indicated his interest in research on Nazi–anti-Nazi conflicts within POW camps and his awareness of the situation in Camp Blanding. He has shared some of his notes on American archival materials and a copy of a paper titled "German World War II POWs in America: Cultural and Political Conflicts," which he presented at the Popular Culture Association's national meeting in Philadelphia in April 1995. Materials enclosed with letter to Robert D. Billinger, Jr., from Lewis H. Carlson, May 2, 1997, in possession of the author.

19. Krammer, *Nazi Prisoners*, has a chapter titled "Wrestling for the Tiller," which deals with the conflicts within the camps, and Koop, *Stark Decency*, focuses on the unique situation of an anti-Nazi army camp in New Hampshire. Gansberg, *Stalag: U.S.A.*, 57, stresses that Americans were surprised to find that "*German* and *Nazi* were not synonymous" and that "many Afrika Korps prisoners were not Afrika Korps at all" but members of the 999th Probationary Division filled with men considered "dangerous to the Reich."

1. NATIONAL CONTEXT

1. See table 1, "Monthly Census of Prisoners of War Interned in Continental United States" in Pluth, "Administration and Operation," 438.

2. Krammer, *Nazi Prisoners*, 2.

3. Jung, *Kriegsgefangenen*, 7–8.

4. Krammer, *Nazi Prisoners*, 3. By June 1944 there were 196,948 POWs in the Unitedt States: 146,101 Germans, 50,278 Italians, and 569 Japanese. See table 1, "Monthly Census," in Pluth, "Administration and Operation," 438.

5. Robin, *Barbed-Wire College*, 6. He cites the War Department's final tabulations as published in the *New York Times*, August 8, 1947, 19.

6. Krammer, *Nazi Prisoners*, 26; Jung, *Kriegsgefangenen*, 20.

7. Jung, *Kriegsgefangenen*, 20.

8. The story of German prisoners of war in Florida starts not with military men but with civilians. The first Germans to be housed at the military reservation at Camp Blanding were civilians classed as "enemy aliens." Technically not prisoners of war, they were foreign nationals feared by the United States and Allied governments because their political allegiance might present a danger to the domestic tranquillity of their place of current residence. In the case of the first German internees at Camp Blanding, the residences from which these "enemy aliens" were ejected were various Central American countries: Costa Rica, Guatemala, and Panama. In December 1941 and January 1942, they were arrested and deported to the United States. During the winter, spring, and summer of 1942, they were housed temporarily at Blanding before being transferred to more permanent internment quarters in Texas, Oklahoma, Tennessee, and North Carolina.

In January 1942 there were 152 deportees in the camp: 35 Germans from

Costa Rica and 115 Germans from Guatemala. There were also two Italians, one each from Costa Rica and Guatemala. In April they were joined by 18 German Jews originally interned in Panama. All were housed in tents within a stockade, 110 by 150 yards in area, enclosed by two cyclone fences topped with barbed wire. They slept in pyramidal tents large enough for four to five persons. The enemy alien internment camp was located in Blanding's Camp Stockade Number 2, originally constructed for the purpose of confining American military prisoners. In March 1942, a visiting inspector from the Swiss Legation in Washington described the whole facility as barren. It was located about 100 yards from a coal dumping place, and the area was usually covered by black dust. The scene was relieved, however, by little gardens that some of the internees started in front of their tents. Yet, interned without trial, separated from loved ones, forced to wear blue American army fatigues marked with the letters EA (enemy alien), these civilians faced great uncertainties in the sand hills of northern Florida. What is more, they were guarded by a 30-man military police detachment that had no experience and little understanding of what should be done with or for their charges. See Billinger, "Wehrmacht in Florida," 161–62.

9. For information on Camp Blanding, see "Blanding Observes Fourth Anniversary," *Bradford County Telegraph* (Starke), Friday, September 15, 1944, 8; and "Camp Blanding Opens Fifth Year of Activity Today: Florida's Largest Military Installation Has Trained 300,000 Soldiers," *Florida Times-Union* (Jacksonville), Thursday, September 14, 1944, 6.

10. Capt. Edward C. Shannahan's Record of Visit to Prisoner of War Camp, Camp Blanding, Fla., December 26–29, 1943, RG 389, Entry 461, Box 2656, National Archives (NA).

11. Charles C. Eberhardt, State Department, Report of Visit by Delegates of the International Red Cross and of the Swiss Legation to Prisoner of War Camp, Camp Blanding, Fla., April 6–7, 1944, RG 389, Entry 461, Box 2656, NA.

12. Capt. Edward C. Shannahan's Record of Visit to Prisoner of War Camp, Camp Blanding, Fla., December 26, 1943, RG 389, Entry 461, Box 2656, NA.

13. Ibid.

14. Jung, *Kriegsgefangenen,* 13.

15. Ibid., 15.

16. Ibid., 14. Jung also notes that until June 1943 even prisoner of war camps were still called "internment camps." Thereafter, internment camps for POWs were called "prisoner of war camps." Ibid., 21.

17. See Krammer, *Undue Process.* As Krammer reminds us, these internment camps—those for Germans alone set up in forty-six locations during the war—should not be confused with POW camps or with War Relocation Authority centers, which housed Japanese and Japanese-Americans from the West Coast. See Krammer, *Undue Process,* 82. To these camps for enemy aliens detained within the United States would be added those detained by allies of the United States in Latin America, who removed them from their own territories. It was such detainees who arrived at Camp Blanding in January 1942.

18. Pluth, "Administration and Operation," 210–11.

19. Jung, *Kriegsgefangenen,* 14–15. For a detailed and well-researched description of these administrative developments, see Pluth, "Administration and Operation," especially 18–20.

20. In August 1942 the ASF was divided into ten service commands and a military district of Washington. After this, the internment facilities came under the commanders of each of the individual service commands, who became responsible for the internment camps in their area. Thus the PMGO exercised its influence more indirectly than directly within the individual service areas, because it did not have its own offices and personnel to carry out its business independently of the area commanders.

21. Communications and reports regarding the enemy aliens and German prisoners of war held at Camp Blanding can be found in the Modern Military Branch of the National Archives and in the Diplomatic Branch of the National Archives because of the involvement of the State Department with the War Department in the matter of internments.

22. Krammer, *Nazi Prisoners,* 39.

23. Ibid., 37–38.

24. Martin Tollefson, "Enemy Prisoners of War," is an excellent survey of the POW routine as carried out under the provisions of the Geneva Convention. The author was formerly a colonel, army of the United States, and director, Prisoner of War Operations Division, Office of the Provost Marshal General, then dean and professor of law, Drake University Law School, Des Moines, Iowa,

25. For details of daily life, canteen coupons, and observance of the Geneva Convention, see Maj. Gen. Archer L. Lerch (PMGO), "The Army Reports on Prisoners of War," especially 537–44. See also Krammer, *Nazi Prisoners,* 47–50.

26. In addition to the Lerch article noted above, see John Brown Mason, formerly of the Internee Section, Special War Problems Division, Department of State, "German Prisoners of War," especially 211–12.

27. Krammer, *Nazi Prisoners,* 50.

2. UNCLE SAM'S SMILING WORKERS

1. For additional details on the development of the rules for the employment of POWs, see Lewis and Mewha, *Prisoner of War Utilization.* See also Krammer, *Nazi Prisoners,* 79–113.

2. For good insights on the army's views on POW labor, see Lerch, "Army Reports on Prisoners of War." See also Krammer, *Nazi Prisoners,* especially 81–88. See also chapter 9, "Contract Labor: The Development of the War Department–War Manpower Commission Agreement, August 1943, and Implementing Directives," in Lewis and Mewha, *Prisoner of War Utilization.*

3. Lewis and Mewha, *Prisoner of War Utilization,* 108.

4. See reports of Guy S. Métraux, February 28–March 18, 1945, RG 59, IR9–545, Box 3344, NA, for the French versions sent to the State Department; and

RG 389, Entry 461, Box 2661, and Entry 461, Box 2656, NA, for the English translations forwarded from the State Department to the army.

5. See State List, monthly April–July 1944, Army Service Forces, file in Research Room, MMB, NA.

6. Information on origins of the camp in E. F. Nelson, State Department Report of Visit along with Verner Tobler, Representative of the Delegation of Switzerland to Prisoner of War Camp, Camp Gordon Johnston, Fla., November 14, 1944, RG 389, Entry 461, Box 2661, NA.

7. "German POW Work in Jackson," *Daily Democrat* (Tallahassee), August 15, 1944, 3; "War Prisoners Will Aid Peanut Harvest in Jackson County," *Jackson County Floridian* (Marianna), June 1, 1945, 1; "County's Peanut Growers Allotted 270 War Prisoners," *Jackson County Floridian* (Marianna), August 10, 1945, 1. See also Camps Inactivated List, Labor Reports, Marianna, Fla., RG 389, Entry 461, Box 2492, NA.

8. Camps Inactivated List, Labor Reports, Hastings, Fla., RG 389, Entry 461, Box 2492, NA.

9. "McNutt Certifies Prisoner of War Camps in State," *Florida Times-Union* (Jacksonville), January 6, 1944, 7.

10. April 1, 1944, List, State List, monthly April 1944–July 10, 1945, Army Service Forces, Research Room, MMB, NA.

11. May 1, 1944, List, ibid., for White Springs. The first labor reports from Telogia and White Springs were dated June 15, 1944. See Camp Labor Reports, RG 389, Entry 461, Box 2492, NA.

12. Capt. Jadie H. Brown's memorandum of December 30, 1943, attached to Record of Visit to Camp, Prisoner of War Division, Provost Marshal General's Office, Prisoner of War Camp, Camp Blanding, Fla., December 26–29, 1943, Report filed by Capt. Edward C. Shannahan, RG 389, PMGO Inspection Reports, Blanding, Entry 461, Box 2656, NA.

13. Charles C. Eberhardt, Department of State, Report of Prisoner of War Camp, Camp Blanding, Starke, Fla., visited April 6–7, 1944, by Dr. Marc Peter, Delegate of the International Red Cross Committee, Dr. Edward A. Feer, of the Swiss Legation, and Charles C. Eberhardt of the Department of State, RG 389, Entry 461, Box 2656, NA.

14. Interview with Harry A. Johnston, former executive officer at Camp Blanding, West Palm Beach, June 22, 1977; notes and tape recorded interview in the possession of the author.

15. Charles C. Eberhardt, Department of State, Report of April 6–7, 1944, Visit to Prisoner of War Camp, Camp Blanding, Starke, Fla., with delegates from the International Red Cross and Swiss Legation, RG 389, Entry 461, Box 2656, NA. See also translation of report of International Red Cross visit by M. Peter on April 6 and 7, 1944 to Camp Blanding, RG 59, State/ Decimal File 1940–44, 711.62114 IR 10–6/44, NA.

16. Original French and English translation of Guy Métraux, IRC, Report on Clewiston, Fla., visited March 16, 1945, RG 59, IR/9–545, Box 3344, NA.

17. Ibid.

18. Ibid.

19. Interview with David Forshay, former Clewiston guard, West Palm Beach, May 29, 1978; notes in possession of the author. Former POW internee Gerhard Anklam recalled bringing home a snakeskin souvenir. Interview with Gerhard Anklam, Berlin, June 3, 1996; tape in possession of the author.

20. See IRC report, Leesburg, Floride, visité par Mr. Métraux le 10 mars 1945, RG 59, IR 9–545, Box 3344, NA.

21. For information on government policies regarding the publicity accorded the POW program, and the difficulties that developed in that regard, see Pluth, "Administration and Operation," chap. 9, "Public Relations."

22. "Leesburg Is Site of New Camp for War Prisoners," *Florida Times-Union* (Jacksonville), Saturday, March 11, 1944, 3. Regarding the POW contribution to the southern lumber industry see Fickle and Ellis, "POWs in the Piney Woods."

23. "Harvesting the Citrus Crops by POWs," *Leesburg Commercial*, Friday, March 17, 1944, 1, 4.

24. See IRC report, Leesburg, Floride, visité par Mr. Métraux le 10 mars 1945, RG 59, IR 9–545, Box 3344, NA.

25. Bill Bond, "German POWs Left Their Mark on County," *Lake Sentinel* (an edition of the *Orlando Sentinel*), Sunday, January 23, 1994, 4.

26. Bill Bond, "Residents Recall Days of POWs in Camp Near Leesburg," *Orlando Sentinel*, Wednesday, October 15, 1986, 3, 6.

27. Bill Bond, "German POWs Left Their Mark on County," *Lake Sentinel* (an edition of the *Orlando Sentinel*), Sunday, January 23, 1994, 4.

28. Bill Bond, "Residents Recall Days of POWs in Camp Near Leesburg," *Orlando Sentinel*, Wednesday, October 15, 1986, 6.

29. Regarding the Leesburg camp and its location, see Bill Bond, "German POWs Left Their Mark on County," *Lake Sentinel* (an edition of the *Orlando Sentinel*), Sunday, January 23, 1994, 1, 4. Bond mentions that the operation of the POW camp on the property is detailed in a history of the Lake-Sumter Community College, researched by Peter Kehde. See Kehde, "Early Industries of the Lake Area," in *History of the Silver Lake Area*, compiled by Pat Carr and Betty Snyder, 1993. Copy in the library, Lake-Sumter Community College, Leesburg, Fla.

30. Edouard Patte, Report on Visit to Prisoner of War Camp, Leesburg, Fla., February 23, 1945, RG 389, Entry 461, Box 2656, NA; Métraux, March 10, 1945, Report on Visit to Leesburg, Fla., in original French copy sent to U.S. State Department and received September 24, 1945, in RG 59, 711.62114 IR/9–545, Box 3344, NA; or in English translation as communicated to the U.S. Army in RG 389, Entry 461, Box 2656, NA.

31. Bond article, citing an interview by Peter Kehde with Walter David, a former lieutenant at the Leesburg camp. Bill Bond, "German POWs Left Their Mark on County," *Lake Sentinel* (an edition of the *Orlando Sentinel*), Sunday, January 23, 1994, 4.

32. Métraux, March 10, 1945, Report on Visit to Leesburg, Fla., in original French copy sent to U.S. State Department and received September 24, 1945,

in RG 59, 711.62114 IR/9–545, Box 3344, NA; in English translation as communicated to the U.S. Army in RG 389, Entry 461, Box 2656, NA.

33. Charles C. Eberhardt, Department of State, Report of Visit to Prisoner of War Camp, Camp Blanding, Starke, Fla., April 6–7, 1944, in company of delegates from the International Red Cross and the Swiss Legation, RG 389, Entry 461, Box 2656, NA.

34. "250 Nazi Prisoners To Be Used in Citrus Plants in City," *Winter Haven Daily Chief*, Wednesday, March 22, 1944, 3 and 4.

35. "German War Prisoners," *Winter Haven Daily Chief*, Thursday, March 23, 1944, 1–2, citing the *Ocala Star Banner*.

36. French copy of Winter Haven, Floride, visté par Mr. Métraux le 12 mars 1945, received by Department of State, September 24, 1945, in RG 59, 711.62114 IR/9–545, Box 3344, NA.

37. "Pasco Firms to Use German Prisoners," *Florida Times-Union* (Jacksonville), Saturday, April 1, 1944, 2; "Nazi Prisoners at Dade City," *Daily Democrat* (Tallahassee), Sunday, April 16, 1944, 13; "Nazi War Prisoners Arrive in Dade City," *Florida Times-Union*, Sunday, April 16, 1944, 8. See also report filed when camp closed: "German Prisoners in Pasco Going Home; 200 Jobs Open," *Tampa Morning Tribune*, Tuesday, December 11, 1945, 1.

38. "Nazi War Prisoners Arrive in Dade City," *Florida-Times Union* (Jacksonville), April 16, 1944, 8.

39. J. L. Toohey, Department of State, Report of Visit to Prisoner of War Side Camp, Dade City, Fla., visited November 29, 1945, by Paul Schnyder, representing the International Red Cross Committee, RG 59, Lot 58D7, Box 22, File: Blanding, NA.

40. Ibid.

41. Werner Burkert, "Militärzeit und Kriegsgefangenschaft," photocopied portion of typescript memoirs sent by Werner H. Burkert of Schaffhausen, Switzerland, to the author in a packet of materials received September 18, 1998.

42. "German Prisoners of War Leave Camp at Dade City," *Florida Times-Union*, Sunday, March 10, 1946, 14.

43. Charles C. Eberhardt, Department of State, Report of April 6–7, 1944, Visit to Prisoner of War Camp, Camp Blanding, Starke, Fla., with delegates from the International Red Cross and Swiss Legation, RG 389, Entry 461, Box 2656, NA. See also translation of report of International Red Cross visit by M. Peter on April 6 and 7, 1944, to Camp Blanding, RG 59, State/ Decimal File 1940–44, 711.62114 IR 10–6/44, NA.

44. See Fickle and Ellis, "POWs in the Piney Woods."

45. Shannahan Report of January 7, 1945, Section on Prisoner of War Branch Camp, White Springs, Fla., RG 389, Entry 459A, Special Projects Division, Box 1609, file 255: Camp Blanding, NA.

46. For details on the military installation at Camp Gordon Johnston, see David J. Coles, "'Hell-by-the-Sea': Florida's Camp Gordon Johnston in World War II."

47. Ibid., 3.

48. Eldon F. Nelson, Department of State, Report of Prisoner of War Camp, Camp Gordon Johnston, Fla., visited on November 14, 1944, by Verner Tobler, Representative of the Legation of Switzerland, RG 389, Entry 461, Box 2661, NA.

49. See State List, monthly April 1944–July 10, 1945, Army Service Forces, Office of Commanding General, Prisoner of War Camps, by Location and Principal Types of Work, Research Room, MMB, NA. See also Eldon F. Nelson, Department of State, Report of Prisoner of War Camp, Camp Gordon Johnston, Fla., visited on November 14, 1944, by Verner Tobler, Representative of the Legation of Switzerland, RG 389, Entry 461, Box 2661, NA.

50. English translation of report on Camp Gordon Johnston, Fla., visited by Maurice Perret of the International Red Cross on June 29, 1944 (received by General Bryan from the Department of State March 12, 1945), RG 389, Entry 461, Box 2661, NA.

51. Ibid.

52. There is a March 12, 1945, stamp on the English translation of the IRC report on Camp Gordon Johnston, Fla., visited by Maurice Perret on June 29, 1944, RG 389, Entry 461, Box 2661, NA.

53. Eldon F. Nelson, Department of State, Report of Prisoner of War Camp, Camp Gordon Johnston, Fla., visited on November 14, 1944, by Verner Tobler, Representative of the Legation of Switzerland, RG 389, Entry 461, Box 2661, NA.

54. Ibid.

55. See Geneva Convention. Bevans, *Treaties*, 2:938.

56. Eldon F. Nelson, Department of State, Report of Prisoner of War Camp, Camp Gordon Johnston, Fla., visited on November 14, 1944, by Verner Tobler, Representative of the Legation of Switzerland, RG 389, Entry 461, Box 2661, NA.

57. Ibid.

58. Edouard Patte's Report of Visit to Prisoner of War Camp, Telogia, Fla., March 1, 1945, RG 389, Entry 461, Box 2661, NA.

59. For a schematic of the Blanding camps and a listing of the numbers of German POWs in each of those twenty camps, see "Kriegsgefangenenlager Blanding/Florida," in *POW-Zeitspiegel* (Camp Blanding), Sonntag, September 30, 1945, 16.

60. State List, monthly April 1944–July 10, 1945, Army Services Forces, Office of Commanding General, Prisoner of War Camps, by Location and Principal Types of Work, Research Room, MMB, NA.

61. First report on POW labor at Kendall, RG 389, Entry 461, Box 2492, NA. See also J. L. Toohey, Department of State, report of visit of December 6, 1945, to Prisoner of War Side Camp, Kendall, Fla., along with Paul Schnyder, representing the International Committee of the Red Cross, RG 59, Lot 58D7, Box 22, File: Blanding, NA.

62. English translation of International Red Cross Report of March 17, 1945, visit by Mr. Métraux to Kendall, Fla., RG 59, 711.62114 IR/9–545, Box 3344, NA.

63. Ibid.

64. "Two POWs Escaped from Camp at Kendall," *Miami Herald*, Sunday, September 3, 1944, 5a, with photographs of the two escapees.

65. "Hunger Drives 2 Escaped Prisoners to Give Up," *Florida Times-Union* (Jacksonville), Thursday, September 7, 1944, 7.

66. "Drew Field, with 15 Square Miles, Has 2800 Buildings," *Tampa Sunday Tribune*, May 27, 1945, 1.

67. Edouard Patte, International YMCA, Report on Visit to Prisoner of War Camp Drew Field, February 20, 1945, RG 389, Entry 461, Box 2656 and Entry 459A, Box 1609, NA.

68. English translation of Mr. Métraux, International Red Cross, Report of Visit to Drew Field, Fla., on March 12, 1945, RG 59, 711.62114 IR/9-545, Box 3344, NA; also in RG 389, Entry 461, Box 2656, NA.

69. Ibid.

70. Maj. Edward C. Shannahan's Memorandum for the Director, Prisoner of War Operations Division, January 7, 1945, Subject: Reports of Visit to Prisoner of War Camp, Drew Field, Fla. (among others), RG 389, Entry 459A, Box 1609, and Entry 461, Box 2656, NA.

71. Report of WKU-258, in Jung, *Kriegsgefangenen*, 131.

72. Ibid., 220.

73. French version of IRC report by Métraux, who visited Orlando Army Air Base, Florida, on March 11, 1945, RG 59, 711.62114 IR/9-545, Box 3344, NA.

74. Report of Maj. Edward C. Shannahan, Field Liaison Officer, January 7, 1945, RG 389, Entry 461, Box 2656, and RG 389, Entry 459A, Box 1609, File 255: Camp Blanding, NA.

75. "War Prisoner Labor Keeps Plants Open," *Daily Democrat* (Tallahassee), Tuesday, January 23, 1945, 8.

76. French version of IRC report by Métraux, who visited Orlando Army Air Base, Florida, on March 11, 1945, RG 59, 711.62114 IR/9-545, Box 3344, NA.

77. English translation of IRC report by Métraux, Work Detachment at Eglin Field, Fla., visited on March 2, 1945, RG 59, 711.62114 IR/9-545, Box 3344 and RG 389, Entry 461, Box 2661, NA.

78. Eldon F. Nelson, Department of State, Report of Visit to Prisoner of War Camp, Camp Gordon Johnston, Fla., accompanying a representative of the Legation of Switzerland, November 14, 1944, RG 389, Entry 461, Box 2661, NA.

79. Edouard Patte, an International YMCA visitor to the Eglin camp on March 3, 1945, noted the provenance of the prisoners. See Edouard Patte's Report on Visit to Prisoner of War Camp, Eglin Field, Fla., March 3, 1945, RG 389, Entry 461, Box 2661, NA.

80. English translation of Métraux report of March 2, 1945, visit, RG 59, 711.62114 IR/9-545, Box 3344 and RG 389, Entry 461, Box 2661, NA.

81. Ibid. Also mentioned, with reference to this particular IRC report, in Jung, *Kriegsgefangenen*, 201.

82. "Dale Mabry Inactivated," *Tampa Morning Tribune*, Saturday, December 1, 1945, 2.

83. English translation of IRC report by Mr. Métraux, who visited the work detachment of Dale Mabry Field on March 6, 1945, RG 59, 711.62114 IR/9–545, Box 3344 and RG 389, Entry 461, Box 2661, NA. See also "War Prisoner Camp Established Here," *Daily Democrat* (Tallahassee), Sunday, December 24, 1944, 1.

84. See "POWs Helping Harvest Crops," *Daily Democrat*, Sunday, July 22, 1945, 7; "50 German Prisoners Work on Leon Farms," *Daily Democrat*, Sunday, July 29, 1945, 11; and "POWs Work 8,051 Hours on Farms in This Area," *Daily Democrat*, Sunday, January 6, 1946, 13.

85. September 1945 POW populations for Blanding system camps in *POW-Zeitspiegel* (Camp Blanding), September 30, 1945, 16.

86. IRC report in French, based on visit on March 13, 1945, to MacDill Field, Florida, by Mr. Métraux, RG 59, 711.62114 IR/9–545, Box 3344, NA.

87. "200 German Prisoners Dig Potatoes: Ripening Crops Pose Labor Problem," *Homestead Leader*, Friday, February 9, 1945, 1; Edouard Patte, YMCA report of February 24, 1945, RG 389, Entry 459A, Box 1609 and Entry 461, 2656, NA; French language report on Homestead, Fla., camp visited on March 18, 1945 by Mr. Métraux, RG 59, 711.62114 IR/9–545, Box 3344, NA.

88. Métraux report of March 18, 1945, visit to Homestead, RG 59, 711.62114 IR/9–545, Box 3344, NA.

89. Ibid.

90. State List, monthly April 1944–July 10, 1945, Army Service Forces, Office of Commanding General, Prisoner of War Camps, by Location and Principal Type of Work, Research Room, MMB, NA. See also "407 Prisoners to Ease Grove Help Shortage," *Homestead Leader*, Friday, October 12, 1945, 1.

91. *Homestead Leader*, ibid.

92. Labor Reports, Homestead, Fla., RG 389, Entry 461, Box 2492, NA.

93. J. L. Toohey, Department of State, Report of Visit to Prisoner of War Side Camp, Welch General Hospital, Daytona Beach, Fla., Visited November 26, 1945, by Mr. Paul Schnyder, representing the International Red Cross Committee and Mr. J. L. Toohey, of the Department of State, RG 59, Lot 58D7, Special War Problems Division, Box 22, File: Blanding, NA.

94. "War Prisoners to Work in Daytona Beach Hospital," *Florida Times-Union* (Jacksonville), Saturday, February 10, 1945, 3; IRC visitor Guy Métraux noted in his report of his March 8–9, 1945, visit to Camp Blanding that he had not been able to visit the following camps: "Welch General Hospital at Daytona Beach, Florida (100 prisoners); Dade City, Florida (305 prisoners); White Springs, Florida (244 prisoners). These three camps are rather far from the main highways, and according to the spokesman, no special problems have arisen." See English translation, Report of Camp Blanding, Fla., visited on March 8–9, 1945, by Mr. Métraux, RG 59, 711.62114 IR/ 9–545, Box 3344, and RG 389, Entry 461, Box 2656, NA.

95. Toohey report of November 26, 1945, visit, RG 59, Lot 58D7, Box 22, File: Blanding, NA.

96. French language report on Venice Field, Fla., visited on March 14, 1945, by Mr. Métraux, RG 59, 711.62114 IR/9-545, Box 3344, NA; and J. L. Toohey, Report of Prisoner of War Side Camp, Venice Army Air Base, Fla., visited December 4, 1945, by Mr. Paul Schnyder, representing the International Red Cross Committee, and Mr. J. L. Toohey, of the Department of State, RG 59, Lot 58D7, Box 22, File: Blanding, NA.

97. "Venice Gets 200 Germans," *Tampa Morning Tribune*, Saturday, February 17, 1945, 1.

98. "Army to Probe Report Nazis Replace Vets in Venice Jobs," *Tampa Morning Tribune*, Friday, March 30, 1945, 1.

99. "Venice CO Denies Vets Are Replaced by Nazi Prisoners," *Tampa Morning Tribune*, Saturday, March 31, 1945, 3.

100. French language Report on Venice Field, Fla., visited on March 14, 1945, by Mr. Métraux, RG 59, 711.62114 IR/9-545, Box 3344, NA.

101. Edouard Patte, Report of Visit to Prisoner of War Camp, Fort Myers, Fla., February 24, 1945, RG 389, Entry 461, Box 2656, and Entry 459A, Box 1609, NA.

102. French language Métraux report, Page Field, Fla., visited on March 15, 1945, RG 59, 711.62114 IR/9-545, Box 3344, NA.

103. Ibid.

104. "German POWs to Help Clean up Magic City," *Daily Democrat* (Tallahassee), October 15, 1945, 5.

105. Chart on "Kriegsgefangenenlager Blanding," *POW-Zeitspiegel*, September 30, 1945, 16.

106. J. L. Toohey, State Department, Report of Prisoner of War Side Camp, Jacksonville Naval Air Station, visited November 23, 1945, by Mr. Paul Schnyder, representing the International Red Cross Committee and Mr. J. L. Toohey of the Department of State, RG 59, 58D7, Box 22, File: Blanding, NA.

107. "Group of 500 Captive Nazis Arrives Here," *Florida Times-Union* (Jacksonville), Sunday, June 10, 1945, 13; "Naval Station Gets Nazi PWs," *Tampa Sunday Tribune*, June 10, 1945, 8B. Re: Captain Gresham, see first labor report from Kendall, June 30, 1944, signed by Captain G. R. Gresham, RG 389, Entry 461, Box 2492, NA.

108. Toohey report of November 23, 1945, visit, RG 59, Lot 58D7, Box 22, File: Blanding, NA.

109. Ibid.

110. J. L. Toohey, State Department, Report on Prisoner of War Branch Camp, Bell Haven Branch Camp, Miami, Fla., visited December 7, 1945, by Mr. Paul Schnyder, representing the International Red Cross Committee, and Mr. J. L. Toohey, of the Department of State, RG 59, Lot 58D7, Box 22, File: Blanding, NA.

111. Labor Reports from Melbourne, Fla., RG 389, Entry 461, Box 2492, NA.

112. Edouard Patte's report of visit to Prisoner of War Camp, Camp Blanding, Fla., and Branch Camps, October 14-23, 1945, RG 59, 711.62114 IR /12-1945, Box 3344, and RG 389, Entry 459A, Box 1609, NA.

113. J. L Toohey, State Department, Report on Prisoner of War Side Camp,

Naval Air Station, Melbourne, Fla., visited November 27, 1945, by Mr. Paul Schnyder, representing the International Red Cross Committee, and Mr. J. L. Toohey, of the Department of State, RG 59, 58D7, Box 22, File: Blanding, NA.

114. J. L Toohey, State Department, Report on Prisoner of War Side Camp, Banana River Naval Air Station, Fla., visited November 27, 1945, by Mr. Paul Schnyder, representing the International Red Cross Committee, and Mr. J. L. Toohey, of the Department of State, RG 59, 58D7, Box 22, File: Blanding, NA; report on the Banana River camp by a visitor from the War Prisoners' Aid of the World's Committee of the YMCA: Edouard Patte's Report of Visit to Prisoner of War Camp, Camp Blanding, Fla., and Branch Camps, October 14–23, 1945, RG 59, 711.62114 IR /12–1945, Box 3344, and RG 389, Entry 459A, Box 1609, NA. For the Germans' August arrival and work problems see USNAS Banana River, Fla., Prisoner of War Camp Labor Report, August 15, 1945, RG 389, Entry 461, Box 2492, NA.

115. Phone interview with Charles M. Blackard, Dallas, Texas, June 1, 1983; notes in possession of the author.

116. Compare Guy Métraux, IRC, English translation and French original of Report of Visit to Clewiston, Fla., on March 16, 1945, RG 59, 711.62114 IR/9–545, Box 3344, NA, with Edouard Patte, Report of Visit to Prisoner of War Camp, Camp Blanding, Fla., and Branch Camps, October 14–23, 1945, RG 59, 711.62114 IR/12–1945, Box 3344, NA. See also J. L Toohey, State Department, Report on Prisoner of War Side Camp, Naval Air Station, Green Cove Springs, Fla., visited November 23, 1945, by Mr. Paul Schnyder, representing the International Red Cross Committee, and Mr. J. L. Toohey of the Department of State, RG 59, 58D7, Box 22, File: Blanding, NA.

117. Toohey report on November 23, 1945, visit.

118. Telephone and personal interviews with David Forshay of Lake Placid, Florida, former American guard at Clewiston and Green Cove Springs camps, May 15, 29, 1978. For more details on the Clewiston camp, see chapter 5.

119. Toohey report of November 23, 1945, visit, RG 59, Lot 58D7, Box 22, File: Blanding, NA..

120. Ibid.

121. I am grateful to Dr. Brian R. Rucker of Pensacola Junior College, who pointed out the existence of the Whiting Field camp and supplied me with information on the camp in letters of August 18, September 1, 1994.

122. DeSpain, "German POWs at Whiting Field." This article was shared with the author by Dr. Brian Rucker, Pensacola Junior College.

123. *Santa Rosa Press Gazette* (Milton), July 1, 1993, special ed., sect. C, 14, 20. This publication was shared with the author by Dr. Brian Rucker, Pensacola Junior College.

124. Ibid., 19, 23.

125. Dr. Brian R. Rucker, Pensacola Junior College, to the author, August 18, 1994.

3. U-BOAT MEN AND OTHER NAVAL PRISONERS

1. Capt. Edward C. Shannahan's Record of Visit to Prisoner of War Camp, Camp Blanding, Fla., December 26–29, 1943, RG 389, Entry 461, Box 2656, MMB, NA. The POW camp at Camp Blanding, which had existed since September 1942, was not revealed to the public until mid-1943. Fred Grube, "German Prisoners at Blanding Like Our Jazz and Cornflakes," *Jacksonville Journal*, June 30, 1943, 1.

2. Gannon, *Operation Drumbeat*; Blair, *Hitler's U-Boat War*, vol. 1, *The Hunters, 1939–1942*.

3. For the story of the sinking of the U-352, see Hoyt, *U-Boats Offshore*, 120–24; also Moore, *Faustball Tunnel*, 35.

4. Moore, *Faustball Tunnel*, 67–68. See Lt. Col. Earl L. Edwards, Assistant Director, Prisoner of War Division, Army Service Forces, PMGO, Washington, D.C., to the Commanding General, Fourth Service Command, May 25, 1944, which notes: "The smaller of the two (2) prisoner of war compounds at Camp Blanding, Florida, has been designated for the internment of German Navy Anti-Nazi prisoners of war and the larger compound has been designated for the internment of German Army Nazi prisoners of war. This segregation is required by the terms of AGO letter dated 18 February 1943, file AG 383.6 (2-17-43) OB-S-B, subject: Segregation of Prisoners of War. Consequently, the German Anti-Nazi prisoner of war camp cannot be combined with any other installation"; in RG 389, Entry 457, Box 1419, File: Camp Blanding, Florida, Construction, NA.

5. Capt. Edward C. Shannahan's Record of Visit to Prisoner of War Camp, Camp Blanding, Fla., December 26–29, 1943, RG 389, Entry 461, Box 2656, MMB, NA.

6. Taped interview with Col. Harry A. Johnston, former executive officer, Camp Blanding, West Palm Beach, June 22, 1977; tape in possession of the author.

7. These men were part of Capt. Jürgen Wattenberg's crew. Wattenberg was a former navigation officer of the *Graf Spee*, the German pocket battleship that had been sunk by the British off Uruguay in 1939. Escaping through Argentina, Wattenberg returned to Germany and took command of the U-162. On September 4, 1942, while operating in the Caribbean, he and his crew were subjected to depth charges from three British vessels. After the sinking of their ship, the U-162 survivors were taken into custody by the British and confined at first at Port of Spain, Trinidad, before being transferred to American custody. They flew from Trinidad to Miami, then went by train from Miami to Washington, D.C. After a brief stay in Fort George Meade, Wattenberg, his officers, and his men were interrogated at Fort Hunt, in Alexandria, Virginia. Most of the crew of the U-162 were then sent to Crossville, Tennessee, and later Papago Park, located outside of Phoenix, Arizona. There, Wattenberg and several of his officers would make national headlines when, two days before Christmas 1944, they were among the twenty-five participants in the largest POW escape that occurred in the United States. For more details on Wattenberg, the men of the U-162, and their escape from Papago Park, see Moore, *Faustball Tunnel*.

8. War Department, Military Intelligence Service Washington: Two Memoranda for Colonel Bryan, November 13, 1942, RG 389, Entry 461, Box 2476, file: Blanding, NA. One lists the names of the three prisoners from the U-162 to be sent to Camp Blanding; the other lists the names of eleven fellow crew members to "be transferred to an internment camp at the earliest practicable date." This second memorandum also notes that "a separate memorandum has requested that three men from this crew be transferred to Camp Blanding, Florida."

9. When transferring the three U-162 crewmen to Blanding, Colonel Bryan, director of the Aliens Division of the PMGO, informed the commanding general of the Fourth Service Command: "It is requested that the strictest secrecy be maintained in all matters concerning these prisoners while in your custody, and the greatest possible care be exercised in preventing any communication between them and any unauthorized persons. It is further requested that all communications written by these prisoners while in your custody be forwarded to this office for censorship and information and that the provisions stated in the Regulations for Civilian Internees and Prisoners of War be complied with." Col. B. M. Bryan to Commanding General, Fourth Service Command, November 14, 1942, RG 389, Entry 461, Box 2476, File: Blanding, NA.

10. Roster of Prisoners of War for January 1943, January 31, 1943, Headquarters Internment Camp, Camp Blanding, Fla., signed by Capt. Lloyd H. Lewis, RG 389, Entry 434, Box 405, File 383.6, NA.

11. Several things can be inferred from the Camp Blanding's January 1943 detention roster besides the fact that three were from one submarine and were of interest to naval intelligence. The POW serial numbers of those on the list reveal that they were first registered as prisoners of war in three different American naval districts—areas of the North Atlantic off Newfoundland, off the Carolinas, and in the Caribbean. Furthermore, all of the prisoners were classified as Germans, all were from four U-boats sunk between July 7 and September 4, 1942, and all were naval prisoners. The clues come from the fact that naval prisoners had serial numbers like 1G-201Na. American naval district Number 1, the area where the prisoners were first processed, was the area off Newfoundland; G indicates German; 201 denotes the sequential number of the POW registered into American custody; and Na means naval prisoner. The serial numbers of the fourteen prisoners in the naval compound at Blanding in January 1943 had a tell-tale sequence: 1G-201Na, 1G-202Na, 1G-203Na; 5-1-Na, 5-7-Na; 10G-3Na, 10G-4Na, 10G-6Na, 10G-8Na, 10G-19Na, 10G-22Na; and 10G-1037Na, 10G-1046Na, and 10G-1048Na. From a POW roster at Blanding from September 1945 we see that 1G-202Na was from the U-210 sunk south of Cape Farvel, Newfoundland, on August 6, 1942. It is logical to conclude that 1G-201Na and 1G-203Na were 1G-202Na's shipmates on the U-210. Similarly, since historian John Hammond Moore writes about Capt. Horst Degen, whose ship was sunk off Cape Hatteras, North Carolina, on July 7, 1942, and the Blanding detention roster of January 1942 lists Captain Degen as 5-1-Na, it is safe to assume that 5-7-Na was a crew member. Also, since 10G-6Na appears on the

Blanding detention roster of September 1945 as from the U-94, sunk on August 27, 1942, southwest of Haiti, then probably 10G-3Na, 10G-4Na, 10G-8Na, and 10G-19Na were from the same boat. Finally, there were the three men from Wattenberg's U-162, with numbers 10G-1037, 1046, and 1048. See the September 1945 Blanding Naval Detention Roster, RG 389, Entry 461, Box 2574, NA. For more on Capt. Horst Degen of the U-701, see Moore, *Faustball Tunnel*, 35–36. For lists of German submarines, their captains, and times and places of sinkings, see appendix of Freyer, *Tod auf allen Meeren*.

    12. Moore, *Faustball Tunnel*, 35.

    13. Wall, "German Prisoners of War in Virginia," 208.

    14. Moore, *Faustball Tunnel*, 36.

    15. The U-595, operating out of Brest in Brittany, had entered the Mediterranean and sunk several enemy transports, but it had been bombed and immobilized by British aircraft. Ultimately running aground on shoals about seventy miles northeast of Oran, Algeria, the men set scuttling charges and escaped to shore. Shortly thereafter the entire crew was captured by an American tank and its accompanying GIs. They were driven to Oran for questioning and loaded on the USAT *Brazil* for transport to the United States. Then there was more questioning at Fort Hunt. Capt. Jürgen Quaet-Faslem and several of the officers of the U-595 would later join Captain Wattenberg and his U-162 people at Papago Park and in their great escape. Ibid., 8–11.

    16. Memorandum for Brig. Gen. B. M. Bryan, Jr., February 17, 1943, and Bryan to Commanding General, Third Service Command, Subject: Transfer of Prisoners of War, February 19, 1943, RG 389, Entry 461, Box 2476, NA.

    17. See War Department, Office of the Provost Marshal General, Washington, D.C., Detailed Official List of German POW at Camp Blanding Internment Camp, June 19, 1943, RG 59, 58D7, Box 22, File: Blanding, NA. Compare this list with the June 10, 1943, Transfer of German Navy Prisoners of War list sent to Commanding General, Third Service Command, RG 389, Entry 461, Box 2476, NA. In June 1943, twenty-two new naval prisoners from Fort Hunt were sent to Blanding. All but one of them were from the U-203 and U-569, sunk off Newfoundland on April 25 and May 22, 1943, respectively. Their captains, Hermann F. Kottmann and Hans Ferdinand Johannsen, like Wattenberg and Quaet-Faslem, were also later to figure prominently in the Papago Park escapes. See Office of the Provost Marshal General to the Commanding General, Third Service Command, Re: Transfer of German Navy Prisoners of War, June 10, 1943, Entry 461, Box 2476, NA. A check of the September 1945 Blanding lists of navy men suggests that a seaman with a POW serial number of 1G-250Na was from the U-Kottmann (U-203), sunk on April 25, 1943. Some of the men in the list of June 10, 1943, transferees from Hunt, have numbers close to that number, indicating their capture in the same district at or near the same time—probably from the same boat. However, several serial numbers in the 1G-280s range are identifiable as being from the U-569. For more on Captain Kottmann and Johannsen, see Moore, *Faustball Tunnel*. The one exception to the U-203 and U-569 crewmen was a sailor with the POW serial number of 7G-101Na. He was one of only two

survivors from a submarine sunk off Brazil on January 6, 1943, the U-164. This conclusion is drawn from the fact that the POW's name and serial number recur—and the story of his survival after the sinking of his U-boat off the coast of Brazil is recounted—in connection with the beating by other inmates of his fellow survivor and fellow internee at Camp Blanding. See Extract from Officer of the Day Log, Prisoner of War Camp, Camp Blanding, Fla., March 4, 1944, RG 389, Entry 461, Box 2476, NA. The beaten man was later listed as from the U-164 in a September 1945 Detention Roster for the Naval Camp at Camp Blanding. See RG 389, Entry 461, Box 2574, NA. For information on U-boat numbers, captains, sinkings, and whether there were survivors, see appendix of Freyer, *Tod auf allen Meeren.*

18. A. R. Tiedgen to Commanding General, Fourth Service Command, February 3, 1944, RG 389, Entry 461, Box 2476, NA.

19. Earl L. Edwards, Lieutenant Colonel, Assistant Director, Prisoner of War Division to the Commanding General, Fourth Service Command, February 17, 1944, ibid.

20. Extract from Officer of the Day Log, Prisoner of War Camp, Camp Blanding, Fla., March 4, 1944, ibid.

21. Ibid.

22. Ibid.

23. Maj. W. H. Lowman to Commanding General, Fourth Service Command, July 3, 1944, and a concurrent note from Maj. Henry R. Totten, Blanding Post Adjutant, to the Fourth Service Command, July 4, 1944, RG 389, Entry 461, Box 2476, NA.

24. Lt. Col. Earl L. Edwards, Assistant Director, Prisoner of War Division to Commanding General, Fourth Service Command, Atlanta, July 7, 1944, RG 389, Entry 461, Box 2476, NA.

25. Edwards to the Office of the Assistant Chief of Staff, G-2, July 27, 1944, ibid.

26. John E. Bakke, WOJG, to Provost Marshal General, August 24, 1944, ibid.

27. Lt. Col. Earl L. Edwards to Commanding General, Fourth Service Command, July 26, 1944, ibid.

28. See Moore, *Faustball Tunnel,* 108, for details of the transfer of five naval officers to Blanding from Papago Park because army intelligence considered them to be anti-Nazi.

29. January 13, 1945, Transfer, RG 389, Entry 461, Box 2476, NA.

30. Maj. Howard W. Smith, Jr., to Commanding General, Fourth Service Command, February 26, 1945, ibid.

31. Col. A. M. Tollefson to Commanding General, Fourth Service Command, March 3, 1945, ibid.

32. Lt. Col. Earl L. Edwards to Commanding General, Fourth Service Command, June 8, 1944, ibid. Regarding the segregation of non-Germans at a special facility at Camp Butner, North Carolina, see Gansberg, *Stalag: U.S.A.,* 18.

33. Moore, *Faustball Tunnel,* 108.

34. Ibid., 108–9.

35. Copy of letter to Provost Marshal General, February 13, 1945, with accompanying letter, Maj. W. H. Lowman to the Provost Marshal General, February 23, 1945, RG 389, Entry 461, Box 2476, NA.

36. Copy of POW's letter to PMGO, February 13, 1945, ibid.

37. Lowman letter to PMGO, 23 February 1945, ibid.

38. Memorandum for the Director, Prisoner of War Special Projects Division, Subject: Field Service Report on Visit to Prisoner of War Camp, Camp Blanding, Fla., February 11–12, 1945, by Capt. Robert L. Kunzig, April 4, 1945, RG 389, Entry 459A, Box 1609, NA.

39. Moore, *Faustball Tunnel*, 109.

40. Bruno Balzer, a two-time escapee, port unit, Palmi, Italy, captured September 1, 1943; Rolf Fitzner, merchant marine, captured August 3, 1943; Werner Hilkenmeier, harbor guard, captured August 10, 1944; Arthur Nackenhorst, merchant marine, captured May 8, 1943; Paul Rogalla, SS *Derinje*, captured September 17, 1944; Rolf Schmidt, harbor patrol, Cherbourg, captured June 28, 1944; Hermann Skof, harbor guard company, Cherbourg, captured June 14, 1944. List compiled by comparing names of escapees printed in Florida press during this period with detention roster for the naval compound at Camp Blanding, October 1945, RG 389, Entry 461, Box 2574, NA.

41. See official correspondence regarding transfers to Blanding in RG 389, Entry 461, Box 2476, NA.

42. See "Four Germans Flee Blanding," *Florida Times-Union* (Jacksonville), June 12, 1945, 11; "Fifth German Flees Blanding," ibid., June 14, 1945, 11; and "Blanding German Prisoner Escapes," ibid., October 10, 1945, 10. Bruno Balzer, Werner Hilkenmeier, Arthur Nackenhorst, and Rolf Schmidt were the four escapees reported first, Rolf Fitzner was the fifth, and Hermann Skof was the October escapee. For more details on these men, see note 40 above.

43. Bruno Balzer on requested transfer list, July 3, 1944, RG 389, Entry 461, Box 2476, NA; Balzer on October 1945 Camp Blanding, Fla., Misc. Navy E. M. Detention Roster, RG 389, Entry 461, Box 2574, NA.

44. Edouard Patte, YMCA, Report of Visit to Prisoner of War Camp, Camp Blanding, Fla., and Branch Camps, October 14–23, 1945, RG 389, Entry 459A, Box 1609, NA; also in RG 59, 711.6214 IR/12–1945, Box 3344, NA. Edouard Jean Patte was born in Ferney, France, in 1898. See copy of Patte's credentials provided by the Office of the Provost Marshal General, RG 389, Entry 451, Box 1224, File: 080: War Prisoners' Aid, YMCA Representatives, NA.

4. WHEN THE AFRIKA KORPS CAME TO BLANDING

1. Bryan to Requirements Division, January 9, 1943, RG 389, Entry 457, Box 1419, File: Camp Blanding, Fla., Construction, NA.

2. HQ EDC to CG SOS Attention PMGO, January 11, 1943, ibid.

3. W. A. Wood, Jr., Brigadier General, General Staff Corps, Director, Requirements Division, on behalf of Lieutenant General Somervell, to Provost Marshal General, Washington, D.C., and Chief of Engineers, Washington, D.C., ibid.

4. Jung, *Kriegsgefangenen*, 379.

5. Pluth, "Administration and Occupation," 123–24; Lerch, "Army Reports on Prisoners of War," 546. Regarding an Anglo-American agreement of November 1942 to take German prisoners to the United States, see Jung, *Kriegsgefangenen*, 7.

6. The Secretary of War ordered the establishment of an infantry replacement training center at Camp Blanding, the construction costs of which were to be reduced by the employment of prisoners of war. Brig. Gen. Ray E. Porter's memorandum for the Commanding General, Army Service Forces, Army Ground Forces, September 7, 1943. Specific authorization for the building of the Blanding POW camp came on October 6, 1943, RG 389, Entry 457, Box 1419, NA.

7. Capt. Jadie H. Brown's Memorandum of December 30, 1943, attached to Record of Visit to Camp, Prisoner of War Division, Provost Marshal General's Office, Prisoner of War Camp, Camp Blanding, Fla., December 26–29, 1943, Report filed by Capt. Edward C. Shannahan, RG 389, Entry 461, Box 2656, NA. The transfer of a total of 1,000 Germans from the two camps in Alabama came as a result of an airmail letter of November 2 from Maj. Earl L. Edwards, assistant director of the Prisoner of War Division, PMGO, to the commanding general of the Fourth Service Command in Atlanta. That letter confirmed a telephone conversation concerning the transfer of prisoners "to the new twelve hundred man compound at Prisoner of War Camp, Camp Blanding, Fla., which has been completed and designated for internment of German Army prisoners of war." Edwards to Commanding General, Fourth Service Command, November 2, 1943, RG 389, Entry 461, Box 2476, NA.

8. For the December 1, 1942, completion of the Aliceville camp and the June 1943 arrival of the first German POWs, see Walker, "German Creative Activities in Camp Aliceville," 21–22. For details on the camp, see Parker W. Buhrman, Department of State, Report of Visit to Prisoner of War Camp, Aliceville, Alabama, by V. Tobler, representing the Legation of Switzerland, November 26, 1943, RG 389, Entry 461, Box 2653, File: Aliceville, Ala., Inspection Reports, NA.

9. About 150,000 of them had fallen into Allied hands in mid-May 1943, captured by units of the First and Eighth British Armies, the American Second Corps, and the French Nineteenth Army Corps and so-called Free French units. Most had became prisoners of the British but were turned over to the Americans for the duration of the war. Of the 15,000 who were in French hands, about 5,000 were also turned over to the Americans. For the fall of the Afrika Korps and its arrival and influence on the American camps, see Jung, *Kriegsgefangenen*, 7–9.

10. Concerning the role of the Afrika Korps in presenting the American authorities with severe difficulties throughout the American camp system, see Krammer, *Nazi Prisoners*, chap. 5, "Wrestling for the Tiller."

11. Capt. Jadie H. Brown, memorandum of December 30, 1942, accompanying Capt. Edward C. Shannahan's record of visit to Prisoner of War, Camp Blanding, Fla., December 26, 1943, and his Report of Incidents Occurring at Camp Blanding, Fla., December 22–30, 1943, RG 389, Entry 461, B. 2656, NA.

12. Ibid.

13. Brown's memorandum mentions the speech by the commanding general, but he gives no name. The service of Brig. Gen. L. A. Kunzig as commander of the Blanding post between July 15, 1943, and January 1944 is the topic of the article "Colonel Smith Now in Command," *Bradford County Telegraph* (Starke, Fla.), January 7, 1944, 1.

14. Brown memorandum, RG 389, Entry 461, Box 2656, NA.

15. Shannahan's Report of Incidents Occurring at Camp Blanding, Fla., December 22–30, 1943, ibid.

16. Ibid.

17. Ibid.

18. Ibid.

19. This copy of Gosse's letter was enclosed by Maj. W. H. Lowman with this Request for Transfer of Prisoners of War memorandum, January 4, 1944, RG 389, Entry 461, Box 2476, NA.

20. Shannahan's Report of Incidents Occurring at Camp Blanding, Fla., December 22–30, 1943, RG 389, Entry 461, Box 2656, NA.

21. Ibid. For a proper spelling of Blanding's naval spokesman's name, as "Bargsten," see the State Department's English translation of the International Red Cross Committee's report of the visit to Camp Blanding on April 6–7, 1944, by their representative Marc Peter, RG 59, 711.62114 IR 10-6-44, NA. Information on Klaus Bargsten's U-521 and its sinking in the appendix of Freyer, *Tod auf allen Meeren*, 357. In his report of the conference, Shannahan misspelled the name as "Bargstrum."

22. Shannahan report, RG 389, Entry 461, Box 2656, NA.

23. Ibid.

24. Ibid.

25. Ibid. For a discussion of the October 1943 "No work, no eat" policy, see Krammer, *Nazi Prisoners*, 110–11.

26. Shannahan reported, "While in Atlanta on Monday 3 January 1944, this officer was informed by Lt. Col. Cockrell that the orders transferring the 39 agitators to Alva had been issued on 31 December 1943." Shannahan, Report of Incidents Occurring at Camp Blanding, Fla., December 22–30, 1943, RG 389, Entry 461, Box 2656, NA.

27. Lt. Col. Earl L. Edwards, Assistant Director, Prisoner of War Division to the Commanding General, Fourth Service Command, January 18, 1944, RG 389, Entry 461, Box 2476, NA. At the beginning of April some of the original sixty-five prisoners who had sought protective segregation were still at Blanding. The problems of December 1943, the resulting transfer of thirty-nine troublemakers to Alva and of thirty-seven of sixty-five protected prisoners to McCain, and the likelihood that "most if not all of these 65 men are expected to follow," was noted in a report by a visiting representative of the Department of State. See Charles C. Eberhardt's report of April 6–7, 1944, Visit to Prisoner of War Camp, Camp Blanding, in the company of a delegate from the International Red Cross and of the Swiss Legation, RG 389, Entry 461, Box 2656, NA.

28. Lowman's Request for Transfer of Prisoner of War, January 4, 1944, RG 389, Entry 461, Box 2476, NA.

29. Mixed medical commissions composed of American and Swiss doctors examined and certified Axis prisoners for such periodic exchanges during the war. Between November 1943 and April 1945 they examined a total of 7,941 German POWs in the United States. Of these, eventually 2,181 sick and wounded Germans, along with 102 medical corps men and doctors, were returned to Germany in a total of five exchanges. In return, 886 Americans, of whom 77 were medical corps personnel and doctors, were returned to the United States. Jung, *Kriegsgefangenen,* 244. See also Pluth, "Administration and Operation," 387n.3. This latter source provides a few more details and numbers but comes up with a total of only 1,166 POWs eligible for return. This seems to be an error picked up from the Provost Marshal General's Office, Historical Monograph, 241. Two different numbers appear to be given: "A total of 1,165 German prisoners of war found eligible for direct repatriation by Medical Commands of General Hospitals were sent back to Germany," and a table of numbers for each of the five exchanges, with the final total of German sick and wounded exchanged listed as 2,181.

30. The forms were for the information of the German Armed Forces Research Office for Violations of International Law. It was a legal research branch of the German Supreme Command set up in September 1939 to investigate war crimes perpetrated by enemy military or civilians against members of the German armed forces—and to investigate allegations from abroad regarding the German military. The reports of the four repatriated Germans were found by this author in August 1980 in the Bundesarchiv, Militärarchiv, Bestand: RW2/v. 109, Freiburg, Germany. They are in a file entitled "Oberkommando der Wehrmacht, Wehrmachtuntersuchungsstelle für Verletzungen des Völkerrechts, USA, Kriegsrechtsverstösse gegen Kriegsgefangenen in den Lagern. Lager: Blanding." Information on the German research branch that took the information can be found in Zayas, *Wehrmacht-Untersuchungsstelle.* For another short rendering of the details of these reports, see Billinger, "The Other Side Now."

31. The stories the four wounded men told the Wehrmacht covered the entire period of their captivity. Their odyssey began with capture by the British in Tunisia in May 1943, transfer to American custody in Oran, Algeria, and then transport by boat from Casablanca, Morocco, to Boston, Massachusetts. They traveled then by train to Aliceville, Alabama, and, in November 1944, to Camp Blanding in Florida. Repatriation to Germany in March 1944 came by way of Hallaron General Hospital, Staten Island, New York, and a boat trip to Europe. They sailed on the evening of February 15, 1944, on a Swedish ship, the SS *Gripsholm.* They were among a total of 132 "disabled German military personnel as prisoners of war ticketed from New York to Lisbon." See list of POW passengers attested to by a representative of the Department of State; the Protecting Power, the Swiss Government; the American Export Lines Surgeon in Charge; the American Export Lines Purser; and the General Operating Manager of the American Export Lines, February 15, 1944, enclosed in communication from James H. Kelley, Jr., Chief, Special War Problems Division, Department of State to Brig. Gen. B. M.

Bryan, Assistant Provost Marshal General, February 26, 1944, RG 389, Entry 451, Box 1217, File 014.33 #2, NA.

32. Quote from Report of Capt. Jadie H. Brown, December 30, 1943, with Shannahan, record of visit to Camp Blanding, RG 389, Entry 461, Box 2656, NA.

33. See materials in the Bundesarchiv, Militärarchiv, Bestand: RW2/v. 109.

34. Some Poles, Czechs, Belgians, and Luxembourgers were eventually screened for possible use against Germany. See Pluth, "Administration and Operation," 360–61.

35. See Koop, *Stark Decency*, 44, 46; Krammer, *Nazi Prisoners*, 247.

36. For instances of American military frustration with both anti-Nazi and Nazi elements, see Koop, *Stark Decency*, 30, and Krammer, *Nazi Prisoners*, 165.

37. Pluth, "Administration and Operation," 345.

38. The reeducation of the German POWs in Florida is the subject of chapter 8. The army's national efforts at reeducation are the subject of Gansberg, *Stalag: U.S.A.*, and, more recently, of Robin, *Barbed-Wire College*. But such efforts, both in the camps and later in the confused political atmosphere of occupied Germany, had minimal effects. See Krammer, *Nazi Prisoners*, 224–27, and Jung, *Kriegsgefangenen*, 237–38.

5. THE "WORST CAMP IN AMERICA"

1. Taped interview with Col. Harry Johnston, wartime executive officer at Camp Blanding, West Palm Beach, June 22, 1977; tape in possession of the author.

2. Regarding escape rates, see Krammer, *Nazi Prisoners*, 117. There was a rate of 0.0044 for federal prisoners versus 0.0036 for POWs. Regarding murders and suicides, Maj. Gen. Archer L. Lerch, the provost marshal general, claimed that there were not as many as in a city of comparable size. In fact, he stated that the rate was lower than that shown by insurance statistics for the German public in time of peace. See Lerch, "The Army Reports on Prisoners of War," 547. For similar statements regarding the low suicide rate, see Peter Edson, "Army Treats Prisoners Different Way Than Goebbels," *Palm Beach Post-Times*, September 24, 1944, 2.

3. "German Prisoners in Labor Camp at Liberty Point," *Clewiston News*, February 25, 1944, 1.

4. Original French and English translation of Guy Métraux, IRC, Report on Clewiston, Fla., visited March 16, 1945, RG 59, 711.62114 IR/9–545, Box 3344, NA.

5. Ibid. But others saw the "snake danger" somewhat differently. Interview with David Forshay, former Aliceville, Clewiston, and later Green Cove Springs American guard, May 29, 1978, Palm Beach Atlantic College, West Palm Beach, Florida; notes in possession of the author. According to this American former camp guard, the greatest danger at Clewiston was to the snakes. The Germans loved to capture and kill snakes and then skin them for making belts. They even requested permission to stand at the margins of

cane fields being burned over in preparation for harvesting so that they might spy and kill fleeing serpents. Gerhard Anklam of Berlin, former Clewiston internee, noted that he killed a snake, had ants eat away the flesh, and kept the skin as a prized souvenir (interviewed on tape by the author, Berlin, June 3, 1996, tape in possession of the author).

6. Guy Métraux, IRC, Report on Clewiston, Fla., visited March 16, 1945, RG 59, 711.62114 IR/9-545, Box 3344, NA.

7. Ibid.

8. "German Prisoners in Labor Camp at Liberty Point," *Clewiston News*, February 25, 1944, 1.

9. Forshay interview, May 29, 1978. The Clewiston camp was still listed as a branch camp of Aliceville, Alabama, on April 1, 1944, State List, monthly April 1944–July 10, 1945, Army Service Forces, Office of Commanding General, Prisoner of War Camps, by Location and Principal Type of Work, Research Room, MMB, NA.

10. Forshay interview, May 29, 1978.

11. "Facts Governing Prisoners of War Told by Speaker," *Clewiston News*, June 30, 1944, 1.

12. Milton Sosin, "Arrogant Nazis Still Laud Hitler," *Miami Daily News*, June 8, 1944, 1B.

13. See chapter 9, "Public Relations," in Pluth, "Administration and Operation," for details of the weaknesses and inadequacy of government public relations efforts and the inability to influence the press greatly. Nevertheless, a glance at the limited coverage regarding German POW camps in the local and national press during the war years indicates the extreme caution with which the press proceeded and—even more—the reluctance on the part of army administrators to make the press aware of what was going on in the camps.

14. See chapter 5, "Wrestling for the Tiller," in Krammer, *Nazi Prisoners.*

15. Forshay interview, May 29, 1978.

16. Eliot Kleinberg, *Palm Beach Post* staff writer, invested much effort in investigating the case. He obtained FBI records through the Freedom of Information Act and had colleagues interview a brother of suicide Karl Behrens, who still lives in the family's old home place near Bremen, Germany. Mr. Kleinberg, who has been helpful in sharing his own research with this author, wrote a comprehensive article on Karl Behrens's suicide, titled "Another Lost Soul on Enemy Soil," *Palm Beach Post*, December 28, 1994, D1, D6.

17. The Kleinberg article presents three versions: Karl Behrens's surviving brother in Germany noted their father's own depression and suicide; Roberta Avant, a former clerk at the U.S. Army Corps of Engineers office in Clewiston, wonders if the escapees at Clewiston were fleeing their fellow prisoners; and former Clewiston prisoner and escapee Gerhard Anklam says, "Capt. Dwight Field, a German-hater, demanded under the most adverse climatic conditions ever more productivity in the sugarcane fields." In a taped conversation with the author in Berlin on June 3, 1996, Anklam hinted at some sort of foul play—probably by the Americans. He said, "No one escapes just to

commit suicide. If someone wanted to kill themselves they only needed to run loudly toward the [prison camp] fence."

18. Kleinberg article.

19. Peter Edson, "Army Treats Prisoners Different Way Than Goebbels," *Palm Beach Post-Times*, September 24, 1944, 2.

20. See articles in *Palm Beach Post* of October 18, 19, 20, 1944, especially, "Clewiston Suffers Light Gale Damage," October 20, 1944, 2.

21. Telephone interview with David Forshay, May 15, 1978; notes in possession of the author.

22. "Sugar Cane Crop Being Harvested," *Palm Beach Post*, November 2, 1944, 2.

23. *Palm Beach Post*, December 13, 1944, 1.

24. Edward C. Shannahan, Memorandum for the Director, Prisoner of War Operations Division, Report of Visit to Prisoner of War Camp, Camp Blanding, Fla., et al. from December 27, 1944, to January 7, 1945, RG 389, Entry 459A, Box 1609; and Entry 461, Box 2656, NA.

25. "War Prisoner Hunted in Glades," *Miami Herald*, January 1, 1945, 2A.

26. "Fugitive POW Found Hanged," *Miami Herald*, January 2, 1945, 1.

27. This quotation and the following information are from the Federal Bureau of Investigation report, "Karl Behrens: Alien Enemy Control—G Escaped Prisoner of War," Miami, Florida, 2-9-45, received from the FBI through the Freedom of Information Act and shared with the author by Eliot Kleinberg of the *Palm Beach Post*. Names of the agents were blacked out in the FBI report provided by the bureau through the Freedom of Information Act. However, the author's earlier interview with former FBI agent and later Palm Beach circuit judge Hugh MacMillan, the writer of the report, allows him to fill in some of the names of those involved. Interview with Judge Hugh MacMillan, West Palm Beach, February 26, 1979; notes in the author's files.

28. FBI report.

29. The FBI official report is here supplemented by the author's interview with Judge MacMillan, West Palm Beach, February 26, 1979.

30. FBI report. The name of the captain at Blanding to whom the Behrens letter was sent is blanked out on the copy of the FBI report as it was received from the FBI through the Freedom of Information Act.

31. FBI report.

32. "Nazi War Prisoner Escapee Found Dead," *Palm Beach Post*, January 2, 1945, 1; "Fugitive POW Found Hanged," *Miami Herald*, January 2, 1945, 1.

33. Information received from Eliot Kleinberg of the *Palm Beach Post*, whose own source was the Camp Blanding Museum and Historical Associates, Inc., of Starke, Florida. James F. Bloodworth, assistant curator, Camp Blanding Museum and Historical Associates, Inc., to Elliott Kleinberg, November 11, 1992, with enclosed "Prisoner of War Cemetery" information, copies of which are in the possession of the author. This information was confirmed by copies of interment records for the seven POWs from Blanding who were reinterred at the Fort Benning Post Cemetery. The copies were sent

to the author on September 29, 1997, through the courtesy of Jim Grantham and Brenda Bowser, Mortuary Affairs Assistant, Cemetery Office, Fort Benning, Georgia.

34. Eliot Kleinberg, "Another Lost Soul on Enemy Soil," *Palm Beach Post,* December 28, 1994, 6D.

35. Ibid.

36. "German POW Hangs Self Near Liberty Point after Escape," *Clewiston News,* January 5, 1945, 1.

37. Letter from Gerhard Anklam to Eliot Kleinberg, Berlin, April 8, 1994, shared by Kleinberg with the author.

38. French original and English translation of Guy Métraux, "Clewiston, Florida," March 16, 1945, RG 59, State Department, File 711.62114 IR/9–545, Box 3344, NA, and Hans Bremer, "1250-Meilen durch Florida: Ein Erlebnis-Bericht," *Zeitspiegel* (Camp Blanding), April 1, 1945, 2–7.

39. Edward C. Shannahan, Memorandum for the Director, Prisoner of War Operations Division, Report of Visit to Prisoner of War Camp, Camp Blanding, Fla., et al. from December 27, 1944, to January 7, 1945, RG 389, Entry 459A, Box 1609, and Entry 461, Box 2656, NA. See also French original and English translation of Guy Métraux, "Clewiston, Florida," March 16, 1945, RG 59, 711.62114 IR/9–545, Box 3344, NA.

40. "Facts Governing Prisoners of War Told by Speaker," *Clewiston News,* June 30, 1944, 1.

41. Milton Sosin, "Arrogant Nazis Still Laud Hitler," *Miami Daily News,* June 8, 1944, 1B.

42. Forshay interview, May 29, 1978.

43. Eliot Kleinberg, "Another Lost Soul on Enemy Soil," *Palm Beach Post,* December 28, 1994, 6D.

44. RG 389, Entry 451, Box 1318, File 383.6: Nationalities, NA.

45. For information on Stüttgen and Anklam, see "German Prisoners Are Captured Near Fisheating Creek," *Clewiston News,* January 26, 1945, 1. Regarding Pernull, see "Nazi POW Freedom Doesn't Last Long," *Palm Beach Post,* January 28, 1945, 2, and "Escaped German PW Captured Saturday By Boys' Alertness," *Clewiston News,* February 2, 1945, 1.

46. "Prisoner of War Camp Here to Close Next Saturday," *Clewiston News,* August 31, 1945, 1; "P.O.W. Camp To Be Closed on September 6," *Glades County Democrat* (Moore Haven), August 31, 1945, 1; Clewiston, Florida, Labor Report filed by Capt. D. Field, September 8, 1945, RG 389, Entry 461, Box 2492, NA; J. L. Toohey, State Department, Report on the November 23, 1945, visit to Green Cove Springs in company of Paul Schnyder of the IRC, RG 59, Lot 58D7, Box 22, File: Blanding, NA, which mentions a September 8 startup date.

47. Allen G. Twiddy, wartime barge captain with the U.S. Corps of Engineers, Clewiston, interviewed by the author, Clewiston, May 25, 1978; notes in the possession of the author.

48. Ibid.; James Fountain, wartime civilian employee of the U.S. Corps of Engineers, Clewiston, interviewed by the author, Clewiston, May 25, 1978; notes in the possession of the author.

49. Telephone interview with Rev. Arlo M. Mueller, North Bergen, N.J., November 19, 1977; notes in possession of the author.

50. Interviews with David Forshay, by telephone on May 15, December 13, 1978, and in person in West Palm Beach on May 29, 1978; notes in possession of the author.

51. Interview with Gerhard Anklam, Berlin, June 3, 1996; tape in possession of the author.

52. Interview with Judge Hugh MacMillan, Palm Beach County Court House, West Palm Beach, February 26, 1979; notes in possession of the author.

6. ESCAPEES

1. Lerch, "Army Reports on Prisoners of War," 546. Jung, *Kriegsgefangenen*, 126, merely quotes Lerch and thus the erroneous percentage. Krammer, *Nazi Prisoners*, 117, presents the numbers and the correct percentage rate.

2. Chronological listing of Florida escape attempts reported in Florida newspapers by month of escape, camp fled, and last names of escapees:

May 1944	Dade City	Summerer and Weber
July 1944	Blanding	Klassen and Kunkel
	Winter Haven	Drews
August 1944	Telogia	Bach, Kruetner, Schulze, Weilgohs
September 1944	Kendall	Schenkel and Severitt
	Gordon Johnston	two unnamed prisoners reported
January 1945	Clewiston	Behrens
	Orlando	Dreschler
	Dade City	Fischer and Gabriel
	Clewiston	Anklam and Stüttgen
	Clewiston	Pernull
February 1945	Blanding	Balzer and Rogalla
	Dade City	Hanns
March 1945	MacDill	Klapper
June 1945	Blanding	Balzer, Hilkenmeier, Nachenhorst, Schmitt
	Blanding	Fitzner
July 1945	Orlando	Dreschler
September 1945	Daytona Beach	Jentsch
October 1945	Blanding	Skof
January 1946	Blanding	Dreschler

3. "German Prisoners Flee County Camp," *Palm Beach Post*, January 25, 1945, 1.

4. "Two Escaped Nazis Nabbed in Glades," *Palm Beach Post*, January 26, 1945, 16.

5. "German Prisoners Are Captured Near Fisheating Creek," *Clewiston News*, January 26, 1945, 1.

6. The author is particularly grateful to Eliot Kleinberg of the *Palm Beach Post*, who, while in pursuit of information for his story on the Karl Behrens suicide and following up on an earlier article by this author, successfully contacted Gerhard Anklam in Berlin. Kleinberg's sharing of Herr Anklam's address and Herr Anklam's friendly reception of the author's questions—by phone, mail, and in a tape-recorded personal interview—have provided the author with valuable insights as well as great personal pleasure.

7. This and the following information is from a letter received by the author from Gerhard Anklam, Berlin, November 7, 1994.

8. Regarding Anklam's good relationship with the Afrika Korps men at Clewiston, interview with Anklam, Berlin, June 3, 1996; tape in possession of the author.

9. Anklam's account checks with information on their capture in the *Tampa Morning Tribune*. See "Escaped Nazi War Prisoners Are Caught," January 26, 1945, 9.

10. In requesting the transfer of German naval prisoners to Camp Blanding in early 1943, a memorandum from the Office of the Provost Marshal General noted, "In accordance with a recent directive from the Secretary of War, these prisoners should not be handcuffed for any reason whatsoever." Office of the Provost Marshal General, Washington, to Commanding General, Third Service Command, Baltimore, Maryland, February 19, 1943, RG 389, Entry 461, Box 2476, NA.

11. Anklam claimed to the author that he never really intended to escape back to Germany—an unrealistic endeavor—but only wanted to escape and be captured so that he would be returned to the more congenial surroundings of Camp Blanding. Notes of telephone conversation between Anklam and the author, July 7, 1994. In an interview taped at his home in Berlin on June 3, 1996, he suggested that his escape attempt was his way of saying that he did not approve of the conditions and situation at the Clewiston camp. Tape of interview in possession of the author.

12. Anklam's written account of his odyssey, sent to the author from Berlin on November 7, 1994. Krammer, *Nazi Prisoners*, 142, notes that the army provided that prisoners could be disciplined for escape attempts by being placed in confinement for up to thirty days, fourteen of which might be on a restricted diet.

13. Anklam account.

14. See Detention Roster for Jacksonville, October 1945, RG 389, Entry 461, Box 2574, File 14: Blanding, NA.

15. *Orlando Morning Sentinel*, January 2, 1945, 7–8.

16. *Tampa Morning Tribune*, January 2, 1945, 1.

17. *Daily Democrat* (Tallahassee), January 2, 1945, 8.

18. *Orlando Morning Sentinel*, January 3, 1945, 2

19. *Tampa Morning Tribune*, January 4, 1945, 7.

20. *Tampa Morning Tribune*, January 6, 1945, 5.

21. *Tampa Sunday Tribune*, January 7, 1945, 1, 14.

22. Ibid.

23. Ibid.

24. *Tampa Morning Tribune,* January 8, 1945, 3.

25. Jung, *Kriegsgefangenen,* 126–27. Krammer, *Nazi Prisoners,* 142–46, notes the various disciplinary and judicial punishments available to the army, including a number of judicial punishments for stealing civilian property that ranged from six months of hard labor in a camp stockade for stealing clothes to several years of hard labor at the U.S. Disciplinary Barracks, Fort Leavenworth, Kansas, for stealing civilian automobiles. Article 50 of the Geneva Convention reads in part: "Escaped prisoners of war who are retaken before being able to rejoin their own army or to leave the territory occupied by the army which captured them shall be liable only to disciplinary punishment." While Article 51 does not discount the possibility of prisoners being "given over to the courts on account of crimes or offenses against persons or property committed in the course of that attempt," Article 52 adds that "Belligerents shall see that the competent authorities exercise the greatest leniency in deciding the question of whether an infraction committed by a prisoner of war should be punished by disciplinary or judicial measures." See Convention of July 27, 1929, Relative to the Treatment of Prisoners of War, printed in Bevans, *Treaties,* 2:949–50.

26. *Orlando Morning Sentinel,* July 11, 1945, 1.

27. *Orlando Morning Sentinel,* July 13, 1945, 1.

28. *Tampa Morning Tribune,* July 13, 1945, 1.

29. "Nazi POW Escapee Captured at Tampa," *Palm Beach Post,* July 13, 1945, 10.

30. *Florida Times-Union* (Jacksonville), January 8, 1946, 13.

31. "Carolina Deputy Captures German Prisoner," *Florida Times-Union,* January 18, 1946, 7.

32. In a letter from Frau Jung, Deutsche Dienstelle für die Benachrichtigung des nächsten Angehörigen von Gefallenen der ehemaligen deutschen Wehrmacht (WASt), Berlin, August 23, 1994, the author was informed that little information was available on Herr Dreschler. He returned to Chemnitz after his repatriation. German registration authorities then listed him as departing for Hof in 1962. No further address was available. Perhaps Dreschler had escaped again, this time from the German Democratic Republic to the Federal Republic. Communication from WASt in possession of the author. Regarding the fears of the POWs concerning forced repatriation to other Allies, see chapters 8 and 9. For information on the army's policy of repatriation of POWs to eight specific zones of residence in Europe, see Pluth, "Administration and Operation," 399–400, 410.

33. "Nazi Prisoners Are at Large," *Daily Democrat* (Tallahassee), February 18, 1945, 7; and "Four Germans Flee Blanding, FBI Reports," *Florida Times-Union,* June 12, 1945, sect. 2:11.

34. Entry on "Balzer, Bruno," in Detention Roster, PW Camp, Camp Blanding, Fla., Misc. Navy E. M. Division, (No date, but probably September or October 1945), RG 389, Entry 461, Box 2574, File 14: Blanding, NA.

35. Bruno Balzer's identification number was 5G-5000 NA. See Detention

Roster, PW Camp, Camp Blanding, Fla., Misc. Navy, RG 389, Box 2574. For an explanation of processing and identification numbers, see Pluth, "Administration and Operation," 82, or Krammer, *Nazi Prisoners*, 4.

36. PMGO to Fourth Service Command, May 10, 1944, RG 389, Entry 461, Box 2476, NA.

37. W. H. Lowman, Major, CMP, to Commanding General, Fourth Service Command, July 3, 1944, and appended concurrence by Maj. Henry R. Totten, Post Adjutant, Blanding, ibid.

38. Ibid.

39. John E. Bakke, WOJG, for the commanding officer POW Camp Blanding to Provost Marshal General, Washington, D.C., August 24, 1944, ibid.

40. *Bradford County Telegraph* (Starke), June 22, 1945, 1.

41. Balzer's fellow escapees in June 1945 were all non–U-boat men in a naval compound that started out containing only U-boat men. The escapees were Werner Hilkenmeier, harbor guard, captured August 10, 1944; Arthur Nackenhorst, merchant marine, captured May 8, 1943; and Rolf Schmidt, harbor patrol, Cherbourg, captured June 28, 1944. Rolf Fitzner, merchant marine, captured August 3, 1943, was a later June Blanding escapee. Information compiled by comparing names of escapees printed in Florida press during this period with detention roster for the naval compound at Camp Blanding, October 1945, RG 389, Entry 461, Box 2574, NA.

42. "German Prisoner Found in Hide-Out Near Alligator Creek; Treed by MPs," *Bradford County Telegraph* (Starke), June 22, 1945, 1.

43. "Four Germans Flee Blanding, FBI Reports," *Florida Times-Union* (Jacksonville), June 12, 1945, 11; "Four German PW's Escape from Camp Blanding," *Tampa Morning Tribune*, June 12, 1945, 1; "Flordian Captures 3 Nazi Prisoners," *Miami Herald*, June 13, 1945, 9; "German POWs Are Retaken," *Daily Democrat* (Tallahassee), June 15, 1945, 3.

44. "Fifth German Flees Blanding; Two at Liberty," *Florida Times-Union*, June 14, 1945, 11.

45. *Tampa Morning Tribune*, March 16, 1946, 5.

46. All of this was good detail, based on POW information available at the time at the MacDill Field camp. An October 1945 detention roster from the Drew Field camp lists Johann Klapper, serial number 31G-51859—meaning a German prisoner captured and processed in Europe—as born on November 14, 1896, a private of the 709th Infantry Division, and captured June 26, 1944. See Detention Roster, PW Camp, Drew Field, Fla., of Camp Blanding, Code 14, October 27, 1945, in RG 389, Entry 461, Box 2574, NA.

47. *Tampa Morning Tribune*, June 19, 1946, 7.

48. Ibid.

49. "German POW Taken from Long Hideout," *Florida Times-Union* (Jacksonville), June 19, 1946, 6.

50. "German Escapes from Prison Camp Here; Is Sought by the FBI," *Winter Haven Daily Chief*, July 10, 1944, 3.

51. This further FBI description of Franz Drews was given in "War Prisoner Escapes," *Daily Democrat* (Tallahassee), July 10, 1944, 8.

52. "Franz Drews, German POW, Recaptured at Florence Villa," *Winter Haven Daily Chief*, July 14, 1944, 1.

53. "War Prisoners Flee, Are Quickly Caught," *Florida Times-Union* (Jacksonville), May 28, 1944, 21, refers to the Summerer and Weber escape attempt. "2 More German Prisoners Flee Near Dade City: May Head for Tampa as FBI Seeks 3rd Here," *Tampa Morning Tribune*, June 5, 1945, 1, refers to the Gabriel and Fischer escape as well as to the search for Fritz Dreschler. Summerer and Weber were recaptured within five miles of the camp after a mere two and a half hours of freedom. The bid for freedom by Gabriel and Fischer lasted two days before they were discovered in a sealed boxcar in a railroad yard in Jacksonville. "All Three Nazi War Prisoners Are Recaptured: 1 Caught Near Tampa; 2 at Jacksonville," *Tampa Sunday Tribune*, January 7, 1945, 1.

54. "Another Nazi Prisoner Loose from Dade City," *Tampa Sunday Tribune*, February 25, 1945, 2.

55. "War Prisoner Recaptured at Lakeland," *Tampa Morning Tribune*, March 10, 1945, 2.

56. "Fleeing German War Prisoners Being Sought: One Nazi Is Refugee from Daytona Beach; 2 Others Escape in Georgia," *Florida Times-Union*, September 25, 1945, 13.

57. "Nazi Prisoner Escapes Here," *Daytona Beach Evening News*, September 24, 1945, 1.

58. "Escaped POW Is Recaptured," *Daytona Beach Evening News*, October 2, 1945, 1.

59. Bruno Balzer's name is found on a list of ten navy prisoners who were described as "ostracized by fellow prisoners of war because of their political opinions and differences." Maj. W. H. Lowman, POW Camp Blanding to Commanding General, ASF, Fourth Service Command, July 3, 1944, RG 389, Entry 461, Box 2476, NA.

60. See note 40, chapter 3.

61. "Another Nazi Prisoner Loose from Dade City," *Tampa Sunday Tribune*, February 25, 1945, 2.

62. "Franz Drews, German POW, Recaptured at Florence Villa," *Winter Haven Daily Chief*, July 14, 1944, 1.

63. Telephone conversation between Gerhard Anklam and the author, July 7, 1994. Anklam claimed that he was sent to Clewiston because of his back talk to a civilian supervisor while on a work detail at Camp Blanding. He found the work demands in the sugarcane field near Clewiston too high and decided that an escape attempt would get him not freedom and a return to Germany—unrealistic because of the great distances involved—but reassignment back to Camp Blanding as "punishment." In a recorded interview with the author in Berlin on June 3, 1996, however, Anklam stressed more his protest of the system and did not mention a plan to provoke reassignment to Blanding.

64. "Enemy Prisoners of War under Sentences of Courts-Martial (through August 31, 1945)," PMGO, Prisoner of War Operations, tab. 115, 2d reel. This list contains the details of the names, crimes, and punishments of those

charged with murder and offenses other than murder in general courts-martial and also those tried for lesser offenses by special courts-martial. The only two Florida prisoners listed were Hans Krings, 4WG-4944 and Walter Schultz, 81G-84219, both of POW Camp Gordon Johnston. They were charged with assaulting a fellow POW on December 12, 1944, and with refusal to obey the command of a superior officer on January 31, 1945. They were tried by general courts-martial on March 13, 1945, at Camp Gordon Johnston, and sentenced to hard labor at the Disciplinary Barracks at Fort Leavenworth, Kansas. Krings was sentenced to eight years hard labor and forfeiture of all pay and allowances for that period, Schultz to seven years of hard labor.

65. Krammer, *Nazi Prisoners*, 115–16, explains the official German policy, which the U.S. Army communicated to the Wehrmacht members.

66. For national numbers, see Allan Kent Powell, *Splinters of a Nation*, 147.

67. "In speaking of their services here, the Army guardsmen were inclined to be rather ironical and caustic, and most of them expressed complete satisfaction if they never saw the muck lands of Florida again." Quoted from "Prison Camp Is Vacated by Army and Internees," *Belle Glade Herald*, December 14, 1945, 1.

7. MACDILL MENUS AND BELLE GLADE BEANS

1. Prisoners of War Convention Signed at Geneva July 27, 1929, in Bevans, *Treaties*, 2:938, 940.

2. Edward J. Pluth notes that the War Department's public information policy prior to 1943 consisted of an October 20, 1942, request to editors and broadcasters not to publish anything about the "arrival, movement, or confinement" of POWs except on authority of the provost marshal general. The policy, Pluth believes, was based on adherence to the Geneva Convention's insistence on protecting prisoners from "insults and public curiosity." After April 1944 standards were loosened somewhat, with public relations officers at POW camps allowed to issue press releases concerning escapes, work, and prisoner casualties. They still needed prior approval from the Bureau of Public Relations for information on suicides, riots, or fights. Pluth concludes that the lack of active and positive explanations of the POW program and the nature of the Geneva Convention on the part of the Bureau of Public Relations was responsible for increasingly negative public responses to the program in 1944 and 1945. Pluth, "Administration and Operation," 238–39, 242, 251. When charges of coddling German prisoners in American custody were raised, the army claimed, and the U.S. House Committee on Military Affairs in two investigations confirmed, that Axis prisoners were "treated well but not pampered" and that the Germans were treating American prisoners in their hands in the same manner. Emphasis was always placed on the fact that the provisions of the Geneva Convention were "being carried out to the letter by the U.S. and that in general the German government was doing the same." Quotation from AP article reporting on the first House Military Affairs investigation: "Nazis Treating Prisoners OK," *Palm Beach Post*, De-

cember 1, 1944, 2. In testimony by army officials, printed in the June 1945 report of the House Committee on Military Affairs, the emphasis was placed first on the Geneva Convention as a treaty ratified by the Senate and, thus, the law of the land. However, it was asserted that the Geneva Convention had been and continued to be the means by which Americans in German hands had also been protected. Any abrogation of the convention would endanger American prisoners overseas. See Committee on Military Affairs report on Prisoners of War, June 12, 1945, Union Calendar No. 207, Report 728, Tab 123 of PMGO, "Prisoner of War Operations."

3. Pluth, "Administration and Operation," 252.

4. Krammer notes the letter to the *New York Times* and arrives at this conclusion in *Nazi Prisoners*, 77.

5. Pluth, "Administration and Operation," 259.

6. Ibid., 260.

7. *Palm Beach Post-Times*, September 24, 1944, 2.

8. Ibid.

9. Ibid.

10. "Life of German Prisoner Not Easy, But He's Treated Well," *Palm Beach Post-Times*, October 8, 1944, 20.

11. This explanation, which emerged in later army responses to criticisms of POW menus, was also the one presented to the author by Col. Harry A. Johnston, former executive officer, at Camp Blanding, in an interview in West Palm Beach, June 22, 1977; notes are in the possession of the author.

12. Pluth, "Administration and Operation," 267–68.

13. Ibid., 267.

14. Pluth mentions the influence of these members of the House of Representatives, citing particularly the role of Congressman Harless. Ibid., 267–78.

15. *Tampa Sunday Tribune*, January 7, 1945, 1.

16. *Tampa Morning Tribune*, January 10, 1945, 6.

17. "As Tribune Readers See It," *Tampa Morning Tribune*, January 11, 1945, 8.

18. *Tampa Morning Tribune*, January 13, 1945, 1.

19. Ibid., January 16, 1945, 4.

20. "As Tribune Readers See It," *Tampa Morning Tribune*, January 16, 1945, 4.

21. Ibid., January 17, 1945, 8.

22. Editorial, "German Reciprocity," and "As Tribune Readers See It," *Tampa Morning Tribune*, January 17, 1945, 8; editorial, "Golden Rule," and "As Tribune Readers See It," *Tampa Morning Tribune*, January 18, 1945, 6.

23. *Tampa Morning Tribune*, January 30, 1945, 1.

24. Ibid., February 2, 1945, 8.

25. See Pluth, "Organization and Administration," 268–270.

26. "Army Bans Frills for Prisoners: Tribune Story on Menu Brought It, Says Peterson," *Tampa Morning Tribune*, February 17, 1945, 1.

27. Editorial, "No More Fancy Food," *Tampa Sunday Tribune*, February 18, 1945, 14.

28. *Bradford County Telegraph*, February 16, 1945, 2.

29. Ibid., March 9, 1945, 1.

30. *Tampa Morning Tribune*, March 14, 1945, 1.

31. Parenthetically, it is important to note Pluth's comments in "Administration and Operation," 279–80: "The anti-coddling campaign conducted by columnists and commentators Drew Pearson and Walter Winchell had much to do with stirring up public opinion. Pearson, whose syndicated column, 'Washington Merry-Go-Round,' was carried by some 350 papers, welcomed the opportunity to report sensational news. He was the bane of both political and military agencies in Washington."

32. *Tampa Morning Tribune*, March 14, 1945, 1.

33. Ibid., March 29, 1945, 1.

34. "First Photo of Slain Internees," *Tampa Morning Tribune*, April 10, 1945, 4.

35. "U.S. Accuses Germany of Cruelty to Prisoners," *Palm Beach Post*, April 13, 1945, 12.

36. Ibid.

37. Examples of reports in Florida newspapers of earlier POW strikes: "German Prisoners Strike in Colorado," *Florida Times-Union* (Jacksonville), April 1, 1944, 7, regarding a Trinidad, Colorado, strike; "Army Punished Nazi Prison Mutineers," *Florida Times-Union*, July 7, 1944, 16, regarding a Utica, New York, strike; "280 German Prisoners on Bread Diet," *Winter Haven Daily Chief*, January 19, 1945, 1, regarding a Camp Reynolds, Pennsylvania, strike; and "Nazi Prisoners on Bread Diet," *Winter Haven Daily Chief*, March 2, 1945, 1, regarding strike at Camp Perry, Ohio.

38. "Mounts Calls Farmers Meeting to Discuss Spring Labor Needs," *Belle Glade Herald*, January 19, 1945, 1; "Relief from Labor Shortage Seen in Proposed Activities," ibid., January 26, 1945, 1, 6; "Army Authorities to Inspect Sites for War Prisoner Camp," ibid., February 2, 1945, 1; "Farmers' Advisory Committee Makes Labor Suggestions," ibid., March 16, 1945, 1.

39. "German POW Will Do Glades Canning," *Palm Beach Post*, March 30, 1945, 1. Herman Finke, a former POW at Belle Glade, recalled being sent to Leesburg from Blanding on November 2, 1945, and then from Leesburg to Belle Glade on March 19, 1945. Telephone interview with Herman Finke on July 6, 1994; notes in possession of the author.

40. Telephone interview with Charles M. Blackard of Dallas, Texas, on June 1, 1983; notes in the possession of the author.

41. The information on Finke is from telephone conversations with the author on January 28, February 26, and July 22, 1994, notes of which are in the author's files, and from a recorded interview with the author in New York on June 23, 1997. During the 1997 interview, Herr Finke also presented the author with both his own written chronology of events and his military *Soldbuch* (pay book and identification pass), the notations of which confirmed the details given in the interview.

42. Telephone interview with Herman Finke, February 26, 1994; notes in the possession of the author. Further details in tape-recorded interview with Herman Finke, June 23, 1997.

43. Telephone interview with Herman Finke, January 28, 1994; notes in possession of the author. Details repeated in taped interview of June 23, 1997.

44. Finke asserts that the strike was inspired by the American guards. Author's notes of telephone conversation with Herman Finke, January 28, 1994. In a tape-recorded interview with the author on June 23, 1997, Finke repeated that the Germans were unfairly blamed for the strike, which he said was really instigated by their guards. The local Belle Glade paper said, "Because of no tailor made cigarettes, and maybe no beer, 240 war prisoners refused to work in the canning plant Wednesday." But it also noted that the Germans were only part of an already difficult local labor problem: "All is not well on the farmer's front, leastwise not in the Glades due to the overpaid negro indifference and the German war prisoners arrogance and sabotage." See "German P.W.s Strike for Tailor Mades; Negroes Leave $16 Jobs," *Belle Glade Herald*, April 6, 1945, 1.

45. Both a former guard at Belle Glade and two former workers at the Belle Glade Experiment Station mentioned that the prisoners were made to stand out in the stockade when they refused to work. Notes of telephone conversation between the author and an American former Belle Glade guard, Charles M. Blackard, of Dallas, Texas, on June 1, 1983, and author's notes of interview with former wartime Belle Glade Agricultural Experiment Station workers William Scheffler and Maceo Golson, June 2, 1977. Notes in the files of the author.

46. For the AP report of the strike, see "250 Germans in Florida Strike for Cigarettes," *Tampa Morning Tribune*, April 12, 1945, 1, and the same AP story in the *Winter Haven Daily Chief*, April 12, 1945, 2, 4.

47. Prisoner of War Camp Labor Report, Belle Glade, Fla., April 15, 1945, signed by Lt. Horace C. Smith, Jr., RG 389, Entry 461, Box 2492, NA.

48. Farmers' delays were reported in the local paper: "German P.W.s Strike for Tailor Mades," *Belle Glade Herald*, April 6, 1945, 1.

49. Prisoner of War Camp Labor Report, Belle Glade, Fla., April 15, 1945, signed by Lt. Horace C. Smith, Jr., RG 389, Entry 461, Box 2492, NA.

50. "Nazi Prisoners 'as Fat as Hogs' Are Reported at Arizona Camps," *New York Times*, April 23, 1945, 3. See also Pluth, "Administration and Operation," 282–83.

51. "U.S. Vows to Punish Nazis for Cruelty to Prisoners," *Florida Times-Union* (Jacksonville), April 15, 1945, 1.

52. Pluth, "Administration and Operation," 279.

53. Drew Pearson, "Merry-Go-Round," *Tampa Sunday Tribune*, April 15, 1945, 17.

54. *Tampa Morning Tribune*, Tuesday, April 24, 1945, 1.

55. For a survey of the criticisms and the work of the House Military Affairs Committee in April through June 1945 see Pluth, "Administration and Operation," 281–87.

56. Pluth, "Administration and Operation," 289. See Lerch, "The Army Reports on Prisoners of War," 536–47.

57. Pluth, "Administration and Operation," 287–88. See also "U.S. Forbids Fascist Salute by Prisoners," *Florida Times-Union* (Jacksonville), April 29, 1945, 17; and "Army Insists Prisoners See Horror Films," *Tampa Morning Tribune*, May 12, 1945, 10.

58. Pluth, "Administration and Operation," 283–84.

59. Ibid., 285.

60. Transcript, "Questioning of Brigadier General Blackshear M. Bryan by Congressman Robert Sikes," Hearing of the Special Committee of the House Committee on Military Affairs Regarding POW Treatment, April 30, 1945, in RG 59, files 740.00114 EW/4-145 through 740.00114 EW/7-3145, Box 3623, NA.

61. Pluth, "Administration and Operation," 285. The Report of the House Committee on Military Affairs on Prisoners of War as submitted on June 12, 1945, Union Calendar No. 207, Report No. 728, is in the second reel of the four-reel microfilm of PMGO, Prisoner of War Division, "Prisoner of War Operations."

62. See Pate testimony in the June 12, 1945, House Committee on Military Affairs Report, noted in note 61. See also Pluth, "Administration and Operation," 286.

63. Maurice Pate, director, Prisoners of War Relief, American Red Cross, "Prepared Statement on Relief Supplies for American Prisoners of War in Europe," page 15 of report from the Committee on Military Affairs, "Investigation of the National War Effort: Prisoners of War," June 12, 1945, House of Representatives Union Calendar No. 207, Report No. 728, in "Prisoner of War Operations," 2d reel.

64. The quotations here and in the following paragraphs are from "Concluding Comments" of the House Committee on Military Affairs report of June 12, 1945, 18–19, ibid.

65. Pluth, "Administration and Operation," 292. In an AP story from Washington dated May 11 and printed in the *Tampa Morning Tribune,* it was noted that "German PWs will find no more beer, cigarettes, candy, and other similar items in PW canteens after existing stocks are exhausted." See "Army Insists Prisoners See Horror Films," *Tampa Morning Tribune,* May 12, 1945, 10. See also Jung, *Kriegsgefangenen,* 48–71, and Krammer, *Nazi Prisoners,* 240–4. Telephone interview with Herman Finke, January 28, 1994. In fairness, it must be noted that between June and August 1945 the American civilian public suffered from a major cut in food supplies as well. See "Food Supplies Lowest Since Start of War: Eggs Added to List of Scarce Items," *Tampa Sunday Tribune,* June 10, 1945, 1. The AP story noted, "For Americans, the next two months may be the period of greatest stringency. Some improvement in meat supplies is expected to show up early in August."

66. Press: "More Food Sought for Nazi Prisoners in Kentucky," *Tampa Sunday Tribune,* June 17, 1945, 4. The report noted that the assistant secretary of the Kentucky Farm Bureau Federation said he telegraphed the state senators and congressmen in Washington to ask that POWs doing farmwork be given more and better food so that they could be kept working all day. In

obvious public reply, the War Department responded that its policy gave "sufficient nourishment to insure health and maximum working efficiency": 2,500 calories a day for sedentary POWs, 3,000 for moderate work, and 3,700 for heavier work. This was compared with the standard ration for American troops overseas of 3,900 calories a day but 4,150 if in combat. See "Army Says War Prisoners Get Enough Food," *Tampa Morning Tribune*, June 20, 1945, 2. For continuing complaints of POW food shortages on the national level, see "Reports Nazis Lose Weight as Food Is Cut," *Tampa Morning Tribune*, July 3, 1945, 1. The AP story from Hays, Kansas, said that the superintendent of the Fort Hays agricultural experiment station wrote to his congressman that the Germans locally were losing ten to twelve pounds and could no longer do a day's work because of the sharply reduced food allotments after the disclosure of atrocities in Germany. He protested that it was unfair to those who hired their labor. Herman Finke telephone interview with author, January 28, 1994. See also comments of a Blanding prisoner and others in Jung, *Kriegsgefangenen*, 61. For impressions from IRC reports of Florida camps and elsewhere, also see Jung, *Kriegsgefangenen*, 57.

67. See Powell, *Splinters of a Nation*, 85–86. See also one of the sources that he cites, PMGO, "Prisoner of War Operations," 1:77–78.

68. See Jung, *Kriegsgefangenen*, especially 51, and the report of one former POW in Arkansas who noted the loss of weight among some prisoners was up to twenty kilograms, about forty-four pounds.

8. ON THE THRESHOLD

1. "Nazi Prisoners 'as Fat as Hogs' Are Reported at Arizona Camps," *New York Times*, April 23, 1945, 3.

2. Krammer, *Nazi Prisoners*, 190–191.

3. For details on the development and practice of the reeducation program, see especially the chapters devoted to the topic in Jung, *Kriegsgefangenen*; Gansberg, *Stalag: U.S.A.*; Krammer, *Nazi Prisoners*; and Robin, *Barbed-Wire College*. Gansberg, 116, says the public learned about the reorientation program on May 28, 1945. Jung (217) says it was only decided to make the public aware of the program on June 2, 1945. For an example of public dissemination of information on reeducation, see "Army Gives German POWs Large Doses of Nazi Purging News and Literature," *Palm Beach Post*, July 13, 1945, 7.

4. Letter of Maj. Gen. Allen W. Gullion to Chief of Staff, Army Service Forces, "Orientation of Enemy Prisoners," June 23, 1943, quoted in Robin, *Barbed-Wire College*, 22.

5. A discussion of the PMGO's reluctance to undertake a reorientation program and the delays occasioned by the massive new POW arrivals can be found in Jung, *Kriegsgefangenen*, 210–11.

6. Krammer, *Nazi Prisoners*, 195.

7. Ibid. See also Article 17 of Convention of July 27, 1929, Relative to the Treatment of Prisoners of War, in Bevans, *Treaties*, 2:942.

8. Jung, *Kriegsgefangenen*, 213; Gansberg, *Stalag: U.S.A.*, 63; Krammer, *Nazi Prisoners*, 196.

9. Jung, *Kriegsgefangenen*, 213.

10. Krammer, *Nazi Prisoners*, 197, quoting from PMGO, "A Brief History," 545. Robin's thesis is that "no plan for reeducation would have made any meaningful difference" (*Barbed-Wire College*, 9).

11. Floridians, like others of the American public, would learn about *Der Ruf* in June. See "Der Ruf Interprets U.S. to German POWs," *Daily Democrat* (Tallahassee), June 20, 1945, 3.

12. Gansberg, *Stalag: U.S.A.*, 89–119.

13. Fred Grube, "German Prisoners at Blanding Like Our Jazz and Cornflakes," *Jacksonville Journal*, June 30, 1943, 1, 3.

14. Ibid.

15. Gansberg, *Stalag: U.S.A.*, 105.

16. *Jacksonville Journal* article of June 30, 1943.

17. See Fred Grube, "Nazi Officers Maintain Discipline at Blanding Prisoner of War Camp," *Jacksonville Journal*, July 1, 1943, 1, 2; Fred Grube, "Captured Germans at Blanding Indulge in Favorite Hobbies," *Jacksonville Journal*, July 2, 1943, 1, 3; and Fred Grube, "German Prisoners' Clubs Stage Saturday 'Shindigs' at Blanding," *Jacksonville Journal*, July 3, 1943, 1, 2.

18. Record of Visit to Camp, Camp Blanding, Fla., December 26–29, 1943, by Capt. Edward C. Shannahan, RG 389, Entry 461, Box 2656, NA.

19. Ibid.

20. C.C. Eberhardt, State Department, Report of Visit of April 6–7, 1944, to Prisoner of War Camp, Camp Blanding, by Dr. Marc Peter, Delegate of the International Red Cross Committee, Dr. Edward A. Feer of the Swiss Legation, and Charles C. Eberhardt of the Special Division, Department of State. RG 389, Entry 461, Box 2656, NA.

21. Marc Peter, Report of International Red Cross Representative Visit to Camp Blanding on April 6–7, 1944, RG 59, Department of State Decimal File 1940–44, 711.62114IR 10-6-44, NA; copy also in RG 389, Entry 461, Box 2656, NA.

22. Ibid.

23. Ibid.

24. Ibid.

25. Krammer, *Nazi Prisoners*, 196–97; Robin, *Barbed-Wire College*, 176–77.

26. Maj. Paul A. Neuland, Memorandum for the Director, Prisoner of War Special Projects Division, re: Field Service Report on Visit to Prisoner of War Camp, Camp Blanding, Fla., February 11–12, 1945, by Capt. Robert L. Kunzig, RG 389, Entry 459A, Box 1609, NA.

27. Ibid.

28. Ibid.

29. Ibid.

30. Visit to Prisoner of War Camp, Leesburg, Fla., February 13, 1945, ibid. Capt. Benjamin Painter's first name is not indicated in the Kunzig report, but it is noted in Edouard Patte's report of his visit to the Leesburg camp on behalf of the YMCA on February 23, 1945, ibid.

31. Visit to Prisoner of War Camp, Orlando, Fla., February 13, 1945, ibid. The full name of Capt. E. D. Smith, Jr., is not given by Kunzig, but is found in labor reports from Orlando, RG 389, Entry 461, Box 2492, NA.

32. Ibid.

33. Visit to Prisoner of War Camp, Drew Field, Fla., February 14, 1945, ibid. Capt. L. A. Drewery's first name is not indicated in the Kunzig report, but it is noted in Edouard Patte's report of his visit to the Drew Field camp on behalf of the YMCA on February 20, 1945, ibid.

34. Visit to Prisoner of War Camp, Dade City, Fla., February 14, 1945, ibid. Kunzig does not give Lt. John B. Pike's full name. It is found in the report of the November 29, 1945, visit to the camp made by J. L. Toohey of the State Department, RG 59, Lot 58D7, Box 22, File: Blanding, NA.

35. Ibid.

36. Visit to Prisoner of War Camp, South Miami, Fla., February 15, 1945, ibid.

37. The first issue of *Der Ruf* (The call) appeared in camp canteens on March 6, 1945, priced at five cents. See Krammer, *Nazi Prisoners*, 202.

38. They may have been more important as boredom relievers and as souvenirs of America than tools of reeducation. Regarding the New World Series, see Gansberg, *Stalag: U.S.A.*, 78–79; and Robin, *Barbed-Wire College*, 96–106; Robin denigrates the idea that the books had any real reeducation impact.

39. Edouard Patte, Report of Visit to Prisoner of War Camp Blanding, Fla., February 26, 1945. RG 389, Entry 459A, Box 1609, NA. The camp newspaper that he was referring to was the *Zeitspiegel*, which began publication in February 1945. See the list of German POW camp newspapers published as an appendix to Böhme, *Geist und Kultur*, 276.

40. Edouard Patte, Report of Visit to Prisoner of War Camp Drew Field, February 20, 1945; MacDill Field, February 23, 1945; Venice, February (n.d.), 1945; and Homestead, February 24, 1945, RG 389, Entry 459A, Box 1609, NA.

41. Edouard Patte, Report of Visit to Prisoner of War Camp Gordon Johnston, March 1, 1945; Telogia, March 1, 1945; Dale Mabry, March 2, 1945; and Eglin Field, March 3, 1945, RG 389, Entry 459A, Box 1649, NA. Patte does not give the full names of either 2d Lt. William B. Neil or Lt. C. C. Guetschaw. Neil's name is found March 2, 1945, in a report on the progress of the Intellectual Diversion Program, ibid.; and Guetschaw's name appears later in a labor report from Marianna, RG 389, Entry 461, Box 2492, NA.

42. 2d Lt. William B. Neil to Commanding General, Fourth Service Command, March 2, 1945, RG 389, Entry 459A, Box 1649, NA.

43. Maj. Paul A. Neuland, Memorandum for Director, Prisoner of War Special Projects Division, March 21, 1945, Field Service Report on Visit to Prisoner of War Camp, Camp Gordon Johnston, Fla., March 7–8, 1945, by Capt. Walter H. Rapp, RG 389, Entry 459A, Box 1649, NA.

44. Ibid.

45. For information on the differences between the army and the YMCA in the spring of 1945, see Maj. William B. Gemmill's Memorandum for General Lerch, July 27, 1945, RG 389, Entry 451, Box 1224, File: 080 Gen P/W, NA.

46. Maj. William Gemmill reviewed the situation in a July 27, 1945, memo to Gen. Archer L. Lerch, the provost marshal general, ibid.

47. Tracy Strong, War Prisoners' Aid of the Young Men's Christian Associations, to Gen. Archer L. Lerch, Provost Marshal General, August 1, 1945, ibid.

48. Ibid.

49. Krammer, *Nazi Prisoners*, 212, 217, quoting from Bryan, "Re-Education Program for German Prisoners."

50. Krammer, *Nazi Prisoners*, 217, makes this comment and notes brief articles in *Publishers Weekly*, June 23, the *Fort Smith (Arkansas) Times Record*, July 7, and the *New York Times*, July 8, 15.

51. Peter Edson, "Army Gives German POWs Large Doses of Nazi-Purging News and Literature," *Palm Beach Post*, Friday, July 13, 1945, 7.

52. "Three POWs End Lives Over Trips to Europe," Fort Dix, N.J., AP, *Palm Beach Post*, Saturday, June 30, 1945, 1.

53. Details of these repatriations are the subject of chapter 9, "The Long Way Home."

54. Peter Edson, "Army De-Nazified German Prisoners with Intimate Knowledge about U.S.," Washington, AP, *Palm Beach Post*, Friday, July 13, 1945, 12.

55. Ibid.

56. Capt. William F. Raugust, Field Service Officer, PW Special Projects Division, to Commanding Officer, Prisoner of War Camp, Camp Blanding, Fla., September 3, 1945, RG 389, Entry 459A, Box 1609, NA; and Capt. William F. Raugust, to Commanding Officer, Prisoner of War Camp, Camp Gordon Johnston, Fla., September 4, 1945, RG 389, Entry 459A, Box 1649, NA. For confirmation of the changes undertaken, see Maj. John H. Suther, Prisoner of War Camp Commander, Camp Gordon Johnston, to Provost Marshal General, September 18, 1945, RG 389, Entry 459A, Box 1649, NA.

57. Information on the German prisoner newspapers can be found in Böhme, *Geist und Kultur*, appendix i, 270–76. For Florida camps there is an alphabetical list of newspaper titles, with camps and period of appearance. Here are listed *An der Schwelle*, Eglin Field, September 1945–January 1946; *POW-Zeitspiegel*, Camp Blanding, August–December 1945; *Was bei uns los ist: PW-Lagerzeitung*, MacDill Field, March–November 1945; and *Zeitspiegel*, Camp Blanding, February–July 1945. Copies of some of these papers can be seen at the Bundesarchiv, Militärarchiv, Freiburg, Germany (henceforth cited as BMF). They are also available on microfilm through the Library of Congress, "German Prisoner of War Camp Papers Published in the United States of North America from 1943 to 1946." Blanding's *POW-Zeitspiegel* and *Zeitspiegel* are on reel 1, Eglin Field's *An der Schwelle* on reel 6, and MacDill's *Was bei uns los ist: PW-Lagerzeitung* on reel 9.

58. *POW-Zeitspiegel* (Camp Blanding), July 15, 1945, 7–8, B 205/322, BMF.

59. Otto Haehre, "Kriegsgefangene als Helfer an Wiederaufbau der Heimat," and Erich Reichel, "Über die Demokratie," *POW-Zeitspiegel*, August 12, 1945, 15–19.

60. Hans Rauer, "Warum Vertrauensmänner," ibid., 14.

61. Friedrich Brunkhardt, "Das Leben geht weiter (Life goes on), *Was bei*

und los ist: PW-Lagerzeitung (MacDill Field), June/July 1945, 1–2, B 205/511, BMF; also on reel 9 of "German Prisoner of War Camp Papers."

62. August 1945, 12, ibid.

63. *An der Schwelle,* November 15, 1945, 6, B 205/v. 291, BMF.

64. *POW-Zeitspiegel,* October 14, 1945, 10–11, B 205/332, BMF.

65. Taped interview with former Belle Glade internee Herman Finke, June 23, 1997.

66. Gansberg, *Stalag: U.S.A.,* 103–4.

67. *POW-Zeitspiegel,* September 16, 1945, 25, B 205/332, BMF.

68. Finke interview, June 23, 1997.

69. Jung, *Kriegsgefangenen,* 220.

70. Report of Visit to Prisoner of War Camp, Camp Blanding, Fla., and Branch Camps by Edouard Patte, October 14–23, 1945, RG 59, 711.62114 IR/12–1945, Box 3344; also in RG 389, Entry 459A, Box 1609, NA.

71. Finke interview, June 23, 1997, and copy of *Englisch Wie Man's Spricht,* shared with the author at that time.

72. Patte's YMCA Report on Visit to Camp Blanding and Branch Camps, October 14–23, 1945, RG 389, Entry 459A, Box 1609, NA.

73. Finke's certificates shared with author during interview of June 23, 1997.

74. Patte's Report on October 1945 Visits to Blanding and Its Branches, RG 389, Entry 459A, Box 1609, NA.

75. *POW-Zeitspiegel,* October 14, 1945, 10–11, B 205/332, BMF.

76. Patte's report, October 1945, RG 389, Entry 459A, Box 1609, and RG 59, 711.62114 IR/12–1945, Box 3344, NA.

77. Ibid.

78. Wolfgang Speer and Karl Bartsch (Camp Belle Glade), "Was soll aus den Kriegsgefangenen in Amerika werden?" (What is to become of the POWs in America?) *POW-Zeitspiegel* (Blanding), September 30, 1945, 3.

79. J. L. Toohey, Report on Visit of Paul Schnyder, representing the International Red Cross Committee, and Mr. J. L. Toohey, of the Department of State, to prisoner of war side camp, Bell Haven Branch Camp, Miami, on December 7, 1945, RG 59, 58D7, Box 22, File: Blanding, NA.

80. See chapter 6, "Special Projects," in Gansberg, *Stalag: U.S.A.,* especially 120–21. Later, between February and April 1946, another 23,147 POWs were put through a cycle of six-day courses at Fort Eustis, Virginia, studying the workings of democracy and its potential for Germany before their repatriation directly to Germany. See chapter 7, "Fort Eustis," in Gansberg, *Stalag: U.S.A.*

81. J. L. Toohey, Report on Visit of Paul Schnyder, representing the International Red Cross Committee, and Mr. J. L. Toohey, of the Department of State, to prisoner of war side camp, Welch General Hospital, Daytona Beach, on November 26, 1945, RG 59, 58D7, Box 22, File: Blanding, NA.

82. J. L. Toohey, Report on Visit of Paul Schnyder, representing the International Red Cross Committee, and Mr. J. L. Toohey, of the Department of State, to prisoner of war side camp, Banana River Naval Air Station, on November 27, 1945, ibid.

83. Edouard Patte, Report of Visit to Prisoner of War Camp, Blanding, Fla., and Side Camps, January 20–30, 1946, RG 389, Entry 459A, Box 1609, NA.

84. Ibid.

85. Krammer, *Nazi Prisoners*, 224.

86. See particularly Gansberg, *Stalag: U.S.A.*, and Robin, *Barbed-Wire College*, for contrasting moderately positive and fairly negative evaluations of the program. Krammer, *Nazi Prisoners*, and Jung, *Kriegsgefangenen*, have chapters on the reeducation efforts and reach more cautious conclusions regarding its effects. See Smith, *The War for the German Mind*, for a comparative study and evaluation of the differing impacts of the reeducation efforts of the Americans, British, and Russians. Smith deems the effects of the American effort difficult to judge.

87. The earliest and most positive assessment of the program was written by Martin Tollefson, former director, Prisoner of War Operations Division, Office of the Provost Marshal General: "Enemy Prisoners of War," 51–77, especially 67–73.

88. Ibid., 72.

89. Jung, *Kriegsgefangenen*, 238.

90. Interview of Gerhard Anklam, Berlin, June 3, 1996; tape in possession of the author.

91. Interview of Herman Finke, New York, June 23, 1997; tape in possession of the author.

92. According to Tollefson, "Enemy Prisoners of War," 72: "The results of the poll of the Shanks [Camp Shanks, New York, pre-shipment camp for Europe] group might have been more favorable had it not been for the fact that the morale of these prisoners at this time was not high. Many resented the fact that they had not been selected to attend the special courses at Fort Getty, Fort Wetherill, or Fort Eustis. . . . In addition, many of the prisoners at Camp Shanks shared the opinion that they were destined, upon their arrival in Europe, to serve in labor battalions rather than to be sent home immediately. This opinion embittered them against democracy."

9. THE LONG WAY HOME

1. Provisions of the Geneva Convention that deal with "Direct Repatriation and Hospitalization in a Neutral Country" are Articles 68–74. Article 68 explains the basis of exchange for "seriously sick and seriously injured prisoners of war," and Article 69 describes the use of "mixed medical commissions" composed of three members, "two of them belonging to a neutral country and one appointed by the detaining Power." Convention of July 27, 1929, Relative to the Treatment of Prisoners of War, in Bevans, *Treaties*, 2:953–54.

2. Information on these repatriations in Jung, *Kriegsgefangenen*, 244.

3. Specific dates and numbers involved in these exchanges are found in PMGO, "Prisoner of War Operations," 1:241.

4. See chapter 4, "When the Afrika Korps Came to Blanding."

5. These materials are grouped together with the reply from Col. A. M.

Tollefson, Assistant Director, Prisoner of War Division, May 13, 1945, RG 389, Entry 451, Box 1217, File: 014.33, #2, NA.

6. English translation of the International Red Cross report of M. Peter's visit to Camp Blanding on April 6 and 7, 1944, RG 59, 711.62112 IR/10-6-44, NA, and RG 389, Entry 461, Box 2656, NA, and Charles C. Eberhardt's Report of Prisoner of War Camp, Camp Blanding, Starke, Fla., visited in the company of the IRC and Swiss representatives on April 6–7, 1944, RG 389, Entry 461, Box 2656, NA.

7. Reply of Col. A. M. Tollefson, Assistant Director, Prisoner of War Division, May 13, 1945, RG 389, Entry 451, Box 1217, File: 014.33, #2, NA.

8. See Article 75 of the Geneva Convention, Bevans, *Treaties*, 2:954.

9. Jung, *Kriegsgefangenen*, 241.

10. Ibid., 241.

11. Ibid., 243–44, 252.

12. Ibid., 242–43, 253.

13. While 123,000 Germans from the U.S. camps went to Britain and 55,000 went to France, some may have wound up in Belgium or Luxembourg. The United States agreed to supply POW labor to these last two governments. About 30,000 POWs held by the Americans at a camp in Mons were turned over to the Belgians, and about 5,000 other POWs were given to Luxembourg. However, these Germans appear to have been held in Europe, not the United States. See Jung, *Kriegsgefangenen*, 243. Krammer, *Nazi Prisoners*, 248, notes that of the massive numbers of POWs held by the Americans in Europe, not only did France, Britain, and Belgium receive large numbers, but an additional 50,000 were divided among the Netherlands, Scandinavia, Czechoslovakia, Yugoslavia, and Greece.

14. Jung, *Kriegsgefangenen*, 245–46. Krammer, *Nazi Prisoners*, 250, relates instances of discharges from POW Discharge Center #26 at Bad Aibling, POW Center #15 at Marburg/Hesse, and Ingolstadt, Bavaria.

15. "Was Soll aus den Kriegsgefangenen in Amerika Werden?" (What is to become of the POWs in America?), *POW-Zeitspiegel*, September 30, 1945, 3.

16. Jung, *Kriegsgefangenen*, 248, mentions and quotes some "calming" assertions by the provost marshal general, printed in the July 1, 1945, issue of *Der Ruf*, the national POW newspaper produced at Fort Kearney. Jung gives additional evidence of such American attempts to calm the prisoners' fears, and, by implication, questions the honesty of such attempts. See especially page 247.

17. Krammer, *Nazi Prisoners*, 237–38.

18. Jung, *Kriegsgefangenen*, 246.

19. Semimonthly report on POWs, May 15, 1946, Headquarters Army Service Forces, Office of PMGO, copy in RG 59, 740.00114 EW/5–1546, NA.

20. Krammer, *Nazi Prisoners*, 255. Jung, *Kriegsgefangenen*, 248, mentions the 141 men serving prison terms but fails to note the 134 POWs still hospitalized or the 25 at large as escapees.

21. General Courts-Martial of Prisoners of War, Charges Other Than Murder, Tab. 115 in PMGO, "Prisoner of War Operations," reel 2.

22. Written summary of Gerhard Anklam's odyssey shared with the author in a letter from Anklam of November 7, 1994; letter in possession of the author.

23. Jung, *Kriegsgefangenen*, 253; Krammer, *Nazi Prisoners*, 247.

24. Taped interview with Herman Finke, June 23, 1997.

25. Gerhard Anklam's typed outline of his military and POW experiences sent to the author on November 7, 1994.

26. A copy of Gerhard Anklam's official discharge papers, along with the outline of his military experiences, sent to the author by Anklam on November 7, 1994.

27. Copy of Gerhard Anklam's official registration and health certificate from Russian authorities stamped Erfurt, March 30, 1946, sent to the author on November 7, 1994.

28. Anklam's written summary of military and POW experiences shared with author.

29. Taped interview with Herman Finke, June 23, 1997.

30. Ibid.

31. Regarding dyeing of uniforms, see "Supplement to Historical Monograph," 26–27, appended to PMGO, "Prisoner of War Operations," vol. 1, microfilm reel 1.

32. Typed summary of important dates shared with author and in recorded interview with Herman Finke on June 23, 1997.

33. Jung, *Kriegsgefangenen*, 252.

34. Information and interpretation from recorded interview with Herman Finke, June 23, 1997. Many POWs who found themselves turned over to the French and British found their luggage lightened by British or French guards, but more often it was their fellow Germans in the camp who did the stealing. See Jung, *Kriegsgefangenen*, 253–56.

35. Tape of Finke interview, June 23, 1997.

36. Ibid.

37. Ibid.

38. Ibid. Krammer, *Nazi Prisoners*, 249–50, mentions the American pressure on the French and the resulting "salaried, voluntary worker" status arrangement. He notes that the men had three months to decide, those deciding for repatriation to be shipped home at the rate of 20,000 a month. Krammer concludes that "The vast majority chose to be repatriated immediately, though nearly 10,000 remained to work well into mid-1948."

39. Tape of Finke interview, June 23, 1997.

40. Telephone interview with Lüdeke Herder, September 10, 1997, supplemented and verified by copies of American and British documents pertaining to Herder, sent to the author by Herder from Wiesbaden on September 12, 1997. Information on Werner Burkert is gained from "Militärzeit und Kriegsgefangenschaft," an autobiographical typescript shared with the author in materials, including photocopies of POW identity papers, received from Werner Burkert of Schaffhausen, Switzerland, on September 18, 1998.

41. Lüdeke Herder information was verified by copies of American and

British documents pertaining to Herder sent to the author by Herder from Wiesbaden on September 12, 1997.

42. Ibid.

43. Burkert, "Militärzeit und Kriegsgefangenschaft."

44. Provisional Certificate of Security Clearance No. A 2693, for Lüdeke Herder, dated January 21, 1947, copy of which was sent to the author in Herder's letter of September 12, 1997.

45. Office of the Theater Provost Marshal Headquarters, United States Forces, European Theater, APO 757 U.S. Army, February 6, 1947, concerning former Prisoner of War Herder, Lüdeke, whose British P/W No. was D 891662; a copy was sent to the author on September 12, 1997.

46. Information, including additional official stamps and notations, on Lüdeke Wilhelm Herder's Certificate of Discharge, February 6, 1947, signed by Richard S. Kotite, 2d Lt. Inf., headquarters Dachau, PW Reception and Discharge Center. A copy was sent to the author, of September 12, 1997.

47. Burkert, "Militärzeit und Kriegsgefangenschaft."

48. Ibid.

49. Jung, *Kriegsgefangenen,* 252–57, cites numerous examples of reports of disillusionment.

50. Interviews and correspondence with Herman Finke and Lüdeke Herder.

51. "Former Prisoner of War Makes Visit to Dade City," *Dade City Banner,* October 6, 1960. A copy of the clipping was sent by Werner Burkert to the author in materials received on September 18, 1998.

52. Quotation from the diary of a repatriated German POW, Jung, *Kriegsgefangenen,* 257.

10. EPILOGUE

1. "Solemn Ceremony Marks Graveside of German POW's," *Middleburg Press,* December 14, 1989, 10.

2. For a copy of the Geneva Convention, see Bevans, *Treaties,* 2:932–64. Eliot Kleinberg of the *Palm Beach Post,* who wrote a story on the Karl Behrens's suicide case, "Another Lost Soul on Enemy Soil," *Palm Beach Post,* December 28, 1994, D1, D6, received and shared details on the Blanding Prisoner of War Cemetery—with some details of the seven prisoners interred there up until April 25, 1946. Kleinberg's information was received in a letter and enclosures from James F. Bloodworth, assistant curator, Camp Blanding Museum and Historical Associates, Inc., Starke, Florida, November 11, 1992. Copies of interment records for these seven from Blanding and other German POWs buried at the Fort Benning Post Cemetery were sent to the author on September 29, 1997, through the courtesy of Jim Grantham and Brenda Bowser, mortuary affairs assistant, Cemetery Office, Fort Benning, Georgia.

3. Details on the seven POWs originally interred at the POW cemetery at Camp Blanding and then reinterred at the post cemetery at Fort Benning, Georgia, were sent to the author by the Deutsche Dienststelle für die Benachrichtigung der nächsten Angehörigen von Gefallenen der ehemaligen

deutschen Wehrmacht (WASt) (German Office for the Notification of the Next of Kin of the Deceased of the Former German Armed Forces), Berlin, October 28, 1997.

4. According to interment records at the army post cemetery at Fort Benning, Behrens, Moos, and Sturm are listed as Protestant, Klose as Catholic. The Austrians—Baumgartner, Erler, and Stamicar—have no religious affiliation listed but were probably nominally Catholic.

5. Most details on the seven POWs originally interred at the POW cemetery at Camp Blanding are from materials sent to the author from WASt, Berlin, October 28, 1997. This material was supplemented as the following footnotes indicate.

6. File: Death Lists, RG 389, Entry 467, Box 1514, NA.

7. Ibid.; also Col. A. M. Tollefson, Director, Prisoner of War Operations Division, to Special War Problems Division, Department of State, October 11, 1945, RG 389, Entry 467, Box 1513, NA, which explains the circumstances regarding the Baumgartner drowning. Both reports cite Baumgartner as being at Camp Blanding, but his name is on a list of Austrians in the Belle Glade Camp, which sent men to work on the barges and dikes at Clewiston. See Heinrich Baumgartner, 31G-121592, listed as an Austrian citizen on Belle Glade camp list submitted with other nationality lists by Capt. Charles E. Collins, personnel officer, Headquarters Prisoner of War Camp Blanding, Fla., to Office of the Provost Marshal General, July 30, 1945, RG 389, Entry 451, Box 1318, NA.

8. Official WASt records from Berlin indicate that Rudolf Stamicar drowned in the Banana River, but the drowning is also listed as a "work accident." Charles M. Blackard, a guard at the camp, recalled the death of one of the POWs at Banana River. He said that a number of POWs fell off a truck while being taken to work, and one died as a result. Phone interview with Charles M. Blackard, Dallas, Texas, June 1, 1983; notes in possession of the author. Blackard's memory regarding the death as resulting from a work-related accident is confirmed by a labor report of January 15, 1946, from the Banana River POW camp. Signed by the camp commander, Capt. Eugene V. Joyce, it simply noted, "1 man died due to injury in line of duty." USNAS Banana River, Fla., Prisoner of War Camp Labor Report, January 15, 1946, RG 389, Entry 461, Box 2492, NA. Though neither Blackard's memory nor the labor report mention drowning as the cause of death, the dead man could have been none other than Pfc. Rudolf Stamicar of Graz, Austria.

9. Obituary of Wendelin Sturm in *Was bei uns los ist: PW-Lagerzeitung* (MacDill Field), June/July 1945, 5.

10. German Death Lists, RG 389, Entry 467, Box 1514; details of Georg Moos's death found in Report of Col. A. M. Tollefson, Director, Prisoner of War Operations Division, to Special Projects Division, Department of State, January 16, 1946, RG 389, Entry 467, Box 1513, NA.

11. German Death Lists, RG 389, Entry 467, Box 1514, NA.

12. "Fugitive POW Found Hanged," *Miami Herald*, January 2, 1945, 1. See also German Death Lists, Category of Suicides, RG 389, Entry 467, Box 1514, and details of escape and hanging in Maj. Stephen M. Ferrand, Chief, Legal

Branch, Prisoner of War Operations Division, to Legation of Switzerland, Department of German Interests, Washington, D.C., January 3, 1945, RG 389, Entry 467, Box 1513, NA. For details on Behrens's death, see chapter 5.

13. Quotation and statistics here from PMGO, "Supplement to Historical Monograph," 26.

14. War Department, Washington, D.C., Prisoner of War Circular No. 1, September 24, 1943, 62–63, Tab 7, in PMGO, "Prisoner of War Operations," microfilm reel 1.

15. Col. A. M. Tollefson, Director, Prisoner of War Operations Division to Special Projects Division, Department of State, January 16, 1946, RG 389, Entry 467, Box 1513, NA.

16. Grave numbers and location received in Blanding "Prisoner of War Cemetery" shared by Eliot Kleinberg of the *Palm Beach Post* and in a letter and enclosures from James F. Bloodworth, assistant curator, Camp Blanding Museum and Historical Associates, Inc., Starke, Florida, November 11, 1992. Confirmed by interment records sent to the author from the Cemetery Office, Fort Benning, Georgia, September 23, 1997.

17. Story and quotation from Gerhard Anklam's notes written for author and based on Anklam's memory as aided by reference to the "five-year diary" that he bought at Camp Blanding and has kept as a record of his POW and early postwar experiences. Information shared with author in letter of November 7, 1994.; diary shown to author during visit with Anklam in Berlin, June 3, 1996.

18. Anklam letter of November 7, 1994, and interview in Berlin, June 3, 1996.

19. Interview with Herman Finke, June 23, 1997.

20. Telephone conversation with Herman Finke, February 26, 1994; notes in possession of the author.

21. In addition to Herman Finke, Karl Held, Lüdeke Herder, and Werner Burkert mentioned in this narrative, Martha Knapp, a former teacher in the Dade City area, knows of two other former POWs besides Herder and Burkert who have returned to Dade City over the years. E-mail message from Martha Knapp to author, September 9, 1997.

22. Jerard Thornton, "WWII POW Returns to See Campsite," *Clewiston News*, December 31, 1986, 1.

23. Detention Roster, Blanding, Camp #18 (Belle Glade camp), n.d., RG 389, Entry 461, Box 2574, NA.

24. "Prisoner of War Camp Here to Close Next Saturday," *Clewiston News*, August 31, 1945, 1; "P.O.W. Camp To Be Closed on September 6," *Glades County Democrat* (Moore Haven), August 31, 1945, 1; Clewiston, Florida, Labor Report filed by Capt. D. Field, September 8, 1945, RG 389, Entry 461, Box 2492, NA.

25. "Prison Camp Is Vacated by Army and Internees," *Belle Glade Herald*, December 14, 1945, 1, 6; notes of Herman Finke, telephone conversation with author, July 6, 1994.

26. Notes from author's telephone conversation with Dr. Karl Held, June 2, 1993.

27. Detention Roster, Blanding, Camp #18 (Belle Glade camp), n.d., RG 389, Entry 461, Box 2574, NA.

28. Regarding the similar repatriation of Gottlob Hasel, Horst Finke's friend from Aliceville and Belle Glade, who was selected at Camp Forrest for early return to Germany as part of the postwar denazification program because of membership in the Nazi party, information was found in the taped conversation of Herman Finke with the author, June 23, 1997.

29. Biographical information from copies of letters from Herder to Mrs. Knapp's class, shared by Martha Knapp, September 11, 1997; from author's telephone conversation with Herr Herder on September 10, 1997; and from a letter and enclosures sent to author by Herder from Wiesbaden, September 12, 1997.

30. Copies of letters from Herder to Mrs. Knapp's students sent to author by Martha Knapp, Ridge Manor, Florida, September 11, 1997.

31. Ibid.

32. Facsimile from Werner Burkert, Schaffhausen, Switzerland, to the author on February 11, 1999.

33. Bill Bond, "Residents Recall Days of POWs in Camp Near Leesburg," *Orlando Sentinel*, October 15, 1986, 3, 6; "German POWs Left Their Mark on County," *Lake Sentinel* (an edition of the *Orlando Sentinel*), January 23, 1994, 1, 4. For the stories about the Leesburg camp, see chapter 2.

34. Bond, "German POWs Left Their Mark on County." See Peter Kehde, "Early Industries of the Lake Area."

35. Lori Rozsa, "Oldtimers Recall German POWs Held in Florida," *Miami Herald*, December 19, 1993, 6B; Eliot Kleinberg, "Another Lost Soul on Enemy Soil," *Palm Beach Post*, December 28, 1994, D1, D6.

36. For the story of Karl Behrens, see chapter 5.

37. Interview with Herman Finke, June 3, 1997; tape in possession of the author.

38. Bremer, "1250-Meilen durch Florida."

39. Taped interview with Gerhard Anklam, Berlin, June 3, 1996.

APPENDIX

1. Hans Bremer, NCO, 31 G-51500, is listed as the assistant German spokesman at Camp Blanding. See English translation of Report on Camp Blanding, Fla., visited on March 8 and 9, 1945, by Mr. Métraux, International Red Cross to State Department, September 5, 1945, RG 59, 711.62114 IR/9–545, Box 3344; also found in RG 389, Entry 461, Box 2656, NA.

2. Bremer, "1250-Meilen durch Florida."

BIBLIOGRAPHY

ARCHIVAL MATERIALS

Bundesarchiv, Militärarchiv (Federal archive, military archive), Freiburg, Germany
  Bestand: B 205/322, *POW-Zeitspiegel* (POW times mirror), Camp Blanding, Florida.
  Bestand: RW2/v. 109: Oberkommando der Wehrmacht, Wehrmachtuntersuchungsstelle für Verletzungen des Völkerrechts, U.S.A. Kriegsrechtsverstösse gegen Kriegsgefangenen in den Lagern. Lager: Blanding (Supreme command of the armed forces, armed forces research office for violations of international law, U.S.A. Law of war violations against prisoners of war in the camps. Camp: Blanding).
Deutsche Dienststelle für die Benachrichtigung der nächsten Angehörigen von Gefallenen der ehemaligen deutschen Wehrmacht (WASt) (German office for the notification of the next of kin of the deceased of the former German armed forces) Berlin. Information on seven German POWs interred at Camp Blanding POW Cemetery and reinterred at Fort Benning Post Cemetery.
Federal Bureau of Investigation (files accessed through Freedom of Information Act), "Karl Behrens: Alien Enemy Control—G Escaped Prisoners of War," Miami, Florida, 2-9-45.
Fort Benning Post Cemetery, interment records for German POWs in post cemetery.
National Archives (NA), formerly in Washington, D.C., now in College Park, Maryland.
  Records Group (RG) 59, Diplomatic Branch
    58D7, Special War Problems Division, Box 22, File: Blanding; Box 29, File: Gordon Johnston.
    Decimal File 711.62114 IR 10-6-44, International Red Cross (IRC) Visits by Marc Peter.
    Decimal File 711.62114 IR/9-545, Box 3344, IRC Visits by Guy Métraux.
    Decimal File 711.62114 IR/12-1945, Box 3344, Edouard Patte's YMCA Reports.

Decimal File 740.00114 EW/4-145 through 740.0114 EW/7-3145, Box 3623, Civil Affairs Division, Diplomatic Archive, Transcript, "Questioning of Brigadier General Blackshear M. Bryan by Congressman Robert Sikes," Hearing of the Special Committee of Military Affairs Regarding POW Treatment, April 30, 1945.

Records Group (RG) 389, Modern Military Branch

Entry 434: Box 405, File 383.6—Early Blanding Naval POW Detention Rosters.

Entry 451: Box 1217, File 014.33 #2—February 1944 Repatriation of Sick and Wounded POWs; Box 1224, File: 080 Gen P/W—War Prisoners' Aid, YMCA Representatives; Box 1318, Nationality Lists.

Entry 457: Box 1419, File Camp Blanding, Florida—Construction.

Entry 459A: Box 1609, File 255: Camp Blanding, Special Projects Division Reports; Box 1649, Camp Gordon Johnston.

Entry 461: Box 2476, File: Blanding—Transfers; Box 2492, Enemy POW Information Bureau, Reporting Branch, Subject File 1942–46, Camps Inactivated 4th Service Command: Camp Labor Reports; Box 2574, Camp Blanding Detention Rosters; Box 2653, Reporting Branch, Inspection Reports (Aliceville, Alabama); Box 2656, Reporting Branch, Inspection Reports (Military, International Red Cross, and YMCA Reports on Camp Blanding); Box 2661, Reports on Camp Gordon Johnston POW Camps.

Entry 467: Box 1513, Prisoner of War Operations Division, Legal Branch, Numeric-Subject File 4.1, German Death Lists October 1944 through 1946; Box 1514, German Death Lists.

ARTICLES, BOOKS, AND DISSERTATIONS

Bevans, Charles I., comp. *Treaties and International Agreements of the United States of America, 1776–1949.* 12 vols. Department of State, Washington, D.C.: Government Printing Office, 1969–.

Billinger, Robert D., Jr. "The Other Side Now: What Blanding Prisoners of War Told the Wehrmacht." *Florida Historical Quarterly* 73 (July 1994): 62–78.

———. "With the Wehrmacht in Florida: The German POW Facility at Camp Blanding, 1942–1946." *Florida Historical Quarterly* 58 (October 1979): 160–73.

Blair, Clay. *Hitler's U-Boat War.* Vol. 1, *The Hunters, 1939–1942.* New York: Random House, 1996.

Böhme, Kurt W. *Geist und Kultur der deutschen Kriegsgefangenen im Westen* (Spirit and culture of the German prisoners of war in the West). Munich: Ernst and Werner Gieseking, 1968.

Bremer, Hans. "1250-Meilen durch Florida. Ein Erlebnis-Bericht" (1,250 miles through Florida: The report of an experience). *Zeitspiegel* (Camp

Blanding) Nr. 3 (Sonntag, April 1, 1945): 2–7. See in reel 1, vol. 2, "German Prisoner of War Camp Papers Published in the United States of North America from 1943 to 1946."

Burkert, Werner H. "Militärzeit und Kriegsgefangenschaft" (Military service and prisoner of war captivity). Autobiographic typescript sent to the author by Werner H. Burkert, Schaffenhausen, Switzerland, September 18, 1998.

Carlson, Lewis H. *We Were Each Other's Prisoners: An Oral History of World War II American and German Prisoners of War.* New York: Basic Books, 1997.

Coles, David J. "'Hell-by-the-Sea': Florida's Camp Gordon Johnston in World War II." *Florida Historical Quarterly* 73 (July 1994): 1–22.

DeSpain, Brian. "The German POWs at Whiting Field." *Newsletter, Santa Rosa Historical Society* 9, no. 5 (June/July 1985): 1, 3.

Doyle, Frederick Joseph. "German Prisoners of War in the Southwest United States during World War II: An Oral History." Ph.D. diss., University of Denver, 1978.

Fickle, James E., and Donald W. Ellis. "POWs in the Piney Woods: German Prisoners of War in the Southern Lumber Industry, 1943–1945." *Journal of Southern History* 56 (November 1990): 695–724.

Freyer, Paul Herbert. *Der Tod auf allen Meeren* (Death on all the seas). Berlin: Deutscher Militärverlag, 1971.

Gaertner, Georg, with Arnold Krammer. *Hitler's Last Soldier in America.* New York: Stein and Day, 1985.

Gannon, Michael. *Operation Drumbeat.* New York: Harper & Row, 1990.

Gansberg, Judith. *Stalag: U.S.A.* New York: Thomas Y. Crowell, 1977.

Green, Vincent. *Extreme Justice.* New York: Pocket Books, 1995.

Hoyt, Edwin P. *U-Boats Offshore: When Hitler Struck America.* New York: Stein and Day, 1978.

Jung, Hermann. *Die deutschen Kriegsgefangenen in amerikanischer Hand—USA* (The German prisoners of war in American hands—U.S.A.). Vol. 10, pt. 1 of *Zur Geschichte der deutschen Kriegsgefangenen des Zweiten Weltkrieges,* 22 vols., ed. Erich Maschke. Bielefeld: Gieseking, 1972.

Kehde, Peter. "Early Industries of the Lake Area." In *History of the Silver Lake Area,* compiled by Pat Carr and Betty Snyder, 1993. Copy in the library, Lake-Sumter Community College, Leesburg, Fla.

Koop, Allen V. *Stark Decency: German Prisoners of War in a New England Village.* Hanover and London: University Press of New England, 1988.

Krammer, Arnold. "German Alien Enemies in the U.S. during World War Two." Paper presented at the German Studies Association meeting in Bethesda, Md., October 1993.

———. "German Prisoners of War in the United States." *Military Affairs* 40 (April 1976): 68–73.

———. *Nazi Prisoners of War in America.* New York: Stein and Day, 1979.

————. *Undue Process: The Untold Story of America's German Alien Internees.* New York: Rowman & Littlefield, 1997.

Lerch, Archer L. "The Army Reports on Prisoners of War." *American Mercury* 60 (May 1945): 536–47.

Lewis, George G., and John Mewha. *History of Prisoner of War Utilization by the United States Army, 1776–1945.* Department of the Army Pamphlet No. 20–213 (June 1955).

Mason, John Brown. "German Prisoners of War in the United States." *American Journal of International Law* 39 (April 1945): 198–215.

Moore, John Hammond. *The Faustball Tunnel: German POWs in America and Their Great Escape.* New York: Random House, 1978.

Pabel, Reinhold. *Enemies Are Human.* Philadelphia and Toronto: John C. Winston, 1955.

Pluth, Edward J. "The Administration and Operation of German Prisoner of War Camps in the United States During World War II." Ph.D. diss., Ball State University, 1970.

Powell, Allan Kent. *Splinters of a Nation: German Prisoners of War in Utah.* Salt Lake City: University of Utah Press, 1989.

Provost Marshal General's Office. Prisoner of War Division. "Prisoner of War Operations." 4 vols. Unpublished historical monograph, Historical MSS File, Office of the Chief of Military History, Dept. of the Army, Washington, D.C. August 31, 1945; and "Supplement to Historical Monograph," April 1946. Available on microfilm through the Library of Congress.

Robin, Ron. *The Barbed-Wire College: Reeducating German POWs in the United States during World War II.* Princeton, N.J.: Princeton University Press, 1995.

Smith, Arthur L., Jr. *The War for the German Mind: Re-Educating Hitler's Soldiers.* Providence, R.I.: Berghahn, 1996.

Spidle, Jake W., Jr. "Axis Prisoners of War in the United States, 1942–1946: A Bibliographical Essay." *Military Affairs* 39 (April 1975): 61–66.

Schoeps, Karl H. "The 'Golden Cage' and the Re-education of German POWs in America as Seen by Two Prominent Post-War German Writers: Hans Werner Richter and Alfred Andersch." Paper presented at the Western Association of German Studies, Madison, Wisc., September 30, 1983.

Tollefson, Martin. "Enemy Prisoners of War." *Iowa Law Review* 32 (November 1946): 51–77.

Walker, Chip. "German Creative Activities in Camp Aliceville, 1943–1946." *Alabama Review* 38 (January 1985): 19–37.

Wall, Forrest Burnette, Jr. "German Prisoners of War in Virginia during World War Two." D.A. thesis, Carnegie-Mellon University, 1987.

War Department. *Englisch Wie Man's Spricht: Spoken English, Basic Course, Units 7–12* (English as it is spoken). War Department Technical Manual, German, TM30-1506A. Washington, D.C.: Government Printing Office, 1945.

Zayas, Alfred M. de. *Die Wehrmacht-Untersuchungsstelle: Deutsche Er-mittlungen über alliierte Völkerrechtsverletzungen im Zweiten Welt-krieg* (Armed forces research center: German investigations regarding violations of international law in the Second World War). 3d ed. Munich: Universitas/Langen Müller, 1980.

INTERVIEWS: NOTES AND TAPES IN POSSESSION OF THE AUTHOR

Anklam, Gerhard. Former Clewiston POW; Berlin, June 3, 1996.

Avant, Roberta. Former secretary at U.S. Corps of Engineers, Clewiston; Clewiston, May 25, 1978.

Blackard, Charles M. Former Belle Glade and Banana River guard; telephone interview, Dallas, Tex., June 1, 1983.

Finke, Herman. Former POW at Belle Glade camp; telephone interviews on January 28, February 26, July 22, 1994, and taped personal interview, New York City, June 23, 1997.

Forshay, David. Former Clewiston and Green Cove Springs guard; telephone interviews on May 15, December 13, 1978, and personal interview, West Palm Beach, May 29, 1978.

Fountain, James. Wartime civilian employee of the U.S. Corps of Engineers, Clewiston; Clewiston, May 25, 1978.

Golson, Maceo. Wartime mechanic's helper, Belle Glade Agricultural Experiment Station; Belle Glade, June 2, 1977.

Held, Dr. Karl. Former POW at Belle Glade camp; telephone interview, Munich, June 2, 1993.

Herder, Lüdeke. Former POW at Dade City camp; telephone interview, Wiesbaden, September 10, 1997, and letter and copy of discharge documents sent to author on September 12, 1997.

Johnston, Harry A. Former executive officer at Camp Blanding; West Palm Beach, June 22, 1977.

MacMillan, Judge Hugh. Former FBI agent; West Palm Beach, February 26, 1979.

Mueller, Rev. Arlo M. Former pastor in West Palm Beach and visiting chaplain at Belle Glade and Clewiston POW camps; telephone interview, North Bergen, N.J., November 19, 1977.

Scheffler, Willard. Wartime chief mechanic, Belle Glade Agricultural Experiment Station; Belle Glade, June 2, 1977.

Twiddy, Allen G. Wartime barge captain with the U.S. Corps of Engineers, Clewiston; Clewiston, May 25, 1978.

U.S. NEWSPAPERS

Belle Glade Herald
Bradford County Telegraph (Starke)
Clewiston News
Daily Democrat (Tallahassee)
Daytona Beach Evening News

Florida Times-Union (Jacksonville)
Fort Smith (Arkansas) *Times Record*
Glades County Democrat (Moore Haven)
Homestead Leader
Jackson County Floridian (Marianna)
Jacksonville Journal
Leesburg Commercial
Miami Daily News
Miami Herald
Middleburg Press
New York Times
Orlando Morning Sentinel
Palm Beach Post
Palm Beach Post-Times
Santa Rosa Press Gazette (Milton)
Tampa Morning Tribune
Tampa Sunday Tribune
Winter Haven Daily Chief

POW NEWSPAPERS

Available on microfilm through the Library of Congress, "German Prisoner
of War Camp Papers Published in the United States from 1943 to 1946."
An der Schwelle (On the threshold), Eglin Field, September 1945–January
1946, on reel 6.
POW-Zeitspiegel (POW times mirror), Camp Blanding, August–December
1945, on reel 1.
Was bei uns los ist: PW-Lagerzeitung (What's going on here: POW camp
newspaper), MacDill Field, March–November 1945, on reel 9.
Zeitspiegel (Times mirror), Camp Blanding, February–July 1945, reel 1.

ROBERT D. BILLINGER, JR., is the Ruth Davis Horton Professor of History at Wingate University, Wingate, North Carolina. He specializes in nineteenth- and twentieth-century German and Austrian history.

THE FLORIDA HISTORY AND CULTURE SERIES
edited by raymond arsenault and gary r. mormino

Al Burt's Florida: Snowbirds, Sand Castles, and Self-Rising Crackers, by Al Burt (1997)

Black Miami in the Twentieth Century, by Marvin Dunn (1997)

Gladesmen: Gator Hunters, Moonshiners, and Skiffers, by Glen Simmons and Laura Ogden (1998)

"Come to My Sunland": Letters of Julia Daniels Moseley from the Florida Frontier, 1882–1886, by Julia Winifred Moseley and Betty Powers Crislip (1998)

The Enduring Seminoles: From Alligator Wrestling to Ecotourism, by Patsy West (1998; first paperback edition, 2008)

Government in the Sunshine State: Florida Since Statehood, by David R. Colburn and Lance deHaven-Smith (1999)

The Everglades: An Environmental History, by David McCally (1999; first paperback edition, 2001)

Beechers, Stowes, and Yankee Strangers: The Transformation of Florida, by John T. Foster Jr. and Sarah Whitmer Foster (1999)

The Tropic of Cracker, by Al Burt (1999; first paperback edition, 2009)

Balancing Evils Judiciously: The Proslavery Writings of Zephaniah Kingsley, edited and annotated by Daniel W. Stowell (1999)

Hitler's Soldiers in the Sunshine State: German POWs in Florida, by Robert D. Billinger Jr. (2000; first paperback edition, 2009)

Cassadaga: The South's Oldest Spiritualist Community, edited by John J. Guthrie, Phillip Charles Lucas, and Gary Monroe (2000)

Claude Pepper and Ed Ball: Politics, Purpose, and Power, by Tracy E. Danese (2000)

Pensacola during the Civil War: A Thorn in the Side of the Confederacy, by George F. Pearce (2000)

Castles in the Sand: The Life and Times of Carl Graham Fisher, by Mark S. Foster (2000)

Miami, U.S.A., by Helen Muir (2000)

Politics and Growth in Twentieth-Century Tampa, by Robert Kerstein (2001)

The Invisible Empire: The Ku Klux Klan in Florida, by Michael Newton (2001)

The Wide Brim: Early Poems and Ponderings of Marjory Stoneman Douglas, edited by Jack E. Davis (2002)

The Architecture of Leisure: The Florida Resort Hotels of Henry Flagler and Henry Plant, by Susan R. Braden (2002)

Florida's Space Coast: The Impact of NASA on the Sunshine State, by William Barnaby Faherty, S.J. (2002)

In the Eye of Hurricane Andrew, by Eugene F. Provenzo Jr. and Asterie Baker Provenzo (2002)

Florida's Farmworkers in the Twenty-first Century, text by Nano Riley and photographs by Davida Johns (2003)

Making Waves: Female Activists in Twentieth-Century Florida, edited by Jack E. Davis and Kari Frederickson (2003)

Orange Journalism: Voices from Florida Newspapers, by Julian M. Pleasants (2003)

The Stranahans of Ft. Lauderdale: A Pioneer Family of New River, by Harry A. Kersey Jr. (2003)

Death in the Everglades: The Murder of Guy Bradley, America's First Martyr to Environmentalism, by Stuart B. McIver (2003; first paperback edition, 2009)

Jacksonville: The Consolidation Story, from Civil Rights to the Jaguars, by James B. Crooks (2004)

The Seminole Wars: The Nation's Longest Indian Conflict, by John and Mary Lou Missall (2004)

The Mosquito Wars: A History of Mosquito Control in Florida, by Gordon Patterson (2004)

Seasons of Real Florida, by Jeff Klinkenberg (2004; first paperback edition, 2009)

Land of Sunshine, State of Dreams: A Social History of Modern Florida, by Gary Mormino (2005; first paperback edition, 2008)

Paradise Lost? The Environmental History of Florida, edited by Jack E. Davis and Raymond Arsenault (2005; first paperback edition, 2005)

Frolicking Bears, Wet Vultures, and Other Oddities: A New York City Journalist in Nineteenth-Century Florida, edited by Jerald T. Milanich (2005)

Waters Less Traveled: Exploring Florida's Big Bend Coast, by Doug Alderson (2005)

Saving South Beach, by M. Barron Stofik (2005)

Losing It All to Sprawl: How Progress Ate My Cracker Landscape, by Bill Belleville (2006)

Voices of the Apalachicola, compiled and edited by Faith Eidse (2006; first paperback edition, 2007)

Floridian of His Century: The Courage of Governor LeRoy Collins, by Martin A. Dyckman (2006)

America's Fortress: A History of Fort Jefferson, Dry Tortugas, Florida, by Thomas Reid (2006)

Weeki Wachee, City of Mermaids: A History of One of Florida's Oldest Roadside Attractions, by Lu Vickers and Sara Dionne (2007)

City of Intrigue, Nest of Revolution: A Documentary History of Key West in the Nineteenth Century, by Consuelo E. Stebbins (2007)

The New Deal in South Florida: Design, Policy, and Community Building, 1933–1940, edited by John A. Stuart and John F. Stack Jr. (2008)

Pilgrim in the Land of Alligators: More Stories about Real Florida, by Jeff Klinkenberg (2008)

A Most Disorderly Court: Scandal and Reform in the Florida Judiciary, by Martin A. Dyckman (2008)

A Journey into Florida Railroad History, by Gregg M. Turner (2008)

Sandspurs: Notes from a Coastal Columnist, by Mark Lane (2008)

Paving Paradise: Florida's Vanishing Wetlands and the Failure of No Net Loss, by Craig Pittman and Matthew Waite (2009)

Embry-Riddle at War: Aviation Training During World War II, by Stephen G. Craft (2009)

The Columbia Restaurant: Celebrating a Century of History, Culture, and Cuisine, by Andrew T. Huse, with recipes and memories from Richard Gonzmart and the Columbia restaurant family (2009)

Ditch of Dreams: The Cross Florida Barge Canal and the Struggle for Florida's Future, by Steven Noll and David Tegeder (2009)